THE
BEST-KEPT
SECRET

THE
BEST-KEPT
SECRET

*Men's and Women's Stories
of Lasting Love*

Janet Reibstein

BLOOMSBURY

To Stephen Monsell

Published by Bloomsbury Publishing, New York and London
Distributed to the trade by Holtzbrinck Publishers

All papers used by Bloomsbury Publishing are natural,
recyclable products made from wood grown in well-managed
forests. The manufacturing processes conform to the
environmental regulations of the country of origin.

Library of Congress Cataloging-in-Publication Data

Reibstein, Janet Alese.
The best-kept secret : men's and women's stories of lasting love
/ Janet Reibstein.—1st U.S. ed.
p. cm.
ISBN-13 978–1–58234–309–9 (hardcover)
ISBN-10: 1–58234–309–8 (hardcover)
1. Couples–Case studies. 2. Love–Case studies. 3. Interpersonal relations.
4. Marriage. I. Title.
HQ801.R3345 2005
306.7–dc22
2005017580

First U.S. Edition 2005

1 3 5 7 9 10 8 6 4 2

Typeset by Hewer Text UK Ltd, Edinburgh
Printed in the United States of America by Quebecor World Fairfield

CONTENTS

Introduction:
What Is This Thing Called Love?

W HEN MY BROTHERS and I were little, at six thirty every weekday evening our father would return from his daily commute between Manhattan and our house in Great Neck, a half hour away. His key would turn in the lock and its very sound would still the cacophony of our squeaky, irritable squabbling and our mother's low grumbles. Like we were ending one musical movement and beginning another, my brothers and I would erupt into a chorus of delighted shouts: "Clear the runway!" we'd yell, and jump, one by one, into his arms. Meanwhile, our mother would stand, gently silenced, at the end of the runway (the hallway to the front door) at the entry to our kitchen. She'd watch. A moment earlier her features would have been duller, masked by the scowl of the daily routine of suburban motherhood. But then, her look would sweeten and body uncurl like a cat's under her smudged slacks and billowing cotton blouse blotted by spaghetti sauce. Over our small heads our father, breezing in from the world beyond Great Neck in his camel hair coat and leather briefcase, would grin back with relief, glimpsing her across the long entrance hall. He would put the last of us down and march past—on a mission that ended in their embrace, framed in the kitchen doorway, we children left, on the runway, behind.

We knew our parents were "in love." We knew what the movies meant.

This scene was part of our life, a backdrop and beginning to our evening routines, our wind-down to each weekday evening for fourteen years—until their marriage got sidetracked, overwhelmed above all by illness, drained by the dangling threat of death. My parents' marriage was never easy; my mother was moody, my father easily frustrated. Frayed tempers flared often, especially on rainy weekends. But though they bickered, though my mother lunged publicly at holes in my father's logic, though he rolled his eyes and snapped with hot impatience at her disorganization, they always managed to quickly restore their rhythm of easy enjoyment.

They left me with a yen to know their secret, a quest to discover why some marriages resist the forces that sidetrack others why some act as barricades against the siege of unhappiness, retaining happiness and fortitude between the two partners at their core. The yen has turned into a career as a psychologist with a research and clinical specialty in couples. As a child I thought about my parents' secret and tried to decode it. It wasn't there between the parents of my next-door neighbor and then best friend: they were separate, elusive to each other; fear hung in her mother's eyes and contempt in her father's when around each other. Later, when I was older, another friend tried to live at my house. "I just want to be around your parents," she said. "Mine hate each other." The secret was seductive.

Most of my professional life has been devoted to witnessing, managing, and trying to stem the pain that grows up within partnerships. A decade ago I was researching a study of affairs in marriages.[1] In the midst of both my clinical work and this study—an often painful one to research and write—I came across an obituary I'd saved from the *New York Times* in the 1970s. I'm not a pack rat, but this had survived the various moves across country and then across the ocean since then. It was the obituary of an American actress and wife of a well-known playwright. They had been married a long time, and had had, apparently, a legendarily happy union. Her husband had predeceased her. The obituary noted their marriage as one of her achievements and told of his dying words to her: "Well, darling, it's been a wonderful ride together." I had kept the piece (no longer, sadly, in my files) as a talisman. I'd been struck viscerally by those words. I wanted to know why. Why they'd had it. Why my parents had had but lost it. How I could have it. How others could try. They were both gone now. And their stories—their secret stories—had died with them.

As a commentator on relationships, I periodically am asked the question, usually by journalists hot to write a quick and pithy piece spurred by a new statistic on the rising brittleness of relationships, the decline in number of marriages, or the breakdown of a famous one, "Is there a future for marriage? For committed relationships?" A variant on this has been, "Have we moved into a new norm: that of serial monogamy?" Or, "Should we all expect relationships to be temporary, and also unfaithful?" I find myself shocked—not to mention irritated—that there is such ignorance about the insatiable, ongoing, time-honored, and even animal need to be in a happy, secure, erotic, and deepening union with one other person. We may not be skilled at getting there: we obviously increasingly lack the secret to having them. But the evidence of mounting partnership breakdown does not convince that we do not strive for or want desperately to have lasting and wonderful relationships. We just don't know how. We have lost our way. And, crucially, we even seem to have lost our faith in their reality. But they are still the stuff of most everyone's dreams, and they still drive people to try again, and again, and again, after each disappointment, each relationship failure. *This* time we'll make it. *This* time I'll get it right.

Finally, in the mid-1990s Channel 4 (in the U.K.) commissioned a series based on a small piece of research I was conducting on the happy relationships that I suspected were alive and somewhere out there. It confirmed they were: seventy couples volunteered to be part of a documentary series, in which they'd be filmed at home, showing them "happy." Only five were chosen for the program, but a subset of twenty were filmed briefly and interviewed, while six were interviewed in great depth. For most of these couples—and the myriad of others out there in the world whom they represent—being in a marriage-like partnership (not all were married) is the central, transformational, and ever-replenishing relationship of their lives, as revelatory and prized to them as parenthood or being a child has been (more so, for some). These interviews and tapes confirmed for me that despite the grim statistics, the urge that people have to couple, and couple and re-couple again, no matter the failures of their last relationship, does make sense: some people do manage it. Why shouldn't it be me, or you, or the next person, this time?

"We can finish each other's sentences!" cry Tim and Lorna, one of the couples I interviewed for this book, a working-class couple from Blackpool, now in their early fifties. Indeed, when I talked with them, Tim frequently jumped in to end Lorna's. Sometimes Lorna smiled indulgently, sometimes her smile froze. "He's like a big baby" was her reaction as she tousled his hair, a resigned affection helping her rise above the small annoyance.

Tim and Lorna married with stars in their eyes. They beam from their wedding photos, Tim in his frilled tux, Lorna in her frothy white gown. But when they were young, they did not rise above the small annoyances; resentments flared; violence erupted. Tim was held overnight by the police for domestic violence, then released, a sobering experience. They broke up briefly, not knowing how to save a marriage both ached for. This was their particular marital trial by fire—each partnership will have its own. He and Lorna are now back together. Having faced the knowledge they can't bear to be apart (and also he, in his words, "hurting, for her, for what I did"), they have learned to let things go. Instead of perfect contentment, they strive for pragmatic, imperfect solutions, such as when Lorna gardens—her private passion, her dahlias as prized as children. He feels abandoned when Lorna spends hours digging and cutting without him, so now he trots behind her, "helping," he says; "ruining things," she confides. "He pulls something up and goes, 'Is this a weed?' 'No,' I go, 'Tim, that's not a weed. That's a plant I recently put in,'" she says, laughing. She lets it go, a detail that doesn't fit into the story she is at pains to tell me, that their relationship is wonderful. It is a detail she willingly relegates to the rubbish bin. "It's just a garden. I can put in another plant."

Tim and Lorna obviously enjoy each other, though they also manifestly get on each other's nerves. Their story is what happens after the Cinderella wedding. Just as, finally, after feminism's exposé, the vaunted joys of motherhood are now known to be alloyed—by broken sleep and rage at incessant crying (especially late at night), by disrupted sex lives and smelly diapers—stories like Tim's and Lorna's expose the same about sturdy love.

There are bad tempers, hurt feelings, intermittent ambivalence, irritation, murderous rage, and periods of loss of faith in each other. These coexist with joy, and happiness and contentment are the themes stressed. Just as in motherhood.

Anna is a former graphic artist turned computer analyst. She and Doug have both been in therapy and use its techniques of dream deconstruction to understand themselves better. They have been together for twenty-one years. Every morning Doug comes down and tells her his dreams. This morning it's one about him building a tower that never gets finished, no matter what he tries to do. Anna quietly pours coffee for them, listening, nodding. "Well, obviously you're a megalomaniac who wants to take over the world. Pretty frustrating, isn't it, because, tragically, you can't," she says deadpan, coolly plunking the mug in front of him. Doug runs a major corporation. There is a grain of truth in what Anna says. No one dares to say things like that to him at work. He looks up at her with worry in his eyes. "Do you think so? Really?" Then Anna laughs and says, "Of course it's true. But don't worry, I'm very turned on by megalomania." He responds, "You know, I only love you for your body, not your mind, anyway." And they begin a play food fight, ending in a kiss.

Anna can't put exactly what she loves about Doug into a few words. But I've observed them over the years. I've witnessed the private scenes such as the dream analysis and the food fights. And I've watched them recover as Anna chastised Doug in front of me for criticizing their son. "Enough, Doug," she said, sharply, while Doug bit his tongue and suffered in silence, Anna avoiding his gaze. It was clear the argument was old. Within minutes, though, it was gone; they let it go. Because I saw their private world, I got a privileged glimpse.

For intimacy is not public: real love stories are, perforce, private and secret. Moreover, the rhetoric around intimacy is that it *ought* to be private—unless you're in trouble, and then the troubles ought to be "talked about." So happiness, told in tales that could persuade that relationships are, indeed, happy, gets lived out behind closed doors, while the troubled ones become part of the discourse we, the public, hear.

When my parents' marriage went through a particularly bad patch after my mother was diagnosed with cancer, their sex life suffered. How do I know this? Because out of her pain and the loneliness she felt during the breach from my father, my mother confided her anger, disappointment, and sense of rejection to me. In doing so she broke their implicit pact of privacy and respect for what had been *only* theirs. And as she did so, she began to weave a tale of *un*happiness, laying aside the one she'd lived with my father for years before, of *happiness*. Telling it to me, on her own, without him, was significant in many ways. For in so doing, perhaps, she was beginning to reinforce the tale's growing credibility to herself—through another's listening to it, through telling it aloud. The very act of telling her story apart from him underlined their estrangement at that point, and itself increased and verified it. Indeed, in part, this describes the process of estrangement in couples in general: separate stories growing and told apart from the other, which have as their themes the very estrangement itself.

But when my father became ill a few years later—more ill than she—and she found herself back in the circle of his tenderness, nursing him, she clammed up again. Then, as she watched him become thin, white, and helpless, I'm sure her broken confidence to me was something she wished gone. Their story—now melded together again by their shared commitment to each other, pleasure in their mutual support, their resumed daily conversations and satisfying routines—went underground, bounded off from detailed conversation with the rest of us once again. They were once again a couple bonded together, once again their private world sealed up. The essential secrecy of such a strong bond is why my friend wanted to live inside my parents' private house: she peeked in and spotted it, behind closed doors. The best-kept secret.

Recently, reading Studs Terkel's *The Good War*, an oral history of the Second World War, I found myself resonating with the same pique that impelled him to go out and grab the testimony, the stories of those who'd been in World War II, in order for him to combat, before it was too late, the evident loss of connection among people who hadn't been alive during that war to what was probably the seminal shaping event of the last century. Like Terkel, I didn't want to lose an important record, a record of what is still shaping the dreams and motivations of most people in the Western world at the beginning of this new century, though they may hardly be aware of it: the record of the Great Marriage, the Great Partnership. If questions of the "does it have a future?" sort are so persistently asked, the stories of the Great Partnerships are obviously not being heard above the din of reports of the failed ones. The stories garnered for this book, then, form a record, proof that enduring, real-life love in the second half of the twentieth century, and into the twenty-first century, in the Western world is alive and well.

"All happy families are alike," wrote Tolstoy, but he was wrong. Each story is different; my parents' is different from Tim and Lorna's, which, in turn, is different from Anna and Doug's. Yet most love stories do share themes: redemption through another's love or learning how one can be good to another, renewal through another's dependence or belief in you, wisdom through your own experience of your loved one and his or hers of you, and peaks and troughs of shared experience. Each individual love story today also pivots around the same conundrums: the tension between individual freedom and commitment, the task of regenerating mutual interest and desire in the teeth of predictability and routine, the need for security and stability against the push for novelty, and the sheer difficulty of the economics of time and energy for each other within two complex lives. All these over increasingly long lives.

All happy relationship stories—which are mostly internal, private, and not fully articulated unless called upon to be told (as in this book)—will also share key points as they are being shared. They will (a) emphasize the positive, leaving out or minimizing the negative; (b) be able to draw on past successes and pleasures during times of difficulty or distress so that the story shows an "expansive" time perspective—i.e., remembering the past, despite the distressing present; and, related to this, (c) project to the future as a time in which their past and present strengths will shine, again drawing on the positives in their relationship stories; and (d) be more or less similar "stories," if divergent in small ways, across the couple. These relationship stories are built up over a lifetime together, each day adding data into the bank about what makes the relationship work and gives them pleasure, and what the couple do that gets them through times of stress or crisis. A pleasant day at the beach? A sentence added to the "we do enjoyable things together" strand of the story. A tense time getting ready to get there? A sentence added to the coping one: "we get overwrought preparing, but we know to let it go."

What is unique to each story is *how* each loving couple can live within the tensions of long-term coupledom and still feel satisfied together. Some couples will master the distribution of loyalties between children and partners judiciously, balance work and home equably and equally, sustain the troughs of boredom and restart desire—by any outsider's measure. In contrast, others won't manage anything like such balanced lives—outside observers might spot all sorts of deficits—but still describe themselves as happy. The result, however, is the same: a sense of contentment with their relationship, for it is what the couple tell themselves that is the key, rather than an objective truth.

Moreover, each relationship story contains its own individual twists, which can arise in surprising areas. For example, a theme of contemporary relationship lore is that good sex, done frequently, underlies happy partnerships. It's a risky theme, which has come to dominate current cultural beliefs about sex and how it should operate in relationships. It's risky because couples who find themselves having it infrequently, or who feel lust slipping out of their lives, might start to question their relationship adequacy and begin to weave a relationship story of failure instead. Research shows it's normal for long-lived relationships to have sexual troughs. Relationship happiness can, indeed, coexist within a range of sexual behaviors, satisfaction, and, most definitely, frequency within many years of a partnership. This book adds its own evidence to such research.

The twists in the sexual strands of the stories are varied. Normally, long-lived couples do accept a decline in the frequency of sex, although often the severity of this decline is temporary; some happy relationships (a minority) can even encompass infidelities; while some (again, few) couples dispense with sexual intercourse altogether, often later in life because of physical incapacity, as we will see more fully in chapter 6. One woman interviewed for this study, for instance, claimed she thinks that "sex is when you can't think of other entertainments." Her story is about the relative unimportance of sex and the relative importance of other shared pleasures. Though she and her husband (married eighteen years) have satisfying sex, they do so infrequently, sex being only one among many mutual rewards. They described themselves as "happy, attracted, in love, and vitally interested in each other." In contrast, a couple I spoke with who are in their eighties talk about how their happiness pivots around the importance of their constantly stoked eroticism. Their tale about their happy relationship overlooks elements of their relationship that others—such as their estranged son, bitter at being neglected, feeling always outside their circle of mutual passion—might describe negatively. "I find you embarrassing," he told them, and they are still hurt. Retired to North Carolina, they golf, take walks, ride bikes, and swim, all the while joking and still flirting as if they had recently met. An ideal couple? Yes, they would say, remaining bewildered by their son's remarks.

Tolstoy was wrong. Telling each story reveals something new.

But it turns out Tolstoy was onto something. Happy relationships share something important: they're likely to lie behind most people's happiness with life. People in happy partnerships seem to be healthier, have better incomes, have more sex, greater social networks, higher self-esteem, and report greater enjoyment of life in general—largely because being part of a stable and happy couple is more likely to give you access to any and all of these good things in life.[2] For instance, affluence is more likely: couples usually have more than one income (or at least do at various points of their lives together). Being part of a couple means you have two sources of social networks. And being part of a couple means that someone who sees you daily and who cares about you is likely to notice if you seem unfit or under the weather and to prod you into doing something about it. The other side of this is that you may be more motivated to keep yourself healthy for him or her. After all, if you break down, her life becomes more difficult. Steady access to a sexual partner means more frequent sex, even if that frequency fluctuates over time. And no matter how much excitement you get from new sexual encounters, comfort and intimacy, and the likelihood of working out what most satisfies you, increases over time in relationships. A comfortable and happy relationship is likely to mean "good" sex within a number of important parameters: feeling confirmed you are loved, being physically gratified, and being shown you're attractive. One's self-esteem can't help but rise. Being part of a couple also bestows on you membership in a prized club—the "couples" club. The Western world values that membership highly.

To get the record I wanted, I asked couples to tell me their stories. But how do you get people to do the thing that I'm arguing is unlikely: that is, to make the private public? Fortunately, set against the implicit need for privacy within intimate happiness is something else: the need to tell a story to oneself, to make sense of one's life.

We all have stories—big and small—that accompany our lives. Relationship stories are more or less conscious, and usually only fully articulated when specifically solicited—something that rarely happens, indeed, perhaps only for books such as this one (or when telling a lawyer or marital therapist why you want a divorce or why your relationship doesn't work). One interviewee, a seventy-two-year-old retired businessman, married for over fifty years, said after our session together: "You know, I don't usually talk this way. I don't stop to ask myself questions about 'why does it work?' or consciously, 'what's it been like?' But this was great. *I didn't know I had it all there,* and I've learned something about myself. I think it's great to be forced to look back and think about your relationship. I think everyone should be made to do this!"

Here we need to observe something about "stories" and their construction. Stories silently accompany our lives, elaborating themselves as they do. We all know those voices we hear in our heads (albeit barely registered) that suddenly accuse, "that was stupid," or applaud, "that's great! Well done!" We often find ourselves reliving and savoring pleasurable episodes as if in front of a screen again and again, reminding us how good life and love can be, or the opposite, replaying torturous ones, mistakes or tragedies, until we have some way to tell ourselves what these memories mean, enabling us to go forward and the scenes to recede. Our reveries might even take the form of conscious conversations. How many of us have suddenly found ourselves mouthing words in public, lost in thought, only to realize with alarm that we've been talking to ourselves in front of all those passersby we'd neglected to notice? These scenes, conversations, and fragments of sentences build on each other. And despite those episodes when we catch ourselves mouthing passionate arguments in our heads out loud in public, these words and sentences are pretty much usually unconscious ones. They rise to awareness only when, and if, something unusual happens. A partner starting to do the dishes after years of nagging, for instance, might mean you become suddenly aware of the conversations you've had internally about his "unwillingness" to do this very chore. Now sentences change, descriptions of your partner evolving to fit this surprising new development. Another sentence, this time consciously, is added to your relationship story.

The story of "how we met" is also a story that couples consciously construct, and usually together. These stories commonly extol the delightful, often magical-seeming, sometimes humorous and surprising circumstances and conditions that bring a couple together. They usually emphasize the connection or pleasure between two people and will often leave out—to the point that these other details are effectively erased from memory (until the story is rewritten, perhaps during a breakup)—anything that was also present but which might not fit the story of happiness: the potentially irritating expressions, the deviations from shared politics, the unsettling flakes of dandruff on a shoulder. Such dispiriting details are present but submerged, either at the moment they're experienced or in the construction of the story afterward. And as the story is told and retold, and joins other stories that also confirm its underlying point—that is, that *this* is the person who "fits" me as a partner, a person with whom I'm "happy"—then it also helps to shape, even create, further happiness together. This is especially true if the story is essentially shared, if the point made (even if some of the details may diverge) is the same: "We have a happy life together; we form (at least mostly) a good partnership." So, telling a story of happiness appeals to an understandable and very functional psychological impulse in people. It is part of why people do want to shout their love from the rooftops.

In this book are stories of couples, from the United States and Great Britain, who have nominated themselves as having been in a loving, long-term (at least nine years) partnership. People either sent in their stories, filled out a long questionnaire, which also invited them to write their stories, and/

or were interviewed. They were located by word of mouth, often in a "snowball effect" (one person nominated another, who volunteered another, etc.), or through advertisements in community newspapers, or through calls for participants in articles interviewing me about relationships in major media. As a result, this is not a statistically representative sample, but instead one specifically garnered to tell stories of happiness, and one of people who were willing to talk about their relationships, or to try to put their experience into words. As a record, it can be a resource for further studies of a more scientifically robust design, drawing on clues from these admittedly skewed and rather articulate respondents. As a privileged glimpse into the textures of lives lived with a love that lasts through years and tribulations, it is, I hope, an invaluable and unique document. In most cases the stories and quotes that form the bulk of this book are direct, but in some they have been modified. This is to ensure confidentiality. Exact details of the participants, such as their names, localities, ages, occupations, and other demographic identifiers, in addition to some specific wording and circumstances, have been changed slightly, but, it is hoped, retain the spirit of the participants' stories. That is, as much as possible within the boundaries of the contract for confidentiality and anonymity, the stories try to stay close to or are in the words of the individuals, either as they have written or spoken them.

Couples span an age range between twenty-eight and eighty-three. Each member of the couple was asked to be interviewed or to provide his or her story separately, and, in most cases, though not all, it was possible to receive accounts from both members of a couple. Some are in their second, or even third marriage—these, however, as one person said, are the "true partnerships" for them, or in the case of the man who had been married for thirty years and, after his first wife's death, now for thirteen, it's his second "great marriage." These are all the ones that have lasted. Some are in same-sex partnerships. Not all are married. The rate of marriage is declining, particularly in modern Britain, while the rate of cohabitation is rising, especially when same-sex partnerships are included. The reasons for this are still being debated, but "committed" cohabitations that last, as far as research thus far can tell, are mostly different to marriage in legal status only. I think the record of this book will add to that apparent truth: i.e., that cohabiting couples (including same-sex ones) who both last and stay happy together are essentially the same as those who marry.

The rationale for requiring a relationship to have lasted nine years is that if it has survived these years, in which there are likely to have been transitions or periods that test a relationship's durability, it is likely to be hardy. The nine-year mark is also a watershed when there has been, over the past decade, a peak in divorce petitions. For most couples, children would normally have entered the equation by then as well. This in itself would indicate a strong likelihood that a couple will have weathered an early and major test of a partnership: managing to become a family rather than a couple, while still retaining a couple's strength and lively interest in each other. Even for couples without children, nine years of living together will have produced tests of energy and time for, interest in, and loyalty to one another.

Each chapter includes a discussion of a critical, shared aspect of enduring happy partnerships, followed by either one or two couples' stories, told separately by each partner, illustrating that aspect. Throughout the discussion sections relevant voices of other participants also appear. The interviews and questionnaires specifically focused on what was associated with both happiness and difficulties over people's lives together, as well as the strategies they have developed both to manage the problems and strengthen the assets. But the scope—especially in the very long and wide-ranging interviews—was broad enough to draw out larger life stories, and to meander down paths leading to stories within stories. The aim was to build a uniquely detailed picture of how these couples live and have lived together and to get them to describe what they think has contributed to their statement "we remain in love and are happy together"; what have they changed in their ways of interacting or thinking about their relationship, and what have they retained, and how have both helped to keep such feelings alive?

But what do we mean when we talk about love?

It's a fair question. "Love" is a portmanteau, carrying multiple meanings, suggesting a slew of emotions. Pop songs croon about "caring," "desire," "delight," "longing," "exclusivity" ("you are the only one for me"). Poetry, agreeing, digs deeper, finding "sustenance," and "nurturance," within.

Surveys say people mean "support," "commitment," "intimacy," "good communication," "respect," "being best friends," "sharing," "security," and "satisfying sex"[3] when they talk about love. Theorists talk of "merging" shared well-being, or deepening reciprocal feeling and commitment.[4] Meanwhile, researchers have found that feelings of trust, respect, friendship, and liking; feelings of fairness, mutuality, and reciprocity; and feelings of physical and psychological intimacy distinguish such couples from others—the ones who either don't last or who last but are unhappy.[5]

All these feelings entwined in one word, "love."

So what happens to these feelings in couples who've been together for years? To the exquisite, torturous, dizzy feelings—what one woman interviewee calls "charisma"? Do gray-haired partners still feel ripples of thrills over the breakfast table? What happens to "being one with another," to "finding your soul mate," to "passion"? To feeling you may die if you're too long away from each other, to electric pleasure, to relief at discovering someone who "understands"? What happens to such intensity? Does the conviction that no one else in the room—perhaps the world—really matters decay?

To fall in love, to live in such a state, may be the most intensely pleasurable period of life, so there's a lot at stake in believing it will last. Discord scarcely darkens it. Not because discordant notes don't exist, but because such intense pleasure overrides it. When you're in love like this, you overlook inharmonious details—the slightly irritable word, the white socks with black shoes, the preference for Frank Sinatra records over Bach, or vice versa—that touch off a warning bell. The bell rings, but dimly; at this stage you choose to answer later, and maybe, if you're lucky, you never will. Perhaps Bach takes a backseat to Sinatra during certain moods; maybe with gentle coaching the white socks will be recycled as dust cloths—or, indeed, you'll decide to admire his disregard for style. For, out of the existential island, "across a crowded room," you have found a partner, found your "soul mate."

That discovery ends a quest that began at birth. Psychologists who study emotional processes from infancy, attachment theorists, claim that much of what we call "love" is instinctual. Humans seek a secure attachment, a glomming on to one reliable, central "other." We require it, at the start, for dear life, and afterward, as an only slightly less urgent basic need. The adult caregiver of the infant (usually, in the first instance, the mother) responds to him also as if for dear life: the baby's life is as dear as her own, urgently, she must respond to his cries or coos. The need to attend to the baby overwhelms the mother (or whoever becomes the main caregiver)—it's a period called "maternal preoccupation." In this early period she is pre-occupied with the baby above all else—much like new lovers are preoccupied with each other above all else.

Research is accumulating to support this idea, that our desire for such a singular relationship is innate and lifelong.[6] We eventually leave our parents, or whoever has been that urgent attachment figure, feeling, hopefully, secure, special, and ardently cared for (those who haven't had at least one adequate "primary caregiver" as children remain stuck with the original craving for it—perhaps defending against it, but nevertheless having it). Now "unattached," we leave home with a figurative hunger, an empty space ready to be filled by a new special "other." Interestingly, as we grow up, we also develop a capacity to respond as both caregiver and receiver. Grown-up love means flipping in and out of these roles as situations demand. So the magical discovery of the lover, each partner stuck like glue, as Elvis sang—as the mother was to the infant and the infant to the mother—is not really "magical" at all. It's natural.

The intense pleasure of new love, just as in postnatal intensity, is functional to relationship development. Pleasure glues two into one, with a common purpose: to be together. The very nature of pleasure is that you wish it to continue, impelling a couple toward a future together. Intensity, of necessity, wanes. (Literature and films—for example, *Endless Love*—often describe the impossibility of a continued state of such intense preoccupation: something explodes, or implodes, and destruction follows.) When early love's intensity fades, two lives blending now into each other's reality, bells of discord chime more clearly (perhaps this is why shipboard and summer romances are so brief: encapsulated so fully from reality, the plunge into "love" is extreme, marking the contrast back into "drabness" too starkly). At this juncture the happy relationship story, its introduction so perfect, takes off into a different narrative, no longer about intensity.

Many love stories begin to end around this time. Glue is no longer sufficient, to continue the analogy: bricks and mortar become better metaphors. Real-time demands (projects at work with customary drinks afterward, which send you home late four nights running); real differences (one person tidying the other's underwear strewn on the bedroom floor, the other fuming when pants can't be found); and real other loyalties (the weekly squash game conflicting with the joint yoga class proposed by your lover, the parents' invitation to a dinner on the night of your six-month anniversary) begin to press.

Accommodations, compromises, and negotiations, all while maintaining interest, desire, energy, and time for each other, move into prime position. Processes of living, the bricks and mortar, replace the glue of intense pleasure. But what happens to those wonderful original feelings? Do they wash away? Are they transformed? Or do they crop up intermittently, girding the bricks and mortar?

What these stories often report is that such feelings can, indeed, be restimulated: the description could be from a couple newly in love. You glimpse the boy or girl you met in the middle-age person across the table from you, you touch the skin you know so well but find it suddenly electric again, or you see the familiar profile lit up in a new light, against a different sky, and it looks newly beautiful.

But most often these original electric feelings are transformed, and, it seems, deepened. The original feelings underpin others, cascading layers of pleasures past informing present and future ones. This is similar to how looking at photos of holidays can resurrect the pleasure of the holiday, support the sense of well-being one has as one shuffles through them in the moment, and reenforce the intention to go on another one, sometime in the future, all at once. Or, perhaps a better analogy is that the banking of the original feelings into present ones, over time, is much like the bodies these couples inhabit over the years. To touch your partner's body is to touch the body of now as well as the one you remember from before: literally a body of history. Your partner sees your sags but also holds a sense of the moment you met when the sags hadn't yet formed. The feelings of love that started you off coexist with the feelings of familiarity and deep knowledge of the present, part of the acknowledgment of your shared life, over your joint history.

Couples in this book talk about their early passion with flowery and sensual words, shifting to concrete language when they move into later parts of their tales. This is when they begin to describe how much they talk as a couple, what they actually do day to day (who does what chores and why and how that makes life flow, for example), what qualities each brings to the running of the family and also to their friendship (being an attentive listener, or being very sensible, for example). The early "glomming" on to each other still underlies their present emotional connection: they don't forget it. Instead, they cite a sense of luck and good fortune at having met each other and going on to have had happy lives; some people almost pinch themselves in disbelief at such "luck."

This is more than the tingling feelings or fizz of the beginning.

So there is good news: love can be better, and more intense, over time.

We are about to peer behind the curtains into the best-kept secrets of successful relationships. Each story reveals explicitly, through the wise conclusions of their narrators, or implicitly, through their showing by example, tips, or clues, how to sustain happiness together. They may provide the insight that accompanies recognition: by reading about situations similar to your own, new ways to behave or think about them may emerge. So might assurances that you are on the right track. No single story will provide a map, but each may offer discrete hints for constructing your own. For each path to happiness, as with these couples' and including your own, will be unique.

We love to be told secrets, to enter closed-off worlds, especially if what we're witnessing is entertaining, wise, or novel, which these stories are. People love to talk about things they love, and I wanted to hear them and to tell them in return. The best-kept secrets are being told so the story of how to be happy like these couples can go down in history. With it, the questions "Is there a future for the Great Partnership? Can a partnership of love really endure?" might become history too.

I

Happiness Is in the Eye of the Beholder: Creating Private Love Stories

SUE and BOB FOX

H APPINESS IS IN the eye of the beholder. It lies as much in the sense people make of the details of their lives and their perception that they love and support each other as it does in any objective facts that they do. One person's "healthy" is another's "not in peak form." One person's "solid income" is another's "must make more." One person's "good sex" is another's "not frequent or exciting enough." What would a young couple who make love twice a day, lust and desire compelling each to the other, make of an interviewee's comment that "penetrative sex is on hold" yet whose ensuing remark is that sex is "still important and satisfying"? People choose the details of their stories and give them a perspective. They build and tell themselves a story of their relationship.

What is more, great partnerships are stories told by both partners. They are stories that relate something that is arguably heroic: the triumph of two individuals joining over differences (among others, age, race, culture, gender, backgrounds, beliefs and ideas, styles, expectations, and tastes). These stories are romances in the original sense of the word: they are tales containing "heroes" and "heroines," each of whom have undergone distress, sometimes of the most appalling kind, yet have survived, relationship intact. Serious trauma aside, change, disorder, and disharmony punctuate any normal life course. Heroism, in this sense, lies in how couples complete the tale, managing to sustain loving feelings, able, after distress, to return to them.

> We both believe that time brings new hopes, and in our ability to be happy together . . . Through all this we always retained our sense of humor and the sense that even if we do not have the material things in life we do have the love of each other and our three lovely children (now teenagers). I always say that I did not marry Mick for his looks—he has a crooked nose and is bald. I didn't marry him for his money—he didn't have any. So I must have married him for love.—**Valerie Bright, 52**

Variations on the theme of heroism run through the stories I have collected. We find stories emphasizing that love, heroically, offers "profound comfort," "support," strikes like a mythic-size "thunderbolt," or provides an overwhelming sense of "salvation." An additional piece to this heroism is the fit, or symmetry or complementarity, between the two people's versions: in no serious way do they contradict each other. Instead, they may stress the same points and detail, or sketch in new ones that complement or elaborate the points the other partner has made.

In academia, papers are routinely coauthored, a necessity of laboratory life and intellectual inquiry. In consequence, academia is replete with hot stories of failed collaborations, partnerships broken down over the process of writing up papers together. It is a rather remarkable achievement then that a couple can tell a story that makes sense, each to the other, and that can gracefully accommodate another's details into the narrative each is constructing. And yet, couples who live together harmoniously and richly tell stories that flow and largely verify rather than contradict each other.

Within couples the stories themselves might diverge in the details. The discrepancies in people's stories of the same events (between what the one partner versus the other was doing or seeing during the same period) can be funny, or defy logic, or unfold like layers of an onion. Each partner's different emphasis in relating the singular components of their joint partnership story underscores one of the themes of successful partnerships:

within each couple live two, separate individuals. Sometimes, though, it is the similarity in accounts that can seem eerie.

> I was only nineteen but in another relationship, and we were at a club event—a social club for over-eighteens. I wasn't expecting to fall in love, and was pretty happy with my life, in all. I was instantly attracted to him. He said he was attracted to my red hair.—**Janie Morrison, 49**

> I went to this social club with a group of friends, not really looking to meet anyone. I was in a pretty good state, happy with life, in general. I was taken with her red hair, as well as her all-round good looks and bright, intelligent personality.—**Mark Morrison, 49**

In fact it's diagnostic of unhappiness when a couple tell completely divergent stories, their tales hanging in the air separately, nakedly, testimony of the couple's estrangement. Indeed, one of the striking things about couples who do break up is how differently they relate major aspects of their lives together.

When I was doing Ph.D. training at the University of Chicago, I was assigned to write a "three-generational study of a family." During the interviews, I was to take care to record the story of the marriage (if there was one) at the heart of the family's life. New to Chicago, I asked a friend who was brought up there if I could interview anyone from his family or his friends' families.

I interviewed his mother's school friend, the friend's mother, the friend's fifteen-year-old son, and the friend's husband. Every Sunday for four weeks I would turn into their suburban drive, take out my tape recorder, and sit down with my informant of the day for two hours' worth of questions. The first two interviews with the two women were unexceptional but very simple to do. Each corroborated the other's story of a happy, contented, stable family: squabbles easily settled, kids playing together happily, husband and wife sharing a comfortable family home. "Howie's a very good provider," both women crowed, their stories, at least, matching.

The third week, in a scene reminiscent of *Groundhog Day*, I pulled into the drive again and interviewed the fifteen-year-old son. No, he said, he couldn't say he thought his parents were happy. How could they be? His father was never there. And when he was there, he hardly had a thing to say to them. He once upon a time played ball with him. The boy during the interview was surly; he smoked heavily; and he hated school and sometimes skipped it altogether. Well, I thought, I certainly am going to have a more interesting paper than I'd thought last week.

And then, on the fourth week, I interviewed the husband. It began uncomfortably. He stared at me. I suddenly felt like an intruder, a single, twenty-five-year-old woman alone in a dark, private room, with a man, not a husband and father. I launched into my questions. He brooded for a moment, uncertain how to proceed, and then a flood of confessions erupted. He'd been unhappy for years. There was no place for him in his wife's home, in *her* family. The real couple, he reported, was his wife and her mother. He had virtually no relationship with his children, didn't understand them, felt they didn't like him, and, he finally admitted, he didn't know if he'd be sticking around much longer. I left, the tape full, hardly able to drink the instant coffee proffered when I said my usual thanks and good-byes. A few months later I heard, through my friend, that he'd left and set up house with a much younger woman. My professor wrote wryly on my rather explosive study of a three-generational family, "You've obviously gotten into these people's insides." No, not that. Just an outside witness, or ear, to the estrangement, as shown in the entirely different stories told by the members of this soon-to-be divorced couple.

The stories of happy couples, on the other hand, sound like elaborations of each other, two voices blending in one story.

Sue and Bob Fox

Sue is an attractive, warm, and outspoken seventy-two-year-old. A retired academic in northern California, she has been married for fifty-one years to Bob, a robust, good-looking, modest but powerful businessman. They live in a large, comfortable old house in a leafy, prosperous but unostentatious neighborhood. There are family photos covering the spacious entrance hall. A large, old dog affectionately lumbers up to sniff you out once you've been admitted entry; artifacts and artworks—sculptures, paintings, crafts, and a large array of family photographs—are displayed in their airy and relaxed sitting room. One is struck within moments of meeting what their stories each bear out: theirs is an energetic relationship, based on a shared vision—of a family, of a just society, of a way to make a contribution to it together, and of many pleasures they still enjoy and the past pleasures they've banked.

Perhaps the most striking thing either partner says is that a single question focuses them on why they stay together, through ups, downs, compromises, and frictions: "compared to what?" When or if they've had the urge to flee, to give in to despair, overwhelming anger, or resentment, this question brings them back. "Compared to what?" Throwing in the towel, Sue notes, can bring misery and loneliness, and hardship not envisaged. But more important, in a relationship there will always be compromises, always clashes, always disappointments in each other, no matter who that other person is. And so the question, "compared to what?" stops them short. They get a glimmer of an alternative story—the "what"—and it doesn't look good. That returns them to their "good" relationship story: their strengths, their history, and their future. "Compared to what?" reinstates a story of happiness, with more chapters to unfold.

Sue Fox:

When we met, early on—well, there wasn't much Sue before Bob, really. I was in high school, and it was the big football game at Stanford, where he was a student, and he played football. It couldn't have been more "fifties": he had a friend coming in from out of town that he wanted to fix up, so my friend who knew him was on the phone to him saying names, and he'd seen me once and asked my name, so when she said my name, he said, "Yes." So I was fixed up with this guy . . . We were sitting at this place where everyone used to hang out. It is really funny how he first came to notice me. A huge mess of us sitting at this table, you know, steaks for one, two, or three dollars, and somewhere someone in the restaurant yells,

"Orgasm!" and I said, "What does that mean?" I guess that got everyone's attention.

Later on Bob wanted a glass of milk—he'd just played his first game—and the waitress didn't want to give him a glass of milk for some reason, so I said, "Give him a glass of milk!" I was his advocate. The next day, he was staying at a friend's house near mine and they came over . . . they stopped and talked for a while and then he called and asked me to a dance. My mother wouldn't let me go steady—I was sixteen—so Bob would ask me for dates in six weeks: "What are you doing Saturday in six weeks?" But we talked on the phone and would see each other. I was dating other people all the time. One guy asked me to marry him. I was hooked on Bob, though . . .

I was an only child. I think my father was a manic depressive, but he never went over the deep end. He was very kind and loving . . . a successful lawyer . . . My parents were born in America and so were my grandparents. My folks had a very unhappy marriage but stayed together. They couldn't have separated—they were symbiotic. At one point when I was a grown-up my mother tried to have my father committed, only she tried to get me and Bob to do it. We got as far as the parking lot in the hospital before we realized that if anyone had to be committed, it wasn't Daddy! . . . She was always angry at him. He was depressed. But knowing my mother, she would have had anyone committed who was not paying attention to her. If I could do something for her, then I was okay. But she—well, "abuse" is such a trendy word and I wouldn't use it, but there was a lot of "Oh, my dear, don't you think that dress just makes you look like you have a sack tied around the middle?"

I guess there was a competition. My father loved me—I mean he was crazy about me. And my mother, she went by that psychologist who said, well, you had twenty minutes to eat a meal, and if you didn't, your food was taken away. And if not, then you had nothing until the next meal. I am sure that a lot of my weight problem comes from that . . . although not all of it. I am through blaming my mother for everything! But when I was an infant, it was that the child could only be fed on schedule . . . And there was no touching.

I spent a lot of time—the summers—with my grandparents, my mother's parents, up the coast at their summer house. My parents would drop me there on the last day of school and leave me there and come and get me when school started again. But then my father had a really big fight with my grandfather and they didn't speak for ten years. So that [the routine of spending time with her grandparents] was like taken away. And my mother kept having "breakups" with people and not speaking to them. I was always scared of being that kind of person . . .

I was a good student. I was good at everything. That was a necessity . . . I was thinner too!

I went to college at Stanford, even though I was going to go to Vassar or Bryn Mawr, because I thought if I left, that would be the end of the relationship with Bob and I wanted it. It was important to me. So when I was at college we didn't have my mother there to say you can't go steady, and I just stopped seeing other people, and he stopped seeing other people.

But it was like a Doris Day movie then. Sex was something that didn't happen—kissing and petting, yes. I was on the cusp of the feminist movement. Contraception—that hadn't happened yet. It was that kind of thing. Nice girls didn't do that. If you did, then he wouldn't like you . . . Sometimes it went on and got heavy but there wasn't pressure from Bob.

When I married Bob it was like I walked out on my family. We came back to where he'd lived, which is down the coast from where my parents and their families had settled . . . This is who I am—I am of this marriage and this family—Bob, me, and the kids and their kids. Where would I go, in some ways?

When we decided to get married it was because he was graduating and going into the navy, so we had to and I was only nineteen and he was only twenty-one. Both families were against it because we were so young . . . Once they realized we were absolutely going to do it, they got into it. The families got involved and we had a lovely wedding.

My father did very nicely—we were upper-middle class, not rich in any way, but very comfortable. When Bob would visit me at my parents' house when we were dating, he helped me make the hamburgers when I was cooking. I had no clue what kind of wealth he came from. He never said a word. Then during one of our vacations when I was at Stanford, I went down to his parents' with him. We drove in—his parents lived on this estate, with a tennis court and pool, and this big, old gorgeous house, with huge grounds around it, and his father kept animals for tax purposes, and we drove up and the butler opens the door, and—can you imagine? The butler opens the door! I was shell-shocked. It was not comfortable, though it was fun meeting his brother and his friends. But I entered this world of butlers and maids and cooks and a gardener and a cleaning woman.

He had come from a real upper-class family. They had staff! But they also had a real family. Which is why I left my family to enter his. And it was a family and a social circle. It was a real life and I could get into it and be part of it. Who knows what he would have been like if he had married someone different, but I am not part of a social group. I am not a cliquish sort of person and have never been able to maintain a role in a group. We have friends—a ton of people that are friends, very old and very dear and close friends. We don't spend a lot of time together with all of them, and certainly not all as a group . . . The family we've created is more my social group.

We decided to get married at the end of that year, because he was graduating, anyway . . . He went into the service right away, as it was Korea, into the navy, and we wrote lots of letters. I guess I felt passionate about him then—we had a real loving relationship. It was definitely a romantic thing. He'd come home for leave and I'm going, there is nothing like absence and candlelit dinners and that kind of thing . . . so we had babies right away! Our first, and then next was born, and the day he got back from his first leave, I got pregnant on that day—I had a couple of miscarriages. He would be home for only one day and I'd get pregnant. When I went for my three-month checkup after one of our children, the doctor said, "I don't know, Mrs Fox, but I can't believe you get pregnant so quickly!"

We had four kids in seven years, and we were married young. And then ten years after we had a fifth. I didn't have much help in the beginning. And there were [physical] problems with our second child . . . Bob and I just thought they were wonderful. I see my kids now with their kids, so overwhelmed by two children. Bob was wonderful; his own father, the first diaper he ever changed was his third grandchild's. Bob never wanted anyone [outside help] in the house. When our first child was born, we had a little furnished apartment and I got a nurse because I had mastitis. And then, because I was sick and the nurse had another job, Bob had to take over most of the care of the baby for a while. He did the changing, the bathing, and the nurse showed him how to do all that stuff.

So our first baby was born when he was in the navy and the next about a year later, and we lived with his folks a bit when he first got out of the navy. When our second child was born, she was born with a birth defect—it wasn't clear what it was. It looked like there was this stuff growing out of her eye . . . My mother-in-law never liked damaged goods of any sort . . . So I was twenty-two with a one-year-old and this baby with this thing and we didn't know what it was. The eye doctor didn't either. It turned out it wasn't a cancerous condition but it looked very alarming. I would be out shopping with her in the stroller and some woman would come up and say, "What's the matter with her face?" What did she want me to say?

I went to the hospital and stayed with her for about a week. They tried radiation. Meanwhile I was pregnant, but luckily miscarried because I was holding her during the radiation. Anyway, after a lot of operations and things she was all right, though her eye doesn't completely close. But she saw it as worse than it was. Because when you look in the mirror it's like an optical illusion—you don't see yourself how others see you. It looked huge, like the Elephant Man or something, when that's not at all how she looked in person. She lives nearby now, and is a wonderful mother and works as a school psychologist . . . Our third child also had something wrong when he was little—he had to wear a brace on one of his legs. But it was fixed and he went on to become a star athlete . . . And one was a bit hyperactive . . . They were like a litter. They're all very close. Still are. And they all look after each other. The boys had a talent for picking bad women and nobody would let them marry them, so by the time they married, they married wonderful women! Our kids gave us a great time. It was always fun. The fun is what has made our marriage so good.

One of the things about us—we can disagree about whether the government's doing the right thing but we have never disagreed on how to deal with the children. We have always acted as one. When we have decorated, or are buying a piece of glass or something, we always say that the one who hates it more has the say. So you have veto power. I don't think I've ever tried to get the veto over anything. I would have rather that the kids got a much more progressive education. They went to the family school even though my brother-in-law was miserable there. Finally when our youngest went there it was awful and finally when she was in the eleventh grade Bob agreed, so she changed schools.

Bob didn't try to reproduce the upper-class life. The house we're now in looks like an upper-class house but the reason we're in this house is because this is a neighborhood which is integrated and we bought this house for thirty thousand bucks, and the same house out near his parents would have been double at the time.

When Bob got out of the navy he had a small trust fund from his grandfather, and he went into the family business. He had wanted to be a journalist. He had an application for a job in journalism ready to go when I was pregnant and he never said a word, except to me, and he put it in a suitcase and then wrote a letter to his father and said, "If it is available, I would like to come and work in the family business." He was an English and philosophy student. Probably because of those things he became a fantastic businessman. We moved back to California and he took this job; then I finished my B.A. and eventually began to work on my Ph.D. after a while. Meanwhile he worked at the family business and took it out of the family and made it public, and then built up another and took that public.

Emotionally Bob and I have always been very connected. The sex itself was never really warm and emotional—our warm and emotional caring for each other had not much to do with that. I think the fact that it has pretty much stopped now bothered me because I felt that I was no longer attractive, and it wasn't that he was no longer interested, period, but that it was something wrong with me—because I was fat, or ugly, or whatever. We have sex now maybe once a year—but there are [medications, and blood pressure] problems . . . He doesn't talk about difficult things, so I could get enraged, and I would feel let down. But I adapted. I adapted to it; I was having my own physical problems, anyway . . .

[There was a time when] things were difficult and he wouldn't go to see someone with me; his idea is that "if anyone is crazy, it is not me," so, when it was recommended to go to a family therapist to help [when one of the children was having social and physical difficulties], he wouldn't, so I went alone. And I had a weight problem and I wanted him to help me with it; I was up and down all the time and I was getting to the age where it was starting to affect my health. I thought this issue was mine, but also a relationship problem. The therapist was going to recommend someone we could see together but he wouldn't go. So I was thinking that it would be too bad if we split at my age, but if we did, that was okay too. I thought, "I have to get rid of this; I can't go around feeling like this . . ."

The relationship healed when I understood what I was doing to myself. And I understood that Bob is what he is. I love him dearly. I knew what he was when I married him. I didn't get any bona fide guarantee. And he has had to put up with plenty from me. I am not the easiest person to deal with—I'm pretty much an all or nothing person . . .

What we've always shared is a sense of humor. When the kids were growing up it was a great time, exuberant . . . fun. Anything can become a funny story—like the time we walked out of a hotel in Cape Cod with Davie pooping down my clothes. That's a story that we both tell together, though I would get annoyed because he wouldn't tell it right!

And we are together about most important things. At the moment we are having trouble with our eldest child. I don't know if it's the menopause or what with her. We haven't spoken in a year. She is in a terrible state. We were always very close; she would phone in the mornings and we would talk for an hour, an hour and a half. But the others keep in touch with her, which is wonderful . . . We had problems with all of them at first with our deciding to sell our beach house, which they all loved, and which she lived in for a while with her husband when they were first married . . . She lives on the east coast now and hasn't used the house in years, but still. The kids were all angry, and upset at first. I had been displeased with the house and where it is for a number of years, and the place and neighborhood were changing. We sold the house; I'd become unhappy with the kind of community it was becoming—too moneyed, snobby. It finally got to Bob, too, when the people next door knocked down two houses and built a huge house with a tower. The kids were unhappy too, and we'd talked about it a lot but I don't think they thought that we meant it. But we did.

We buy things for our kids; we are generous, I think, to a fault. We pay for big things—schools, education—and they get money of their own from funds set up. I think the problem [with their eldest daughter] has something to do with the distribution of money that the kids get every year. It's not clear. But the kids organized a fiftieth wedding anniversary for their father and me and she didn't turn up. When I said I was worried because she didn't turn up, she just said, "good." That was the beginning. There was a tirade but I don't think she understands what the situation was . . . As Bob says, with her we've come to realize that it is always about money . . . We are together on how we're dealing with this. There isn't anything that we are not together on.

We got very rich, which was a drama but it didn't change anything about how we lived at all because the fun thing when we got very rich was giving it away. We share a political base and social conscience. He was in a businessman's group for peace during the war in Vietnam, and I was involved too. I'm a socialist person but when it comes to education I am a conservative dinosaur in many ways. I think there is more than one way to skin a cat, and we will fight things through till we agree. He was supportive, totally, of my going back to do a Ph.D. He sits on the board of the city orchestra, and we've set up a cultural center, that he's the chairman of, and we both support the arts in town, and I've been on the board of the Historical Society, chairwoman of our cultural center, and he's been on the university board. Our interests are the same but we have sometimes done them in different places.

I still cook: one time we experimented with having our housekeeper stay and make dinner. That was not a success because she likes to get out of here. I've never had to do the heavy cleaning and stuff. But we both never took on much of that part of life that was having money; that was a choice we made and shared—no fancy vacations, clothes, or cars. In the end we enjoy each other's company, and we have fun.

I mean, our morning routine: he gets up at six and takes the dog out and gets the coffee, and I get the bedroom cleaned up. He comes back up, we get on the bed with newspapers for about an hour or whatever, and talk about them. We never get tired of that . . . We both love getting in the car and riding up the coast to our vacation house, we both like the dog, sports. There is nothing that one does that is of total disinterest to the other. I have always been interested in business. We are both just curious about everything. We both have that. The same things strike us as funny—not like jokes, like, "there was this man that got off the train . . ." but things that strike us as funny, and we tend to be struck the same way by the same kinds of things.

We used to have a cartoon hanging in the kitchen. One man is saying to the other, "How is your wife?" and the first guy answers, "Compared to what?" One is asking how she is and the other takes it to mean what kind of wife do you have, but to us, I mean, everything we take as a "compared to what?" From my standpoint—I'm not saying it has not been positive, and I would do it all over again. But there have been moments, times when I've wanted to—not stay. There was that time when I was very unhappy. I got my Ph.D. and had a ten-year academic job and I'm proud of my academic record, but my joke has always been that I wanted to prove that I could make it on my own if I had to, and if Bob had ever decided to run off with a bimbo, I would not have to eat dog food. I won't become one of those statistics. But I haven't ever really considered leaving because, "Compared to what?" We're both smart. We both have the capacity to reason. I think a lot of people don't stop to think, "What's it going to be like afterward?"

And now, we've bought a new vacation house, with a dock, where you can go sailing, and we've got new projects and we're enjoying it all so much.

Bob Fox:

I'm a native of northern California, the San Francisco area. I've always lived here with the exception of four years when I was in the navy. I went to college nearby, at Stanford. I led a very sheltered and nice childhood in a comfortable home. I was sent to good schools where I was tolerated probably more than I should have been, because I was totally self-centered and self-assured after a certain age. I was the oldest of three children and I was much favored by my parents. They were busy with other things but when it came to paying attention to the children I'd say that both my parents enjoyed my company. They were not at all children-centered. My mother was more involved with children through some of the boards she sat on—the Child Study Center, the Youth Center—things like that. I was sort of an example of her interest and when she had time she enjoyed what I did— especially my accomplishments. I think she was very much involved with the business of child-rearing, as opposed to simply kicking back and enjoying it. She was a hardworking, well-educated woman. I always felt my parents protected me and also prevented me. I suppose this is classic; I'm not the only kid who ever felt it. I decided unconsciously that it was better simply to just walk the path I had been given. Because I was good at it and because that would not cause any trouble. So when I went away to college I really felt emancipated.

My parents treated me well and I did well in school, and I was a very good athlete. I felt different, though, to what I looked like. When I graduated from high school and went to Stanford my main aim was just to get away. I'd been in the same school for thirteen years and I'd been very much sheltered at home. We lived far enough from school and it was difficult with gasoline rationing—this was during World War II—for me to see other kids, so I did a lot of reading. I had a slightly limited social life because of the distance. I wasn't able to walk to other kids' houses. I was always on a team so I was practicing until late in the evening and would get home late. But I didn't feel in the least bit deprived. I felt very comfortable and fortunate and happy; I was relatively pleased with myself.

When I went to Stanford—well, in those days it was a place that paid very close attention to you until you're accepted. Once you were, they didn't care whether you lived or died: you were on your own. Nobody paid attention to you or nagged you. I loved that. That to me was good. One of my kids went there and it was the wrong thing—he would have benefited from more attention. But to me that was what college was for: Leave me the hell alone! Let me do my own thing! I took courses I wanted. I never took a course because somebody thought it would make sense. I would read the whole coursebook and take whatever one interested me. I took the least number of courses in my major that you could possibly take because I wanted to take so many other ones. As a result I had a rather nondescript time academically, but a wonderful four years at college. I did sports. I was captain of the soccer team and played football. Of course I met Sue in my sophomore year, so if you're talking about my time before her, there wasn't much! I was eighteen and she was sixteen.

She was a blind date and it was an amazing experience. I dated lots of people. I always enjoyed it. We had good times. But I never met anyone I had the slightest interest in spending the rest of my life with. Five minutes after I met her I just stopped looking. I can't explain it. I mean there is something chemical or whatever that must explain that. I'm sure it happens to lots of people. But that was the single biggest thing to change my whole approach to life at that point.

I think what it was, was the glimmer of intelligence. Most of the people I dated . . . weren't people with whom I could have a mental sparring session. And Sue was the first one who could give it back to me as well as I could give it to her. I could see it first in the look in her eyes. When I first saw her on the street—I'd had a few drinks but I could still recognize that this is somebody good. And she kind of looked at me quizzically and humorously, and I kind of looked at her. And a couple of days later I called her up and said, "I'm the guy who staggered out onto the street; you may not remember me but my name is Bob Fox and so, so what are you doing next Saturday?" I think our first date was at a soccer match. Her mother wouldn't let us go steady—it felt like an awfully long time. And she went out with other guys and I was just enraged. I said, "I don't want to hear about it. Don't tell me about it." Of course, I was going out with other people back home too. I did it only because of this enforced thing. I wasn't interested in other girls. We sent each other telegrams. It was very romantic. I think we're both still romantic.

We had a wonderful time. We were very fortunate. We spent our college years together, our navy years together, and the whole bit is a cumulative thing. We have thousands of pictures and letters and memories that we share right from the start. That may sound boring to some people, but one of the things that's happened—and it happened when I went away to college and when I was in the navy—I need, and I think Sue does too, change. I'm not the kind of person who says, "Ah, now I have everything in place, and all I have to do is keep it the way it is, and everything will be fine." I do not believe that for one minute. Life is not static, but dynamic, and you are balanced on top of the wave, surfing it, and when you get to the beach you better get out of there because the next wave is coming and then you paddle out and pick up the one after that and come back in again. But you are never . . . you can never assume this wave is here and you can stay on top of that forever.

When it came time in my career and war broke out [the Korean War] and it was time for me to decide what I was going to do, I investigated every branch of the service—the marines, the army, air corps, the coast guard, and the navy. I decided on the navy. My father knew an admiral and he got him to write a recommendation for me and I went to Officer Candidate School and spent four years on the same ship in the navy all over the world.

Sue and I decided to get married earlier so we'd spend some time together before I took off, because I'd be away for most of the next four years. It was all an adventure, I consider. I didn't waste any time. A lot of people say, "Oh, you gave up four years of your life to the service." But I never felt that way. I think I was very fortunate that after thirteen years at school, four at college, I got whipped into shape by the U.S. Navy.

As a junior officer on a ship no one cares about your background, nobody cares about the fact that you went to Stanford or a private school. They care whether you can fulfill your responsibilities on the ship. And I loved that. I was on my own and had to figure it all out for myself. I had to figure out how to work the system. I was very interested from the start in organizational dynamics, the way people relate within an organization. Which is why I went into business when I came back. It was very challenging. We were all over the world—the Far East, in Korea and Japan.

When we had our first kid I was in the navy and I took some days off to come home and look after the baby. Sue was sick for a while. It's amazing because when we got home from the hospital my mother-in-law said, "Let me carry the baby into the house." Well, I'd never carried a baby before in my life. But I just said, "No way. It's not your kid." And I figured out how to handle a baby, and that night I had to get up and do the feeding, you know— and fell asleep at the bottom of the baby's cot. But that to me is what life's all about—it is continually probing and exploring new things, and taking risks, not playing it safe, but extending yourself. And sometimes failing. Failure happens a lot.

One of the questions in any marriage is what things do you share and what things are his and what things are hers. I always cut the grass and she always cooked the meals—there are a variety of things like that. But as far as bringing up the kids, I was a diaper-changer, I was a feeder, and I was a bedtime storyteller. Yes, when I was away on business she had to do it, but when I was home we shared it. She cooks the meals, I clean up, and so we would work in the kitchen together. As far as discipline with the kids, we both were involved. As far as mentoring them, we both were. Sometimes one of us will be very busy and the other one will have to then fill in, and that happens. I'm sure the other doesn't particularly like it, but we understand and we do it. We both get our hands dirty and we both handle lots of things together. If I'm not around and we need a new stove, she doesn't have to wait for me to go to the store—she'll do that . . . I look back at our twenties with having these kids then and I say to myself, "Man, these people who are doing this in their forties—how the hell can they do it?"

We do disagree on things and during this time we used to yell and scream at each other. Still do sometimes. But then the next time we're in the kitchen together one of us will put an arm around the other; we'll make up because we need each other. We still need each other. We need to have a hug. And we realize that in spite of these momentary things—and they are momentary things—there is something solid that transcends them.

We had our kids close together, one right after another. We never said, "We want to have this number of children" and we did use birth control. I don't know. You know it's one of the things that's unclear, how we ended up having so many kids! We had four really close together and then ten years later we had the fifth. The one thing we used to do, and insisted on it for many years—on Thursdays at dinnertime we would have a sitter. And the two of us would take off. We used to spend a lot of time at a bar-restaurant in town where there would be these local colorful characters. Sometimes we would go to a movie, sometimes we'd just drive. We had three or four hours—from six o'clock to around ten on Thursdays—when it was just us. We also took some trips just to take time off and have a holiday. It worked.

We had great times. Later in life we used to take trips with the kids. For our big birthdays we would have these ridiculous gatherings at some resort. We realized we didn't want to spend 100 percent of our time with the kids. It wouldn't be good for us or for them.

I think I was an okay father. I don't think I was a great father. Sometimes I was a little too harsh. But I think Sue was a great mother. When they were little, when they were going to school, when they were all at college at the same time, her priority was the kids, and the family, which was including me, but I was only part of it. I think I always placed her above the kids. Sometimes that bothered me but not enough to make me change or to try to change her. I had this idea that the kids will grow up soon and we'll have our time together and I was looking forward to that.

We were doing our own things then, while the kids were growing up. Sue was doing her Ph.D. and then teaching and writing. I came back into the family business when I came out of the navy. My father had a guilt feeling about business—that his real role in life was to be a philanthropist so the purpose of the business was to give him the freedom to do that. Kind of a communitarian. I was always very competitive—in sport and in life. To me business was a game. I wasn't satisfied with the family business, which I'd been fortunate enough to come back and be a part of. So as soon as I could, when my father retired and I became the president of that company—up to that point there were three family businesses and they were all privately owned, no public stock. As I began to learn not only about business but the family situation, I realized that if we just waited for the older seniors to die and pay out their share to their widows, these companies were gone. So that started a plan to develop a vision of the future and make them public companies. And one thing led to another and then we came up with an innovation which became a much bigger thing than any of the original companies and that put us onto the Stock Exchange. That was the thing that started out as a tiny little venture.

I gathered my family together one day when I decided to do this because I was very comfortable, I had this nice job and all. I was in my early forties and the kids were somewhere in their teens, most of them. So I gathered them and Sue. I told her, I said, "Sue, I've been drinking myself to sleep for the last few months. Something's got to change. I can't be doing this—the old business. It's just using me up. What I want to do is this new one but it's a big risk." And she said, "So what's the problem? Just do it!" And the kids all said, "Go for it, Dad!" My brother—who died young—also was behind me on it. I had total support and was fortunate enough for it to work out. But it was a wonderful demonstration of my partnership and family.

My brother who died—we were tremendous rivals as kids. We used to beat each other up. But when we separated into the service and college and he married and I married, we were fortunate enough to be able to reintroduce ourselves to each other and we became absolutely the best of friends, and he was with Sue, too. We would take vacations together and if we had a problem we would talk to each other. He lived in Seattle. We went to places together as couples and had a good time when we were together. His death was the most major setback that I've ever experienced because it was this horrendous thing that was happening to my best friend. And I wasn't able to do anything about it. I called up every doctor, every clinic, and I was the one who bore the brunt of it—doctors not telling the truth—and I would have to tell the rest of the family. Sue did all this with me. She felt the same way about him. My mother was so upset that she started to drink heavily. She was about seventy. It was twenty-one years ago. My dad was someone who kept it all inside. He didn't share his emotions, even with my mother. He was low-key, honest, wonderful, and everyone thought of him as a saint, which they don't think of me as! But my mother lost it and so did I.

It was the only time I ever cried in front of family—both while he was dying and afterward. I was just devastated. Sue loved him as much as I did. When he was sick we would spend every other weekend up in Seattle. He had a giant tumor at the base of his spine. He was diagnosed at the point that his condition was incurable, and in the end he was on increasing doses of morphine to kill the pain. . . . His seventieth birthday would have been tomorrow and they're all kind of wondering how we'll be. It was the only bad thing that's ever happened to me. That's how good a life I've had.

But how I got through the next part, after he died—I don't know; that part of me never healed up. We got through it together—we felt the same. I got through by refocusing. I plunged back into things—the business was sort of shaky then, so there were things I had to do. I just kept active. So did Sue. It was just instinctive that we both did this. We didn't talk about that we were going to do this. But Sue and I, hundreds of times, will say exactly the same thing. Which means sometimes we don't have to say things because we know the other person is thinking that same thing. That's one of the things about this chemistry thing—this ESP thing. Because when we're doing a crossword puzzle we'll often say the answer at exactly the same split second. And we know this. It no longer amazes us that this happens. When we're involved in something of intensity we know that we are both thinking the same way about the same thing at the same time.

We have been very lucky in that nobody else has died. But as far as our family unit is concerned, with its ups and downs, conflicts and confrontations and difficult relations, all our children, all our grandchildren—we have been healthy, we have been able to do things, we've been fortunate in that we've gotten involved in a lot of things we enjoy, but it's only because we're never really sitting still.

The business really took off from the mid-eighties—that was after my brother's death—to the mid-nineties. It was wonderful, rewarding financially, competitively, satisfied a lot of my instincts. I'm a delegator, not a hands-on manager. Otherwise I wouldn't have had time for the family, as I did. I never allowed the business to dominate even though it was a prime interest. We got lucky.

That thing about her mother trying to take over: there wasn't much of an issue there because I was very pigheaded. Because I felt that her family in a couple of instances tried to interfere. One time Sue had a cold and her mother was on the phone and she said, "How's Sue?" and I said, "Well, she has a cold." And her mother said, "I'll be right there." From two hours away! So I said, "No you won't. What are you talking about?" And that was a sort of watershed moment, a declaration of independence. I don't think Sue particularly enjoyed my family, apart from my brother and sister-in-law; I didn't particularly enjoy hers—not because there was anything wrong with them, particularly, but simply because we had our own family.

My family was a part of our life because we lived nearer to them. We used to go to their house on certain occasions but Sue went along with it because it fitted. They had tried to stop our marriage. They took us out to a restaurant kind of privately. Both sets of parents. And then they reasoned with us and we were at that age if your parents take you out to dinner, you go. And they explained rationally why we should wait. And after about an hour of this sparring my mother turned to my father and said, "Well what would have happened if you had married the girl you were going with when you were twenty-one?" I was then twenty. And he thought for a minute and he said, "Well, the kids would have had red hair." And I just thought, okay, at least Dad's on my side. He's not going to put up with this any more than I am . . . About three days later I called my mother from college and said, "Sue and I have thought about it, and instead of getting married in June, like we were planning, we're getting married in March." Because we then figured that if I was going into the navy by June, we ought to get married even earlier than we'd told them.

I think that whole incident is the kind of thing that our lives have been made up of. Continual declaration of independence, continual deciding about how we're going to play this, together.

We play things together. We have a problem now with our eldest daughter. A couple of our other children have said, "Swallow it. Suck it up to her." You know? And we said, "No way. Nobody gets away with treating us and talking to us like that. You or anybody else. If you don't have manners, we're going to call you on it. This is a civil relationship. We're now all adults. You may be our children but you're not kids anymore. You're in your forties, we happen to be in our seventies. We are all mature human beings and we can act like them. And if we don't act like them, we're going to have to pay prices." Now a lot of our friends and some of our relatives shudder at that because they realize we are taking a chance. But that's the way we play the game, both of us.

I think the only thing that's really got in our way has been our parents. Both of them. I didn't realize Sue was bothered by mine for a long time till she finally began to tell me. And I began to realize she was right, that she was seeing things in a way that I had never seen because I was too close. There was an example about their attitudes toward race. I forget what the incident was, but Sue pointed it out and said, "Do you realize what they are doing and how they are behaving?" And she explained it to me and I said, "Yeah. I never looked at it like that." And from that point on I did look at it. And the same thing happened with her parents. I always felt, regardless of how unpleasant her mother was to her or us, that after her father died we were her mother's caretakers—her mother, who was an unbelievable piece of work. I always used to feel that it was proper if we had a big party that she should be invited, for instance. And Sue complained about it. "Why do we have to have her? She's just going to screw it up." Which she usually did. Finally I realized. A very confrontational thing had happened; I guess it was at my sixtieth-birthday party. We got the whole family together at a hotel and she just totally destroyed it. And the whole family sat around and tore her to ribbons. To her face—it was a sensitivity session par excellence. She called it "The Inquisition." I realized I had been the one who had been insisting. The only one in the family who felt it was right to have her around. That was the end of it. We never did it again.

Whether or not we were able to persuade each other about things, we listen to each other, and it does have an effect. For instance, right now we are looking at the Israeli situation. And I'm not saying one person's right and the other person's wrong—our personalities are a little bit different and that has caused differences . . . I have always felt a little bit more than Sue that there are some issues that cannot be resolved by peaceful means. Which I hate to admit. I hate to admit that because you're saying, "War is okay." But there are times in life when you have to put your foot down, take a stand and face the consequences. Sue agrees with that also. She's not a complete pacifist. In the Israeli situation it's a matter of degree—the degree to which we are willing to accept the way the Israeli government is behaving. So we have discussions about this and we take different views. And we keep at it. Because it's quite possible that I'll come round to her point of view or vice versa.

I've been thinking about, in anticipating this meeting with you, how do you explain it—a good relationship? There were three things that came to mind. Number one: You can sing with her. And I actually mean singing. And you could write a book about what that means. That we liked the same songs. On trips back and forth in the car our kids used to laugh because Sue and I used to sing. Secondly, you can laugh about things. And you laugh often. Life is a humorous, fantastic experience. A lot of it is just fun and . . . if you have two people who don't see it the same way, that's a problem. There's a lot of giggling and laughing. And, third, you can do the *New York Times* crossword together. I didn't discover that until relatively recently. What I mean is you can have an activity that's an intellectual exercise and meet it at the same level, which is very rare. I have a lot of people I like and a lot of people I'm friendly with who are smarter than I am or are beyond me in some small area but the thing Sue and I can do is we can commune with each other at an intellectual level over inconsequential things. Or consequential things. But doing the *New York Times* crossword together—I know a lot of people who do the crossword together but very rarely do they do it with a spouse. We do it together and we are very happy when either one of us can get a word. There is no competition whatsoever. There probably is competition in some things—she has her things and I have mine and we both have very busy schedules and occasionally they will compete.

One of the problems we have now is if and when we want to go to the beach house we have to sit down with our books weeks ahead just to draw a line through a week. We both love going up there. It's an adventure each time . . . We get there and we just breathe a sigh of relief because we're away and it's quiet and beautiful. And we spend the next week or whatever it is up there living unlike the way we live down here. Very open days—if we have work to do, we do have a computer up there and can e-mail, but it's at our beck and call. We like being together, doing ridiculous things, inconsequential stuff.

I retired a few years ago. I believe strongly in the fact that the old guy with the dead head should get out. I did that with all the people who were older than I am. I got rid of them at a certain age: sixty-five. And I said, "You don't have to go, you can sue me if you want to, but I feel like business flourishes better—no matter how good the old guy is—if you allow the young blood to rise." And, secondly, there were things I wanted to do, other things, lots of them.

I wanted to manifest my presence in the community. Instead of just being a name on a list I wanted to actually get involved in cultural activity. I was on boards and I was known and I was a financial supporter of things but I wanted to get into those activities the way I got into the business. My interests were in educational and artistic fields—music and theater. All locally. And Sue wanted to do this too. So it was joint, although we do it in different areas. She's into the historical things and museums. We decided together on where we want to invest our energies and money. There are institutions that needed to grow up, to change, to strengthen, and we've given time and money and energy to them.

Whenever we've given money, we've given it in the name of Bob and Sue Fox. I've wanted the community to feel that we were the ones, not me or she, but we were the ones doing this together. I had this dream in the back of my mind that if I do that and we do become known as a team, we will be treated as a team. So, in fact, just today we received a call from the head of the main library in the city and he wants us to chair jointly their annual charity ball. So they see us as Bob and Sue. That's how I see myself at this stage of life.

I could not live the single life. I haven't the slightest bit of use for it. It is teamwork and it is companionship and sharing. "Sharing" is one of the words I use a lot. If you can't share, go away, because I'm only interested in sharing.

I think as separate people we both believe in romance, but I think I do more than she does. It comes out in little surprises. Occasionally just a hug. Driving up to the beach house singing. It takes a variety of different forms. I think we both appreciate that a lot of the things, when I look back, that were heavy, if we didn't have each other, it would have been practically impossible.

At my seventieth birthday Sue put on a party. She paraded out a theaterful—it was held at a theater in the city—of people that represented all the community groups I was involved with. Our kids were there. I don't think they had any idea of our involvement and recognition. I think they may have known it intellectually but not emotionally. We don't go out of our way to tell our kids what we do here in the city. But they were sat down like they were on display in the front row of this theater and I was up on the stage and all these myriad performers came out to pay homage to me. I wasn't particularly comfortable about it, but it was something, really. And then we went out to a restaurant. Sue did this all, and it was a surprise. A total surprise . . . I'm telling you, if I had a weak heart . . .

Sue and I didn't have much of a life together before we had kids and now we're having our life as a couple. We have a right to that. We're still in good shape, still involved in a lot of things. I play two vigorous games of tennis a week, we sail a lot. And our kids—we're still close to them. David—the second boy—he's the closest thing to the role my brother had in my life. I wrote him a letter a few weeks ago telling him that he was too goddamned busy; he should get off some boards or something because now is the time of life we should enjoy one another's company! He was very appreciative. He's started a business—there are a lot of commonalities . . .

I am more of a risk taker than Sue. She has come to appreciate it . . . I think both of us have gotten more trusting at doing things that may seem like a whim, or going along with the other. I had a plan for her seventieth birthday because she gave me this fantastic party . . . So I planned this huge thing where we were going to visit her old house where she grew up, her old school, her college, her graduate school, and as I got into this plan I sort of dropped a few hints to make sure this was going to be well received. And it wasn't. So I gradually backed off on doing that and said, "Well, we can have dinner in the same restaurant where our folks tried to tell us not to get married and there are other things like that." So we did that.

If I'd done that original birthday thing for her, we would get there and she would say, "Why in the hell did you do this?" or maybe she would have been nice and not said so. Knowing her, she probably would have said so. So that's one of the things that you get better at. If you're paying attention.

Over the years when we'd have these fights and I would go away mumbling to myself, "Jesus Christ!"—those sort of things lasted, like, five minutes. But during that time, of course, it occurred to me, "I could leave her! I could have a different life!" But there was never a protracted period when I seriously held that notion—and I'm sure she had the same. I'd come back from that horrible moment by realizing I had gone too far, that I was not serious about this and that I had allowed my emotions to run away with me. And I would put my arm around her, and sometimes I would say I was sorry, though sometimes I wouldn't have to say I'm sorry. It would just be obvious. It works exactly the same in both ways—she does the same . . . We both realize that we have to get along. That it was an unpleasant, short interval and that we can move on. Pretty much now when we're having a disagreement like that—we still have them—we both realize that there's something much more powerful in staying.

We're engaged with each other by the start of the day, when we get the papers—when I get the paper and make the coffee and I get back in bed and dump the two papers on the bed between us. By then she's awake and she's sitting up and we sit there, the first hour and a half of our day is spent reading the *Times* and the local city paper and sharing from the editorial page. If I'd been smart, I'd have had a tape recorder on our bed for the last thirty years. I'd bet you that that would make the most fascinating political, social, community conversations. We have the most fantastic intellectual discussions about the Middle East, and the Catholic Church, and local politics . . .

We don't talk in detail about our emotions, though. I'm not good at that. Sue is better at that. I feel restraint is a major tool to be used often in personal relationships. Sue almost always feels "say whatever you mean." That is something we have differing opinions about. I've gotten through a lot of things more easily by keeping my mouth shut in certain situations. She feels that I just get into trouble that way but I feel sometimes she gets into trouble by talking when she should have kept her mouth shut. It's true about our interactions to an extent, but not so much now . . . I don't know if it's a gender thing or an individual thing. I think we are conscious of the fact that . . . that there are certain things we could say that would wound the other person and we don't want to do that. I think we're consciously trying not to use certain weapons, like having ground rules.

I think you have to have that crazy feeling for a relationship to last but also you have to do your homework. You have to really think about it and understand that this is something very special, unique, rare, pleasant, wonderful. A kind of miracle. You have to be able to enjoy it but to be able to properly place where this thing is in your priorities. For me it is number one. If you stop thinking that, if you start thinking, "Nah, I'll get around to this or that eventually," that's not good . . . I was right to think we'd have our time together. It is terrific. At our fiftieth-wedding-anniversary party, which we had at the beach house, my sister-in-law, the wife of my brother who died, came up to me and she said, "Bob, you have to know you're lucky." And it's true. I'm one of the luckiest guys—in business, in family, in my relationship . . . Good things have happened to me, but it's really a matter of perception. It's how you perceive things, as good or not good. It's something you can decide. You can think, "No matter how much I have, I want more." Or you can think you're incredibly lucky and happy to have what you've got.

2

The Time Line of Love: Remembering Positives, Past, Present, and Future

DEBBIE and JIMMY GOLD

WHAT HAPPENS WHEN the heroic love story hits the proverbial bump in the road? What keeps successful couples from leaving each other? Perhaps the crucial difference between those who stay and those who go is perspective. People who stay happily tend to frame present resentments, frustrations, distress, sadness, or anger within a perspective that includes the past and projects into the future they want—that is, to take a long view of the relationship. When in the grip of anger or desperation, summoning up a memory, a feeling, or an image of when things were not like that is crucial for intending to go on together. Getting a balance of past, present, and future is a gift, or skill, for being happy in life, in general.[7]

The happy relationship story, as we will see, integrates past pleasures, past episodes of safety and security, and past events that opened up flexibility and growth for both partners. Happy couples also tell stories that extend into the future by mentioning or implying plans and expectations. In contrast, disengaged couples tend not to look before or beyond present distress. Rather than view a current frustration within the context of a long, happy life together, these couples use failures of the moment to feed negative expectations and to serve as reminders that they have not mastered the art of happiness together.

Prior research on hardy, happy couples has found that they look on arguments or issues that keep recurring as inevitable.[8] They accept that there will be recurring differences or dilemmas that present them with the opportunity to learn a bit more each time they occur, rather than be fixed once and for all. They draw on the past during present distress to learn more about each other and expect the future to provide greater opportunities for understanding.

> When we have difficult moments I remind myself that our relationship is cyclical, or, more aptly, helical. We come back to places of conflict or tension and recognize them: we start to know how to approach them and deal with them and the cycle is broken and we move on, as in a helix upward toward the next cycle. For us, recognizing these patterns and realizing it is not the end, but a situation awaiting resolution, has been a real help in dealing with any misunderstanding. I remind myself, "I often feel like this if I'm stressed," or "It's just how Rich deals with his pressure of work," and so that helps redefine the situation as less serious and something to be worked at and remembered.—**Leah Banks, 34**

Moreover, happy couples are "proactive"—they create the positives; they fit themselves to the situations rather than expect the situations to change to suit them. In one moving story I heard, the wife suffered from extreme shyness while the husband was handicapped by having only one lung. But rather than finding his wife's shyness crippling, her husband embraced it as a shared challenge. Instead of finding the single lung a hindrance, each remarked that they have discovered that living with one lung is surprisingly easy. Neither had a sense of entitlement to another kind of life or to easier circumstances, or expected the other to be the one to make changes—an expectation often voiced by estranged couples. Each has fitted to the circumstances and reframed negatives as opportunities, discoveries, or challenges. In this way each has grown individually, as has the power of their relationship. The husband boasts, "Our love for each other prevails . . . My wife makes my partnership special. She tells me she loves me every day, always has time to listen to my moans and groans, and cooks supreme meals. My marriage is special because my wife is my best friend, a wonderful lover, a superb cook, my confidante . . . What more could I want in life?"

Highlighting positive details above less-affirming ones helps maintain a perspective, or state of mind, that values being "loving," or generous, toward each other. Maintaining this disposition steers couples' thinking positively about events that can affect, rock, or threaten to displace their relationships.

> Our eldest child's mental development has not been normal. It seems to have been caused by a defect before birth. Although not severe, she has been a very late developer and consequently it has been challenging . . . Had our marriage not been such a good one, I can imagine a child with disruptive behavior, as we experienced, being the cause of a breakdown . . . We also had twins, who were three years younger. Life with the three children in those early years really was difficult for me . . . We had no proper help or advice and no useful relations near at hand. But my husband was a rock to lean on and was always willing to play his part fully . . . I could not have managed without him.—**Suzanne Brightman, 58**

A joint history of feelings and events is like a shared memory bank. Divorcing couples find it keenly painful to leave behind that history of shared jokes, vacations, and triumphs. When my best childhood friend died at twenty-six, one of the poignant losses was not being able to recall things with her, to verify the odd, often blurry, details of our childhood selves, of things only she and I would know. Only she had heard my nightly telephone rants about my "unreasonable" mother or "hurtful" friends, and only I would have remembered hers. When couples divorce, dividing photos can be more painful than divvying up the silver. When they split, each partner carts away his or her own shoal of memories. If they plundered it together again it would produce unbearable sadness. Quiet, ongoing pleasure and joy can come from staying together and sharing seminal events, enterprises, and emotions. Gardening, for instance, is one shared activity mentioned by a number of interviewees, a convenient metaphor for continuity, regrowth, and change together.

> Through hard work we restored a semi-derelict farmhouse in the remote part of the Welsh Borders. Living conditions were awful at times; no heating, no proper kitchen, dust and dirt, which drove me mad at times. I kept my sanity by gathering animals around me: rearing calves, keeping a small flock of sheep, rearing Tamworth pigs, ducks, chickens, and helping when I could with the building project on farmhouse outbuildings . . . It was worth the struggle *together.*—**Claire Hoxton, 56**

And, of course, a shared history projects toward a shared future, the past being the best predictor of the future.

Debbie and Jimmy Gold

Debbie Gold is an artist and journalist, her husband, Jimmy Gold, an endocrinologist. Jimmy, a lanky, soft-spoken, thoughtful man, is forty-nine while Debbie, bubbly, with wild, flowing hair and a dancer's way of moving, is forty-eight. A youthful-feeling, attractive couple, they live, with their two teenagers and a large, energetic dog, in Brookline, just on the edge of Boston. Their rambling house is cluttered with photographs of family and from some of Debbie's favorite journalistic assignments; their entryway is filled with bikes and skates belonging to them and their children. Debbie is high-energy and warm, while Jimmy is quieter, welcoming, and a calm and dignified presence. Their life is lived at full tilt, with phones ringing and activities humming around them.

Amid this activity, Debbie alludes again and again to how "good" a person Jimmy is; she reminds herself that one of the continual struggles they have had over their life together—that is, the fact that he is routinely overworked and overstretched—itself stems from his conscientiousness and ethical professionalism. Jimmy's account returns often to the theme that the demands his mother has made have impinged on his partnership and hurt Debbie: his delicate concern for his mother's feelings seems pitted against his admiration and adoration of Debbie, and Debbie continues to nurse the hurt and anger she feels from his mother's behavior toward her. Neither of the dramas told in each story ends neatly; this couple picks at them, like a bone, as they recur, gaining a bit more insight each time, as they say. Their story is one of gentle acceptance of each other. It highlights how each attributes positive motives to the other, even in the face of the same frustrations. Their tales are not Pollyannaish, yet, within the strains each separate narrator manages to communicate a perspective that happiness has been theirs, and it is likely to continue.

Debbie Gold:

We got married in 1980. I always get mixed up about whether it's '79 or '80. But we were together from, I think, '76. My parents, and his, were children of immigrants—first-generation American Jews . . . My mother's still alive; she's eighty-one. My father died when he was sixty-eight, about twelve years ago . . . They stayed married. Jimmy's parents are both still alive. His mother comes from a family, very vain, where nobody knows anyone's age—and they've both had facelifts! I'm not kidding. But we think he's about eighty-two and she's about eighty-five. They've been married a long time. Forever. Intact marriages—everyone. My sister's married with two kids, and her kids are also married. All those photos out in the hallway . . . Jimmy's an only child. But he grew up with all these cousins. His mother had four siblings and everyone's died except for one aunt who's ninety-five. She can travel alone— she's in better shape than I am. She humbles me . . . And our kids are fifteen and nineteen.

Jimmy's parents have a good marriage, but it depends on what the definition of "good" is. They love each other. You know, his mother had a stroke about seven years ago—I kind of joke about it—she's a very difficult woman and it's almost like that part of her stroked out, and she's a much nicer person now. She really did not like me from the get-go . . . She did not like me before she even knew me! I wasn't from the stock she wanted for her son—upper-middle-class stock. I came from a middle-class family . . . My parents were totally—I mean they probably had a lot more money, when it came down to it, than Jimmy's parents, but they were very nonmaterialistic.

I would say that my parents had a good marriage but they fought a lot and my mother was more of the subservient nurturer—very loving, warm, but not very strong—and my father was very much the patriarch of the family. My mother was suffocated by my father in many ways . . . He went to Brooklyn College in New York, an intellectual from the 1940s . . . he was a very interesting character. I've carried on a lot of his characteristics. Sometimes it worries me . . . The reason my father went into children's toys was that he couldn't sit in an office. He had to be traveling around and fiddling—he had so many hobbies. He was good at his job, which is amazing to me. He was a good salesman because he got along with these manufacturers so well. He was a very good provider.

I grew up with a real work ethic; I was working when I was fourteen years old. I lived in a fancy neighborhood—everybody had Cadillacs and house-keepers—but my family had a Pontiac and my father couldn't care less about clothes.

My mother didn't work. She did not go to college—she wanted to but couldn't. She wanted to be a dentist, my mother. We don't understand that one! My mother was very quiet. Her parents didn't have a good marriage—her father had a girlfriend on the side and he died at about fifty—and my mother knew that. They had a marriage and they stayed together, but they fought a lot. My mother and sister were much closer and they even look alike. Now, though, I'm very close to my mother, I mean she relies on me for everything. But I always maintained boundaries whereas my sister didn't. I was much more independent than my sister from the word "go."

It was weird because I was always, till I met Jimmy's parents, the kind of girl that the mothers liked. With Jimmy's parents, I had to be checked out by Cousin Ruthie from Scarsdale—the rich one, with the mink coat and just the right kind of silverware, and car, and house—whose values I wasn't too crazy about. His mother was a "fancy lady," you know? It's just that they didn't have the money. But they wanted elegance and "good taste"—materialistic things. My family is much more down-home, really mundane almost. When I breast-fed my kids, his cousins and aunts and mother would say, "How can you breast-feed? Your boobs are going to sag!" So Jimmy and I have become kind of the outcasts of his family, the "bohemians."

What I respect about his mother is she's a woman of her word; she's a strong female and so there are positive things about her. But she also wasn't nice to my parents. So even after my father died and she tried to be nice to me, I guess I never really forgave her for not being nice to my parents . . . Jimmy likes good things—he buys Italian suits and shoes . . . But his values are in the right place. I mean, he doesn't have to have things—and he won't buy anything for himself if he knows we're pulling in our belts. He's not materialistic, but he does have good taste. I respect that in him. His mother has good taste too. She does have some strong points, as opinionated and close-minded as she can be . . .

I wanted to go to Smith College, but I went to the state university because it was cheap, which was actually a great place to be at the time, with great scholars and a really activist atmosphere. It was just after Cambodia, Vietnam, all that when I started. I got enough of the Vietnam stuff to be politicized. Jimmy went to the same university, but he had just left when I started. We didn't meet till afterward.

I went to college for four years and in my senior year I didn't know what the hell I was doing: "Do I want to go to medical school? Do I want to be a doctor?" So, this is amazing: I was a biology and psychology major and one of my roommates was studying nursing and I said, "Well, maybe I'll be a nurse." I had no idea what nursing was about. So I started taking nursing classes, and I said, "This is a good way of life . . . until I decide what I want to do." So I went to Columbia for the summer and I took a whole bunch of courses in nursing and because I was a biology major, I had every science that you needed and I graduated six months later. And then I did nursing.

I actually became a head nurse within two months. And I was very political and here I was in this all-girls environment . . . it was fertile for feminism. It was a fascinating time in my life. I took up cross-country skiing then, and also found out a lot about the history of the city my university was in. That was a good year for me.

Then I moved back to New Jersey and got a job at a teaching hospital near where I grew up. I almost took another job but my father said I shouldn't—there were safety issues in it. He was a "safety" person—we had to have fire drills, I mean, when we were growing up. He would never have worked in the World Trade Center. He never, ever would have . . . It's interesting because my fifteen-year-old's reaction to the World Trade Center, her first reaction when she came home was, "They should have had parachutes on the roofs there." She said at least then they would have had a chance of escaping. "And every five floors," she said, "they should have had walkways between buildings for an outdoor escape." And then she said, "They should have had trampolines for people who had to jump out of the windows."

Anyway, I got a job at that teaching hospital and went back and did a master's at Columbia at the same time in public health. I was twenty-three and I was still with my college boyfriend, Peter, who I loved a lot. I met Jimmy during that time. He was a resident . . . I was head nurse and I had to deal with the doctors and I was also on these committees where I sat with doctors . . . so when Jimmy rotated through my floor I would have to be taking orders, asking questions, and somehow in our conversation—he was quiet and very professional, not at all flirtatious, and I didn't date people at the hospital, even if Peter hadn't been around—we found out we'd both been to the same university. So we both had the same reaction—excited; we both still have friends from our college days.

We began having lunch together. Peter was in medical school not far away at the time. I didn't think this relationship with Jimmy was going to go anywhere, but it was. It was starting to get—well, we were getting titillated with each other at work, which, remember, I said I'm not letting that happen at work . . . So we started having lunch more often and I found myself starting to think about him more and more and then we started seeing each other, so I was seeing him really behind the other one's back, which—I feel so guilty when I talk about this. I still feel like I totally betrayed somebody by doing this. It came to a head. I was making all sorts of decisions then, I mean not just men . . .

It was really at a point when I knew I had to let Peter go. And I loved, him, you know. I just knew he wasn't right for me. He was much more of an eccentric . . . he was in medical school but he was an artist. He was difficult in some ways and Jimmy was not that. Jimmy was very easygoing and very easy. Peter really took me from being kind of middle class, uninteresting, cloistered, you know, not having done very much in my life before college. He was one of those kids who at thirteen or fourteen was down in Greenwich Village playing guitar. He was a musician. So he got me into the Village and that kind of life. My world started opening up through him. He was instrumental in changing my life . . . sexually, everything. At college, too, he was a big deal. He was one of those people who got up in front of thousands of people. He was part of the march on Washington, getting people to go, very political. I learned all different ways of looking at the world that you don't get from growing up in this little middle-middle-class suburb.

But Jimmy was more centered. He was more my soul mate. I kind of knew that immediately. I was immediately attracted to Jimmy . . . Although there was someone else—Jimmy's chief resident . . . we had a little flirtatious thing going.

But Jimmy did somehow win out, even though I had this rule, and I didn't go out with his chief resident. Jimmy is very tender and he's lovable on many levels. The first time we got together we went to a park and sat down and I think he told me about some book he'd just read, so I read it. And we sat and talked about it and he told some stories and I loved the way he told stories. I was mesmerized by his storytelling and still am. I'm still mad about him. He's a really good person. I respect him. He is one of the most honest people I know. So he was really uncomfortable with this secretiveness. I was holding him on a rope too. I wasn't giving him any kind of commitment. Here I was, kind of playing the middle, because I was a coward in terms of letting Peter go, because I still loved him in some ways and I didn't want to hurt him. I was so involved with his family too, I mean his family loved me. Not like Jimmy's!

I can't remember the exact time when I finally told Peter I was seeing someone. I think it was maybe a year. I would go to Jimmy's apartment, or we would go for dinner, when Peter wasn't around, because he was nearby and that's what made it tough. At this point he was more sure of me than I was of him. I drove him crazy. He told me. It went on too long.

But I think I knew from the beginning it would be Jimmy. I always feel like you kind of know it from the beginning. It's like soup in a restaurant: you get great soup, you know it's an indicator; if you get terrible soup, it's not going to be such a good meal!

When I did finally break up with Peter, Jimmy and I didn't move in together. I'd stay weekends and in my own place during the week.

It was when we took a trip to Guatemala together, that's when it happened for me: that's when I knew I was going to spend the rest of my life with him, and we decided to get married. That was probably a year and a half later. We decided we were going to get married and run off somewhere. We weren't engaged. We just decided to get married and we did, six months later. I fell in love harder with him in Guatemala. I guess before that I had some ambivalence because of Peter. How do you go from loving someone that you've been with for so long and you have so much history with and what you're feeling—is it right? I don't know whether I've ever really thought about it, but I know that trip, the fact that I made it, the fact that I wanted to do it with him . . . Well I just loved Guatemala and being there with him. He had been to Central America already with friends who went to where the Beatles went up to the mountains where there were magic mushrooms . . . We flew there and rented a car and did, like, a cross-country trip, and he knew Spanish somewhat and got us out of a lot of messes we were in.

And then I got majorly sick—like I almost had to be flown home—and he took care of me. I think I had food poisoning from eating chicken on the beach. It was like a Fellini movie: there we were on the beach, eating, and these animals came by. In the middle of nowhere and this entourage of animals, like in a circus . . . And I got so sick!

Then we decided we were getting married. So . . . that's what we did. We went to Nantucket for our honeymoon. Then we spent the whole summer traveling because that's when he finished his training . . .

We moved to Pennsylvania and I was still completing my master's. It was crazy and I didn't like being in the rural, or sort of suburbs, place where we were. It was a nice area, but not for us . . . He was working a lot. I mean there was a lot of work time that I wasn't used to when I had to be alone. It's where I started fooling around with journalism and art; it was such a beautiful area. It was always just a hobby for me, and it began to grow, so now it's my job, but that's where it started. We took up sailing because we were near water, and we did that together every day, and we watched the sunset everyday. He had a great job, with a great group, with great hospitals. It probably would have been fine if we'd had kids then. But we weren't really happy there. We wanted to be back in a city, so Jimmy looked for jobs in cities and we ended up in Boston.

That was great—we lived in downtown Boston and had our first kid there, and he loved the neighbourhood—but Jimmy took the job that's been our biggest problem since. That's been the biggest problem in our marriage, this practice he joined.

That and, I guess, his parents. And you know, I don't think they ever really cared about me. And I know that. So I'm not one of those who dotes on them and calls every week. It bothers Jimmy. He is just so good-natured.

He understands my side. He understands . . . he would love me to move, to shift, sometimes. You know, sometimes I'm more generous about them; I know they're getting older . . . And Jimmy knows his mother is very difficult, even though she's his mother. But, you know, the guilt that we should be seeing them more is bad. If he doesn't call them once a week, you know they come down on him, like, "How come we don't see you?" when we just saw them the weekend before.

When Jimmy was looking for jobs to get out of Pennsylvania, he almost took an academic position in New York. He would be a great teacher—that's really his forte. Not that he's not a great clinician, but if he had to explain something to you, like anthrax, you'd quickly understand it. But he went for this other interview, which turned him onto this private practice, and that's the private practice he ultimately joined and that's really been the biggest problem in our marriage. Because the people in his medical practice are not good people, they're not good people at all, and not conscientious doctors and not as good a doctor as he is, and Jimmy is such a good person that even in his practice he's had to compromise a lot of stuff . . .

It's gotten in the way for us in a very big thing in our life: because of his sense of duty and commitment, he works all the time, and he wasn't around enough, even the time when my father died or when he was coming to the hospital to pick me up when our first child was born—you know he was supposed to come at ten, but he didn't till four because he had to work and I had tears in my eyes when he came. But on the other hand I do know that he tried to assert himself then and he couldn't help it.

And he wasn't around when my father died. He was busy working. I resented it a little. I thought he was in the middle again. He was pulled. He's always in the middle, even with me and his parents. But I took his part then. So rather than being angry with him, I take his part and it tempers my anger . . . I have had to deal with a lot of stresses myself . . . But that probably has made me into a stronger person. I think I'm kind of the emotional anchor. But Jimmy's much steadier than me, so I should qualify that. I defer to him for more steady stuff. He's very good at consultation. I trust him. He's so steady and stable and has such a good take on things.

Because he is so fair and patient, he is in this bind at his work, and also he feels he can't let down his patients when the others are letting them down— you know, like, Jimmy is the high-integrity person in the practice. He hasn't been able to stand up to these people, and I understand it, because they are not trustworthy. Having a practice is like being married to someone . . . But he's pulled through all these years, and they've been together for about twenty years. Jimmy had thought when they interviewed him that he should have the security to know he can go off and have his own practice. But doctors who start their own practices are very different from doctors who join practices. To start a practice you have to be much more of a businessman, aggressive, know how to wheel and deal—you know, it's a business. So, he joined a practice because he knew he couldn't do that on his own. He wasn't that kind of a person. It's just unfortunate he joined up with people like them.

Jimmy is not the kind of person who is confrontational. We've had to give up weekends, vacations, because of things his partner, one in particular, the senior one, has done. Jimmy has much more power than he knows—he's very humble and self-deprecating and doesn't realize who he is. So we have different positions. Mine is "you have a lot more power than you think you do." I have made it clear to him that I would give up the money, move to a smaller place, downsize to get rid of that particular "evil partner" from our life!

I know I want to go for the jugular every time this partner does something. Like, he . . . gives himself two [extra] days off a week because he works at the hospital. Now, they all work for the hospital but he always had an extra day off a week, which was outrageous to begin with, and then he takes Fridays off too. Now Mondays and Fridays are the busiest days in the hospital. Plus, he's not a good doctor . . . Jimmy has certain principles and will go over the medicines for every patient every day. This guy never does it because he knows Jimmy is going to pick up the slack for him. So that's where Jimmy and I differ. I am a much more confrontational person. I don't let shit go down as much as he does. He tells me all this stuff because we're very close and I kind of pump information from him. It's almost like I have to hear this so I can say, "He's doing that again!" I guess sometimes Jimmy feels bad when I do this.

Other times he knows, he thinks, it's something he wants to change in himself. So if I know he feels bad about something, it's almost like it's defused and we can work on it together. But if I feel like he's taking this garbage from that guy and not fighting back . . . I get angry with Jimmy, but I know it's displaced anger. Like I wish I could be the one saying something to his partner! And now he has two partners like this—one who started out okay but has become more corrupt over the years!

And also he doesn't want to risk . . . changing things . . . He's the main provider. That's the most important thing to him, that he's a provider for his family. I think he's kind of amazed how successful he's been. I mean, I help, but I mainly am only providing our vacations and our perks, because it's only in the past few years I've really begun working a lot. I am beginning to do well. So that he's been the main earner is the reality.

And you know, he didn't help me that much when we were younger, and it all comes back to that partner: he would be demanding so much of Jimmy's time. I essentially had the kids on my own a lot—Jimmy had to work weekends. So that's why I couldn't work a full-time job. That was my work—I had to keep the house running. So maybe I had some resentments from that. But then it was similar to now: my resentments were to that partner, not to Jimmy.

We didn't plan for when we had the kids—in fact, I was up for a really good job and found out I was pregnant during that interviewing process. It was in public health. I didn't take it. I became, like, a professional mother. I had an amazing support group, because everyone I knew was having kids. You're not bored when you live in a city. There's always something to do . . . I did more art and some beginning journalism . . . I started doing more and more community stuff, and writing that up, and then we had a close friend who's an artist and he wanted me to write some stuff up for him, and I said, "I'm not a professional," and he said, "You can do this." At that point I needed to be validated . . . I began to get some freelance assignments mostly when the kids were finally in school.

The conflicts don't occur that often. That tells me a lot—that there's not much for us to fight about. It only comes out when something outrageous happens—maybe a few times a month. Sometimes all I say is, "I can't believe he's doing this." And maybe sometimes Jimmy will hold back from telling me things. We're pretty good fighters with each other, though. Jimmy gets sarcastic, not mean or angry. I know his style. I'm more emotional. We recently witnessed a fight with my sister and her husband and I saw how, in contrast, Jimmy and I have very reasonable fights with each other! They're usually pretty honest and "on-topic." And, anyway, we both hate that partner. It's not like we're fighting about someone he loves and I hate!

Our arguments can be constructive—there are ground rules because we respect each other. We come out of our arguments feeling somewhat satisfied afterward. The same argument, again and again, about this partner and the practice, and it feels like we've done a little bit of work on it each time. It's still there. This man is still in our life. It's just that it always has to be expressed when he does something wrong, because it's almost like I have to, and I think we both accept that.

Taking his part tempers my anger and then it makes it go away so I don't have any grudges. Although, I will never forget sitting and waiting for him when our first child was born, and when my father was dying and he wasn't there to be with me. I remember these things but I don't have a grudge.

But we are very different—I have to try to back off and try to understand how he isn't like me, and accept this. I have to get everything out . . . He lets me do that. He lets me be that. We have different neuroses. He agonizes, like, if he thinks he made a mistake in medicine—so I'm always the person he'll go over the whole case with, because I know what he's talking about. And I'll be honest with him if I think he really messed up somewhere, because he'll know if I'm just trying to make him feel better. For the most part, he's truly—he shouldn't feel bad about things. He sees the bigger picture, like now, that he's gotten a better lifestyle, with more people working so he doesn't have night call when he used to. But there are still inequities about how much work is done . . .

In the cold light of day we both think about the other person's point of view, even if we might have felt upset. I see us as a bond. I see us as being a permanent bond. I see nothing breaking that permanent bond.

In the last year [since the older child has been gone and the younger one is now a teenager] it's different. I think the percentage of time alone together has changed . . . You know, we'll go out to dinner, just the two of us, now . . . I have a very big social life myself, apart from Jimmy. I have all these things going on in my life and I'm not sure he doesn't need me to be so social—he works so much. I have two reading groups going on, I have friends who come over all the time; I meet this one for lunch one day, that one in between assignments working . . . I'm just more social than Jimmy is.

We also do dinner. You know we have this family—the idea that we as a family always have dinner together. And Jimmy would be coming home at nine or ten o'clock and people would call up and I'd say, "We're eating." And people would say, "Oh, the Golds—they eat dinner at eleven o'clock at night!" We always waited for Jimmy for dinner. The kids would have to snack beforehand.

Now that our older child is away, it's hard; he's going through separation because we were so close. Sometimes he just attacks me. I get angry with him but he's also incredibly sweet-natured and I never forget that. It blows over. Because Jimmy's been the worker bee, I'm the person the kids will call and ask for things. I know this venting, this attack, is something he has to do. But he never attacks Jimmy—they're best friends. Jimmy minds his business when my son and I have this—he knows it's between the two of us. I tell him about it. I need to spill; I can't hold it in!

But we have got friends we see together at our weekend house. When we go there we see people, but we don't always. We don't have to see people. We have the choice. . . . Every evening we usually end up on the couch at night now, which we never used to do—he's not a TV person at all. He's a major music, jazz, person. So most of the time he used to read and listen to jazz. But it's changed and now I'm usually on the couch watching *Charlie Rose*, *Nightline*, and he's been joining me on the couch. So now we snuggle on the couch; we're more physical at night than we have been . . .

But we have one day off a week and that's usually our time together. I never do anything on that day except with Jimmy. It's usually Wednesdays—that's our day together. We can eat out, or we can be physical together, we can go out and see a movie, go to a play. We go for lunch. This woman's just asked me to work on Wednesday and I won't: Wednesdays are out. It's "Jimmy Day." Also, every weekend we're together, though often the kids have been with us on that, and we do see friends then too.

A lot of what I've been talking about in the problem of the job, I need to point out, is that he is principled, as a doctor—he feels he must be there, working, doing the right thing as a doctor for his patients and not burdening another doctor by not being there . . . He is a good doctor and he has a job that he takes very seriously . . . I remember these important things about him and how principled he is, and how good a person he is . . . I see nothing breaking that bond. I don't lose the past and the future.

We're very touchy—we touch each other a lot. I'm very tactile. He is too. It's always been that way. He'll zone out sometimes and I'll know it's because he's thinking about work, and I respect that. But when he zones out I'll go, "Hello? Are you here?" And he comes back.

I think at this point he wants sex more than I do. I'm in a reading group with about twelve women and we joke about it, that it's like, we're all that way now—we were talking about the book *Colette*, which is a very sexy book, and all we wanted to talk about was menopause and men!

But Jimmy still feels the way he did about my body in the beginning. He makes me embarrassed because I don't feel that way about myself. I'm definitely in the last couple of years going through something where I feel like I'm over the hill . . . He's still attracted to me like he was, you know . . . I don't know how! I looked a lot better then!

I don't think sex now is as important to me as to him. But we are physical with each other. Like on the couch every night.

I always liked sex. I wasn't ever . . . you know, this isn't something I've ever spoken, even to women, about. I'm an orgasm person! It was great. I like reaching orgasm with a man together. And we have that. To me that's an almost symbolic union: we have perfection. And usually, if that can't happen, there's a reason. There's some distraction or something. You know he wants to please me and I want to please him. There's still that feeling in our sexual life: it's not just about me and it's not just about him; I'll wait for you, you wait for me. The only thing that's changed over the years is the frequency. As I said, he would like it more often. And, you know, I'm too tired. Sometimes it's almost, or seems almost, like work, which it shouldn't be. The day he's off, that's why it's perfect: we're wide awake, it's not at night when we're tired, and you'd just rather curl up with a book or something else. And I tell him it's not personal. You know, for a while I think he was taking it personally.

I think through a marriage there's always the idea of having another sex partner in your life, you know, just for sex. Just to have stayed with one person your whole life is pretty amazing. So that becomes your fantasy. I'm sure he has had that, and I've had that too. But there are times when I've had no sexuality at all. I think I'm like ground zero for sex. My girlfriend called the other day and said that and I told her that sometimes I'm like that too. You know, even walking past an attractive person on the street doesn't do anything to me. Whereas the other day when I was with this friend, and this guy was next to us and was really attractive, and I said, "Mmmm!!!" I wouldn't do anything, though!

Jimmy and I do flirt. When I was younger I took it, if he stared at another woman, I took it a little more personally. But not for a long time. Becoming monogamous was never an issue. But I do remember in the beginning thinking, "The same person for the rest of my life?" I do remember being a little scared of that. But, you know, the time has gone so fast. I guess I didn't miss anything. You live through it in other ways . . . your fantasy, you read novels.

We've talked about this, but he just says he fantasizes about me! Probably because I've kept myself from him too much! This menopause—I think I'm beginning it—my sex drive has been really low.

Through the years it's been like—we share so much. We talk when he's at work and we always do dinner—even if it's really late. We share everything. I don't think there's anything—well, maybe some secret little stuff, but that's normal. But in terms of our lives, we share everything. Our children—the deepest—medicine, my journalism and art. He shares my excitement over work and I share his.

Jimmy Gold:

Before I met Debbie I had never felt that way about anyone. I'd had girlfriends in college but I never felt I was in love with any of them. When I met Debbie it was really something completely different.

I grew up an only child, with a lot of uncles and aunts who lived nearby. My parents owned a shop. My father went to college but didn't finish. My mother had a sister who lived in a much richer, more successful style, and my mother very much admired that. This aunt set a lot of the family values. We got together with the family a lot on weekends, and I had cousins who were my age, so it wasn't like I was a classic only child. But I was a pretty lonely child, probably a lot because of where I lived and went to school—I also had a stutter. My parents were good people but I don't think they completely understood what I felt. I didn't fit in with the kids who lived near me and went to my school, because they were mostly much rougher.

We had an apartment, and my father's shop was downstairs. Where we lived was a small city, near New York, mainly lower- and middle-class residents. I was the only Jew in my elementary school, but then after that my parents sent me to a Jewish school, where I also didn't fit in because we weren't very observant, though I did make some more friends during that time. I wasn't particularly athletic, but I wasn't bad. Now I play tennis and do sports quite a bit, in fact.

It wasn't till I went to college—a state university—that I began to feel that I fit in. My stutter pretty much went then. I had a girlfriend at college who I was with for a few years but I didn't really think I was in love with her.

In fact, I knew that she wanted it to go further: when I met her parents it was like, what are your plans? I knew that I wasn't going to marry her . . . but we were together for a few years. Then I went to med school, though I spent one semester at dental school first—a mistake, and I applied to med school and got in, thankfully. I dated, and had girlfriends during that time.

I was a resident at the hospital where Debbie was a nurse. I was attracted to her but she had a boyfriend. I asked her if she wanted to get together on a number of occasions and each time I felt she, on the one hand, said, "no," but on the other, left the door open a little bit. It was never, "I'm sorry, I have a boyfriend, I cannot." I asked several times and each time I felt like there was some opening but the end result was always "no." So finally I remember telling her that I don't want to embarrass myself anymore by asking her if she's interested: "you bring it up to me." And she was like the hospital queen—everyone was after her. She used to wear these really short skirts that were of that time, not shorter than other girls' skirts, and she had long hair, and I was really attracted to her. I remember one day I was standing in the hallway and she was talking to a family and I was walking by. And she interrupted her conversation to say, "Just wait a minute, I want to have a word with you." And she came over and said she'd like to get together.

She continued to have a boyfriend. I have to admit that at first I had a snooty attitude. "Snooty" is not the right word. "Arrogant." I didn't think she'd be the one for me because she was a nurse. That goes back to my family: they didn't have the money but they did have the aspirations. We had a very close-knit extended family, and the head of it was this aunt who lived in Scarsdale, and she and my mother, they just used to shop at Lord and Taylor . . . And her son, who died tragically young in a bike accident—my cousin, who I'd really looked up to when we were growing up—was at an Ivy League college and all that. That's what I'd been brought up like. This was about class.

I wasn't sure, personality-wise, if we were going to mesh in the very beginning when I didn't really know her. After a short time, though, I remember she was sitting in my apartment and the light hit her in a certain way and she was smoking a cigarette, as she used to do, and she was saying something and it just hit me, "My God, I'm in love with her!" I thought she was beautiful and from what she was saying I realized, "What's the difference what she does, what I do: We are soul mates. What were you thinking?"

Then, when I fell in love with her, I became infatuated to the point of distraction and this issue of her having another boyfriend became a real horror for me. I remember being in a clinic at the hospital looking in someone's eyes with the ophthalmoscope and thinking of her. I couldn't get her out of my mind. It was torture! It took a long, long time for her to break away from him and it was with the understanding that she would commit herself to me. I thought she was moving in that direction while we were together and I hoped she was but I couldn't be sure. This lasted an interminable amount of time! There was a period when the frequency of our seeing each other went down just after she broke up with him, because that was so disruptive. But then it began to slowly increase and we went to Guatemala for a few weeks and we had a great time. I'd asked her to marry me before we left. I was clear.

When I told my parents that's who I wanted to marry, I got a lot of flack from them, or, really, my mother. Because she was a nurse—this is where I got it from. There is an uncomfortable situation between my in-laws and Debbie and my parents to this day, though Debbie's father died. Debbie resents them still. I know intellectually I should but I don't. I'm in the middle. They're old now and want to spend more time with me. Not with Debbie, me.

Debbie doesn't make it so easy because she resents spending time with them. They pulled things when we were first married. Like, come the Jewish holidays they would put pressure on me to have the first night with them and their family, and not with Debbie and hers, and my mother would say things that were never true, like, "Oh, you were always so religious!" Debbie's family were always very cordial and understanding about it. They were easier-going and didn't want to make any trouble. My parents do not realize the degree to which they've created this themselves. I don't think they intellectually or psychologically can really understand this kind of conversation. I mean, when they have been sick at various times, Debbie's come through—she would go and spend time with my mother when my father was in the hospital and would help. But you do have to tug at her because she resents that they never embraced her. I understand that. She feels in a way that I didn't stick up for her. But they tried to put the kibosh on the marriage in every way they could and they got nowhere . . . I would say, "Don't you think she's beautiful?" and they would have criticisms! She wasn't the Lord and Taylor package.

The fact of the matter is that I don't want the Lord and Taylor package. I never could have related to anyone like that. Instinctively I didn't want that; I wanted the opposite. I was always attracted to someone with a great head, especially psychologically oriented, someone astute about life and people and motivations. That's what turned me on. But I feel a torn loyalty because of all this.

This came out again—this not standing up and being loyal to her and what she believes in, if not to her, has come out in other ways. I joined a private practice in Boston after we'd been in Pennsylvania for the early years of our marriage. I was making more money than I had ever dreamed of making. We bought a house in the country in addition to our Brookline house, and we go there for weekends and it's a culturally rich area and we do a lot of outdoor and cultural things there and we've got a lot of friends who also have houses there . . . Actually, Debbie and I have a good time whatever we do. We tend to remember the good times more than the bad—even when we were in Guatemala, Debbie was so sick she almost had to be flown home, but what we remember are the driving around, seeing things, very simple things.

It was never, has never been, that one of us has had to morph into the other's taste. It's always been very simple. We are both late for things, and that often irks other people: We were recently supposed to go with another family to Washington, D.C., on the auto train. We got there fifteen minutes late and missed the train, so we drove there, but it was okay; no one got really angry or irritable. We missed the train but we went down anyway and had a great time. I do lose it sometimes though—we missed the train going back and I was really fuming then because it's a long drive! Time repairs it. I get sarcastic; I blow off steam and then it's more painful to be upset than not so I calm down. But Debbie goes, "I know, I know." We let it go after a while.

She actually has a shorter fuse than I do. She's more insistent on things being a certain way—she won't let things pass that shouldn't pass . . . she has no fear of making enemies if she tells the truth. She tells it like it is even if she risks the end of a relationship and almost invariably she's respected for it— there hasn't been loss of friendships—and I think that's great. Though she's never really confronted my parents—she does it through me, blaming me for not standing up for her. And I guess to a degree she's right. My mother is now friendly, but friendly in her stroked-out persona, so it doesn't mean the same thing, and my father, he doesn't understand her sensibility. She has eased off in her demands on me to confront. It's now water under the bridge. The early years are gone and it really was the early years. Now there's not too much impact of my parents on our lives. We don't see each other that often.

But my medical practice is the other thing. It all comes back to work coming between us. The biggest thing we had in our marriage was when our first child was born. Debbie had preeclampsia, which means she had high blood pressure related to the pregnancy. Her doctor said they wanted her to have bed rest for a day or two after the delivery, so she had to stay overnight and she told me she wouldn't be able to leave till the next day. So my recollection is somewhat dim but I thought she wasn't going to be discharged till noon or after so I went to work in the morning and I didn't get there till the afternoon. In fact she could have gone home at nine and all the mothers she was with were getting picked up and she was sitting there by herself and it was very painful that I wasn't there for her.

That I've chosen work over family—that has been our only serious problem . . . our ongoing problem. I think she has a fair point to some degree, that I could have taken a stand. But it has eased off to some degree because we have other people in our practice now, so we have other help. Whereas before I felt that it was a real burden to take time off for the other person—but that other person would take time off whenever he wanted. You know, I didn't think it was right. And Debbie would say, "It's fine, as long as it's upheld on both sides." But it was just too hard for me to behave in a way that I didn't think was right—to take time off which would burden others. But I do see that family ultimately suffered.

I've begun to shift, though. I always have recognized the thrust of the matter but I was almost a prisoner of my own maybe warped sense of responsibility or work ethic . . . I think during the early years of my

practice—it was a murderous life in those early years—it would be like eight
A.M. to ten or eleven P.M. every day. The senior partner is less inclined to
work than anyone else and he has been looking for ways to do less work for
many years now. He's a problem within our relationship . . . But we have
become so busy that we had to ultimately agree to take on more partners, so
now we've got that plus ancillary moonlighting help at night. I think that
during the early years Debbie wasn't as happy as I because I was so busy
working. She might have felt that she was bringing the kids up on her own
during that time, but I think that's unfair: I've got lots of video to prove my
point! But I think she would have liked more input from me . . .

But I think that I'm not painting it as positive as it is and always has been.
There's a lot of positive to offset this. You know when you talk about these
difficulties, it seems to color the relationships a grayer color than it is. We
had a good time together in that we have had a deep, abiding love for one
another, and we have a good time laughing together. We still really laugh: we
haven't become jaded with each other's sense of humor. We still get a kick
out of each other and take pleasure in each other and really have a similar
take on so many things that it really feels comfortable: politics, humor, types
of movies, types of books. She like classical music a bit more than I do, I like
jazz a bit more than she does. And with people—it would be surprising for
her to really like someone I don't and vice versa. Just the idea of taking trips
together . . .

The other manifestation of the positive flavor of our relationship is that
doing something that is relatively simple and without frills, we always enjoy.
We always find a way to have a good time when we're together, and when I'm
not thinking about work and when I don't have any of that on my mind . . .
We can have a good time—it doesn't matter what we do. We went to
Chicago for a weekend the other week and had a great time, and there was a
day when all we did was not much—we can walk around, look in a store, go
to a movie, have breakfast in a great place. Just the joy of life, nothing special.

That's what I wanted to say: we're on a similar wavelength in terms of
what we're doing; our goals are kind of the same. I think all these things I've
mentioned we enjoy doing together would be very lonely if I was doing them
by myself. I have a cousin who enjoys spending time by himself—hiking,

reading, going to a movie. I find that lonely. I'm not sure that the capacity to enjoy would be there without Debbie and I'm not sure it would be there for her alone either, but I'm just guessing. But she is a lot more social than I am and a lot more socially skilled, so I don't think loneliness has ever been an issue for her. She's never lonely! I've spent chunks of my life feeling loneliness and so when I'm exposed to it I don't like it . . .

Our sexual relationship—remember it started when I knew I was incredibly attracted to this woman—has changed over time only in terms of the infatuation part. What I mean is that there's an infatuation when you're first with someone that over time changes to something different and . . . probably more profound. Maybe less superficial. Maybe less intense in a certain way, but more profound in another way. And part of the infatuation is the sexuality—it's a new person, it's a person you're attracted to, that over time is no longer new, in terms of it being like the first time. But the ease and comfort and the enjoyment is just the same as it's always been. We're still physically attracted to each other and still enjoy it very much. I don't think it's really changed other than, perhaps, frequency.

The frequency goes down. It kind of dropped off after children because of practical considerations—time and energy, and our second child stayed in our bed for a long period of time when she was very young. We had trouble getting her into her own bed. Just practical considerations like that. And I guess hormones. More for Debbie than for me. That has decreased the frequency, yes, but we still enjoy it . . . I think there's some drop in libido with age too.

That's part of the pleasure of having a day off. And sometimes weekends in the country alone. We still take our family vacations all together. Now that we have the one weekday together, the frequency graph has gone up a bit. It's just as pleasurable now—not that much different. Different only in that it's not brand new. That excitement of what it's like to be with someone that you've idolized in a way physically, and actually can be together—that part of it isn't there. But that's the way it's different.

If I see a sexy, attractive woman, I recognize that physically they're attractive, but I would never betray Debbie. That's what it would be— betrayal. No one night of sex would be worth that even if she never found out. I think I've gained the understanding that I can have an attraction to other people but not have a desire to act on it because of this wisdom about what it can do. When I was younger, in college days, and there were girlfriends, I wasn't that principled. But with Debbie I always was.

The no-turning-back moment for me, the falling in love, was the moment I saw her in the light and realized I was in love with her. I had, I guess, a small internal anxiety when we were going to get married: I saw her through a friend's eyes who saw her as "a little Jewish"—there was a touch of that about her—and that was what had put me off in the past about a girlfriend in high school, when I started to hear "Jewish" expressions coming out of her mouth. And that didn't appeal to me. In fact, the girl I was with in medical school was Baptist. But that was too far! . . . Then I started to look at that, and you know, Debbie is Jewish, as you know, and every once in a while there's something that comes out, and that, coupled with the fact that this was a commitment for life—I had some secret—I don't think Debbie knows this—I had some anxieties about this, at that point.

They were short lived, and the very powerful other stuff about her that I found lovely—something I may not have verbalized that fits in here now—that I loved about her, and that I have enjoyed in other women, is how perceptive she is . . . being perceptive about other people, about what motivates people, about what's going on, always appealed to me. That kind of intelligence—not necessarily someone who can name facts, but someone who is intelligent about humanity, people, about me—really turned me on.

I think a construction that makes sense is that this was something that was missing from my family relationships. I had a friend in high school who was very perceptive and talked about these things when no one else was talking about anything other than getting a girl. And I was attracted to that and I thought Debbie had this. It was that—really that—that turned me on about her when I realized that not only was I physically attracted to her, but she also had this. Then I said, "Wow! She has everything I want!" And that more than squashed these other concerns. It comes up from time to time but it means less and less to me because I see it as just being a superficial issue that really is so unimportant relative to the deeper stuff. If there's ever anything— I don't have to go back to remembering what's positive about our relationship: it's always there. If one day I'm having any questions or doubts or any negative thoughts, the next day they'll be blown away by something. I can have a moment of being down, and then it just goes away—is washed away by true love.

I have thought from time to time about one of us losing the other, through death—that will happen, but I don't dwell on it. I'm pretty good at not dwelling on something I have no control over—no, I shouldn't say that because I do worry about money issues and things like that that I have no control over—but I think I'll be pretty lonely if I happen to survive her . . .

I think it's pretty simple. It hasn't been hard for me. It hasn't been a struggle, being married. I think you have to work at a marriage but it's not hard work for us. We both accept that we're going to be angry with each other from time to time. But that it's so often in a deeper sea of love. I think that Debbie has some resentments about me that I can never undo now—I think they're, in a large part, well founded. I don't have any resentments about her. I'm sorry for those things: I would have been a better person had I come through on those occasions; maybe I came through in other ways. It seems like she's still there, anyway!

3

Love and Partnership:
Who Does What and Why

SARAH STODDARD and STU MILLER
MARIANNE and MICHAEL JONES

THE WORD NOW in vogue for "committed relationship" is "partnership," along with "partners," rather than "spouses." "Do you have a partner?" we now tentatively ask, careful not to make any possibly embarrassing assumptions about either marital status or sexual preference. The noninclusive "marriage," with its "husbands" and "wives," has made way for something new. At once the practical is elevated. At once romance is stripped away.

"Partnership" summons up images of nuts and bolts, functionality. But it is just such functionality that either adds to a couple's happy story, or else changes it to one of unhappiness. Indeed, the nitty-gritty—how comfortably people manage to live together, day after day—is often overlooked as a factor in how happy they are. Can an "odd couple" ever succeed? How do they negotiate cooking, cleaning, washing the car, and cleaning gutters? Who looks after what? How do they, with equanimity or a sense of fairness, stem the tide of lives that not only never lets up, but also keeps accumulating with what can feel like unremitting speed?

My research on how couples divide tasks, and how they feel about that, gives a partial answer: the daily give-and-take, the feeling that each partner gives equally, or that the balance or reciprocity is in place, is key to feeling happy in relationships.[9] Of course, there is a huge variation in how people do this. Couples without children are more likely to say they divide as much as possible straight down the middle, while couples with children, particularly heterosexual couples, find themselves falling back on, to a degree, old gendered roles. Time, energy, and finances become stretched and smoothly running the household rises to a matter of urgency. Getting clean and fed are prioritized over political principles. This can be a source of tension and a major issue for couples who began with progressive, egalitarian-style relationships—for the women, mainly (for statistics bear out the fact that women do more household work and child care than men in such partnerships), though, men, too, find themselves troubled by this retreat to more traditional roles. However, even these couples, who do not claim such division of labor is exactly preferable, in the interviews conducted for this book maintain that they have found other ways to settle a sense of "fairness" and equality of contribution to the relationship and family life—particularly, if the concept of "fairness" is extended over time, with both change and adaptation in responsibility for the particular tasks as situations evolve and demands and circumstances shift. For example, a change or loss of a job, or a long-term illness, can limit or alter the nature of the contribution a partner can make.

> The biggest change has been in who does what, as a result of my illness and also my [early] retirement [on health grounds]. I'm around now, but I can't do most things. I still manage financial affairs. We still garden together, as we'd started to do, but instead of me doing the heavy gardening, as I used to, Gill does now. She does everything around the house. I manage the easy planting—growing things from seed, for instance. We still take pride in each other and in this shared home.—**Howard Evans, 48**

Domesticity is, and always has been, an arrangement around practicalities. Shifts that have derived from changes in women's roles mean that how that arrangement is lived out looks different from one generation to the next. The time in which a couple meets, their age, and the dominant cultural ideas about how couples ought to "do" their relationship are crucial. Instead of erupting over domestic routines, disputes or dissatisfactions in earlier generations tended to revolve more around loneliness and alienation— gender division in roles meant less emphasis on shared worlds, including sexual and emotional intimacy. But for a happy couple, during any genera- tion, mutuality, however defined, is stressed. So while older couples may consequently look different, they feel no less happy.

> We were separated for about eight months, until Alastair's fellowship ended, and then the children and I joined him to travel. The separation was very hard. The household was, obviously, run by me, while Alistair was the breadwinner. But the marriage was central. Alistair, good as gold, has always shared the chores when he was around. There were no washing machines, fridges, dishwashers, or freezers in those days! But he shared in doing the chores even then. And now of course we share them still . . . Our mutual love and affection sustain us, along with a shared interest in cultural activities, tolerance, and a readiness to "kiss and make up."—**Evelyn Crawford, 83**

How everyday life gets arranged is a more critical question for relation- ships now—now, that is, that women, central to most domestic roles, are no longer mostly at home, most of the time, most of their lives. As a result, roles for "partners" are, in theory, negotiable: chores are put up for grabs depending on who likes to do what, who does what well, and who has the time. But as roles move from being more or less strictly gender defined, couples are finding themselves in murky territory. And that has happened just when efficiency *needs* clarity, when there is a clutter of demands on both domestic partners. More often than in the past, it is on just this seemingly boring, mundane issue—who does what, and why, and is it fair, given that it's supposed to be a partnership that's equal—that relationships flounder.

> Early on, when I wasn't around, Claire did resent being landed with all the running of the home and children with little daily input from me. We chose this arrangement, but it doesn't mean it made us that happy.

I have and had nothing but admiration for her for creating a home, with loving care.—**Simon Hoxton, 56**

It is therefore striking to find that even in the midst of talking about what is standardly a more difficult issue for them, the couples in this book frequently mention how each partner's effort in the relationship is appreciated. There is a sense of cooperation and a commitment to each other. Forgoing a tally sheet, they have worked out a routine—sometimes not getting it right for a period (as Simon Hoxton's testimony indicates), then adjusting it in another period—that flows, often demonstrating necessary flexibility. Their arrangement feels fair, each partner feeling recognized for his or her effort—even if an outsider might not be able to point to exactly where the fairness lies.

Tim had a pretty good job but he'd given it up to start on his own business. His financial income didn't materialize. Money was short. I got offered a promotion at work and my earning potential was greater than his, so he became a househusband to look after the kids . . . and suddenly I was pregnant. Again. He didn't speak to me for weeks!— **Sharon Oberland, 45**

It is worth noting, however, that many couples inadvertently report what research still finds: there remains, in most partnerships, a gender-related division within the efficient and smooth running of lives lived together.[10] This makes some sort of intuitive sense: if you leave things to who does what best, one of the main determinants of how roles get allocated, then those who are better trained or have more experience and knowledge of something are more likely to take that "something" over. And it is the case that we are still gender defined in how we're socialized. Girls still do learn to cook more often and earlier than boys, even if Jamie Oliver and Anthony Bourdain are superstars of the stove.

Of course, when there are no children, domestic tasks can be assigned according to who is most willing and across gender categories with greater ease. Such couples often split the housework, cooking, and daily tasks down the middle. And in so doing, men and women can use this opportunity to acquire new, cross-gender skills. The man can become a better cook, the woman a better car mechanic, should each so desire. But when time and energy are in shorter supply—as certainly happens if children become part of the equation—such couples may find themselves foregoing the opportunities to take the time and energy necessary to learn new things. An accident or illness might also make taking on old, much less new, chores impossible.

My illness doesn't allow me to do anything safely, so Tim does everything—cooking, cleaning, stuff for the kids—all the time. For the first time Tim is in control. I think in a strange way he likes it, though we both have learned that I am a strong person.—**Sharon Oberland, 45**

And then there is the question of how same-sex couples "do" their relationships, especially those with children. Without gender roles to conveniently fall back on, how do they carve up domesticity? How do they make it seem good and fair? The same-sex couples participating in this study point out that what has evolved over the years for them is a combination of who likes to do what and who has more talent and interest in particular things. One couple, now in their early fifties, each brought two children into a relationship, which began twenty years ago, when the oldest of these children was seven, the youngest eighteen months. Both women have careers and have worked through the years when children were still at home. Indeed, they divide things according to predisposition and practical demands, but also are able to be flexible, each assuming the other's tasks as situations fluctuate.

I have had three knee surgeries and one shoulder surgery since we got together. It has deepened our relationship, because I've been able to see that the household still runs even when I'm out of commission because Patty does it all till I'm up and moving.—**Jenny Dahlstrom, 52**

Obviously, there is flexibility and adaptability throughout a lifetime together that seems to underscore the best relationships, over any age group or any sexual preference. That seems to be what "partnership," in its best sense, means.

Of course, as noted, when children arrive on the scene, the dividing of housework often changes. It also, predictably, changes the relationship itself. The participants in this research who have children all mentioned that having them has been their most profound shared experience (whether in grief, pride, or joy). This can even include sharing children who may not belong to both from the start (whether through divorce, widowhood or death of a spase, or adoption).

> We both have children from previous relationships and sometimes this has caused problems. Issues have included jealousy and time constraints, with not wanting to stint on time and attention for our respective children, and also personality clashes between ourselves and our children and the children between each other . . . The issues around the children and being all together obviously sometimes cause problems, but on the other hand, the fact that we both have children gives us a common ground: we understand what it involves—the joy and the problems.—**Joanne Long, 40**

A divorced, single mother I know confessed her only regret about divorcing the father of her children: "It was only when I went to the graduation of our child a few years after our divorce and I saw him and his new wife there that I felt the wrench: no one to share with me so utterly the joy around our child, though I knew that he would be experiencing it as I was—in fact, the only other person in the world who was." So the opposite is surely true: those who do stay together become further joined, even as their children grow and leave, through having shared this most intimate project together.

Children can both join couples and drive wedges through them. Partnership-breakdown statistics bear out the latter. The frequency of and desire for sex declines, (for women, particularly, usually during the early years of child rearing). As a couple's focus turns to the children, in addition to work and the nuts and bolts of running a household, the time one spends with the other diminishes. New information about each other gets lost in the jumble and the vitality of the original relationship fades.

The other side of the story is the intense intimacy engendered by sharing the deep, unimaginable love for a child. Taking pleasure and pride in people they have helped to create deepens a couple's enjoyment of each other. Shared grief and distress over children's failures or disappointments strengthens a couple's intimacy and anchors their mutual support. Respect for each one's contribution in child rearing augments mutual respect. And that respect serves to deepen and sustain their emotional connection, that magical sense of "fusion" and passion that started them off and made them want to be together in the first place. Raising children together is a task so much "bigger" than either one of them as individuals and is part of what keeps that heroic, epic sense of love, which fills everyone so powerfully in the beginning, alive.

> Our children have been our delight . . . It has given us reason for togetherness over and above other things. We have tried to use our strengths cooperatively. It was difficult when money was scarce . . . We both tried to balance family commitment with earning extra income. I did part-time work. Jack even tried to start his own wastepaper business while also working as a railway porter. But family came first, for us both.—**Ellie Darling, 72**

Partnership, in the end, constitues much of what we mean when we talk about the "work" of relationships: how couples hammer out reasonable, fair, and feasible routines that support their joint lives, how they design systems flexible enough to be reinvented, free from rancor, as those lives move through time.

Sarah Stoddard and Stu Miller

Sarah Stoddard, twenty-eight, teaches secretarial skills at a business college. Stu Miller, thirty, is an accountant. Sarah and Stu live in rural northwest England and work in the market town nearby, close to where both of them spent most of their childhoods. Sarah, a strikingly pretty woman, is reserved and diffident, while Stu, a small, athletic-looking, wiry, gregarious man, is the one who volunteered them for the study.

Over nine years of cohabitating, they have worked out household duties, financial practices, and a sense of fairness toward each other by trying, where possible, to, in their words, "divide things down the middle." At the point of our interview they were facing the first of two watersheds. One was their upcoming wedding. The second is still putative: within the foreseeable future they plan to have children. Though they cannot be sure exactly how, they know that children, in particular, will change routines, income, and how to judge what's fair. Their stories show them trying to predict how something they each clearly wish for might well upset a carefully wrought and satisfying facet of their life together.

Sarah Stoddard:

We met in a pub, when Stu was home on a weekend, from university. I knew his sister. He's easygoing, really nice and warm, and he was easy to talk to. We just got on well, and we started writing to each other while he was away. At first he'd come home and we'd all go out in a group, going clubbing, you know. Then some of the group began coupling off.

Maybe that's how it started—I mean, made us start to think about us becoming a couple. I had thought he was too intellectual for me, out of my league. I wasn't going to university, I was training to be a legal secretary, and I just didn't think he'd take me seriously. But we were spending more and more time together when he came down at weekends, and he was coming down for more weekends. I stopped feeling that way—you know, about him being "better" than me. I got to know him better. I realized he was natural, down-to-earth.

We started to go out for coffee, just to spend time together, talking, apart from the group. I first noticed, when we were out clubbing, or after, when we went out with others, that he would want to stay around talking to me, and then he wrote to me. But it was when he went away to South America once for a vacation and he called me: that's really when I knew! So it wasn't like "love at first sight" but sort of slowly dawning on me and him. And then I could admit that I had that interest in him. I'd stayed away from long-term relationships till then. I was afraid of them. As soon as they became sort of serious I'd break them off.

That was because of my background. I had a really happy childhood here: me, my younger brother, my mother and father. I thought my parents had a good relationship. My father was a self-made businessman. He had his own mechanics business here, and he had bigger ambitions, so when I was nine he moved us all to Australia, where he set up on his own again, and did pretty well. But we were separated from all our relatives. Still, I remember liking it in Australia at first. It was sunny, we had a nice house. My mother didn't work—she never did—she was with us, a really good mum, and she seemed okay, actually happy, with my dad. They didn't have rows.

Anyway, then when I was twelve, she died. A brain tumor. Completely unexpected. We moved out of that house almost right away, and my dad got a girlfriend, also right away, who wasn't that much older than we were—I mean, she was nineteen! We began to make new friends in our new neighborhood, and then he broke up with this girlfriend and moved us all back to the U.K., back to where we started. It wasn't a good time. And then it turned out that he'd been having affairs all along, which was why he'd had this girlfriend so soon after my mother died. It was a good thing we moved back to the area we came from. My dad never looked after us, not from the time my mum died. I did all that.

I don't speak to him now. I'm close to my brother, as I brought him up from the time Mum died. From the time I left school I've tried to have nothing to do with my father. So I guess that's why I really didn't trust men and I wasn't looking to settle into a relationship. I actively didn't want to get married. But I have to say that I do think it was lucky my dad moved us back here, though I certainly didn't at the time. If he hadn't, I would never have met Stu.

Stu, on the other hand, always lived here, except for when he went away to university, and for three years when we were separated during the week, when he worked in Nottingham. Both his parents live here, and two of his four brothers and sisters. His parents broke up when he was thirteen, so actually, our families fell apart at similar points. But his parents are completely different. They're civil to each other. They both have had new relationships, though his mother's has recently broken up. He grew up with more money than I did. He didn't live quite so well after they got divorced, but he always had two holidays, one with each parent, and lots of nice presents for Christmas and birthdays. For a while things were tense, I guess, but his parents do treat each other sort of as friends now. They'll both be at our wedding, and there are no problems we foresee. My dad is *not* invited.

So when we got together, my mind changed. We could always talk. We were always comfortable. We talk about everything: our day, wedding plans, what we're going to do, different things that have come up during the day, things about other people, like if he's had an argument with his sister; we discuss current events. Future—like kids. Yesterday, for instance, the paper had a quiz for couples: how much do you match each other, so we did that on the way home from work together. We just feel like best friends and like equals.

Stu Miller:

We got together through mutual friends. She'd been in a sort of serious relationship but was single when I met her and had been for about nine months before we got together. I was free too. It was pretty low-key at first—just getting together around the pub with a group of friends. She knew my younger sister, and I was home from university, just visiting, and hanging around with my sister's friends at that point. I liked her—she was easy-going—but I didn't think she'd be that interested in me . . . I'm from a family—well, we always had enough, a good lifestyle . . . My parents divorced when I was about twelve, no, thirteen, but my parents actually have managed to be friends. They both remarried, and I think that helped. It's a different thing from Sarah's family.

We've had a lot of separations over the years. Our jobs have meant I've been in a different city. For three years we had a weekend relationship. For the past two years we've been living in a house we bought together.

We've decided to get married, after nine years together. Why? Because it was just the right thing to do now, sort of a logical progression, from living together, preparing to have children someday soon. But mostly I just thought it would sort of bring us closer together. It's like a statement, isn't it? That you're joined together. It's symbolic, marriage—it makes the relationship more of a unit, or team. I want to show that sort of emotional commitment.

In fact, she's going to take my name, though I know that's a bone of contention for some couples. In her case, she wants to get rid of her name: she doesn't get along with her father. She sees it as a new beginning, taking a new name. But it doesn't mean that we're not doing things equally, because we are. We split everything down the middle.

That includes finances. At the moment we earn pretty much the same, so it's pretty easy. When I was working and living in Nottingham my salary was quite a bit higher and that was a bit more uncomfortable, trying to work out a financial routine that felt absolutely fair. I did contribute more, and sometimes it meant I'd want to spend more on myself than she could on herself. Now we put the same amount into a lump sum every month and then out of that pay all the joint bills. Our own individual stuff we pay for out of our own accounts and neither of us is very materialistic so there's not much of a problem with this arrangement. A lot of what we like to do is similar, so the costs of our entertainment are pretty much the same too. And if we're out, we take turns paying for things. It evens out in the end.

She manages our money a bit better, because she's worked out a system and plans and is very practical, so she keeps the accounts, but we do discuss things.

We spend a lot of time together—have a lot of joint friends. We drive to and home from work together because we work near each other. When we get home one of us makes dinner—we take turns—and the other one cleans up. But I do like to cook—I've gotten into cooking lately. On Tuesdays she works late, so I go home first and always cook then. I also do the heavier stuff—like in the garden, cutting down a tree, which just makes sense. I actually like home repairs and painting and stuff, but we do tend to share most things.

On the weekends we go to the gym, sometimes to yoga classes together. Some nights she'll go out and meet friends and some I will, but usually after we've cooked and cleaned up. We do the major house cleaning and shopping on the weekends together. We talk about everything: we both tend to analyze things and people. I've been in my job, for instance, for a few months, and she knows all about the people in it, and I know about the job she has down at the college. Sometimes we'll talk about the future, and about when we should have kids, and what that's going to look like . . .

I think she'll take some time off work at that point, but go back part time, and, yes, I think then things will change a lot. We'll have less money, and have to do fewer things on the weekends, and I think she'll probably do more of the cooking and housework, because she'll care about how the house looks, and she'll be around and I won't, so she'll be more likely to do it.

We've been watching to see what friends of ours who are having babies do. We're discussing it at the moment. We've talked about my staying home and looking after the kids. I took my nieces out this past weekend swimming—I like kids; I feel quite comfortable with them. But so does she—I like watching her with other people's kids. It's pretty certain that she will take a bit of time off work, rather than me. I don't expect her to take time off work, but she wants to—not long. Neither of us would feel challenged staying home all day, staring at the cat. I need her to be mentally challenged, just as she wants to be, because I like her as an interesting person, not bored with life.

When we do have kids I'll try to do what I can. It's no sweat: I just see something that needs doing—if I see it, I'll do it, or if she asks me, I don't mind doing whatever.

We're both really easygoing, and we don't have heated arguments. Other people have said this about us. We don't have those horrible silences after disagreeing. We might disagree when we're debating a point, for instance, but then we don't go around silent or ignoring each other; we sort it out there and then. We've had that a bit about the wedding—I have wanted to have my say about certain things, like where it will be, or who's invited, or what to have on the menu and what to spend. We were trying to decide between scallops and a pasta appetizer, but we weren't sure how many people would want that, and then how to figure that out, and we couldn't come to an agreement and were interrupting each other because each of us was so sure that we had a solution. Finally we sort of went quiet, and thought—both of us—"Oh, wait a minute, right," and then listened to what the other had to say. I can back down, and so can she.

Marianne and Michael Jones

Marianne and Michael Jones are examples of how you can get it right the second time around, especially if, like them, you are reflective about the factors in the breakdown of your previous relationships, including your own contribution. They met a few years after each had undergone the painful unraveling of a first marriage. What is most moving about their story is how they have come to love and care for each other's children, while remaining clear-eyed about the difficulties around developing that love. Children are often a large obstacle to new relationships working out, despite the best intentions on everyone's part. Marianne and Michael each had two sons from a previous relationship. They also had their own child, a daughter, whose birth helped knit the siblings together. The children have all grown now and are living independently. Marianne and Michael live in a small town on the south coast of England.

Marianne Jones:

Michael and I met at a party and immediately felt the usual falling-in-love stuff: how much we had in common, how good we felt together, passion, finding lots to laugh about together, etc. Two days after we met, he turned up at my house early one morning after walking his dog and the reality of me surrounded by my own children and several that I either child-minded or was taking to school was a bit of a shock for him—not quite such a glamorous vision as at the party. When he moved into my house a few months later it wasn't a carefully thought-out, considered option, but quite rash, and, by rights, should have been a complete disaster. Several friends thought I was completely mad, on the rebound, totally irresponsible, etc., and in their position I would have said the same, but I knew I was right! Time seems to have borne this out, but it could be that we have just been very lucky—I wouldn't recommend getting together as we did!

. . . Within weeks of Michael moving into my home, we had sons aged ten and twelve, his, and three and five, mine, living with us for the entire summer . . . I felt at the time that Michael had fallen in love with my boys as much as he had with me and did occasionally wonder what would happen to us as a couple when the children were no longer needing us so much . . . I think it helped that we both had sons from previous relationships; there was a balance . . . There were evenings when I had to sit quietly at the top of the stairs gathering my strength for a few minutes before I went down and started again. It was exhausting but it did help the boys to all feel they were getting their share of us . . .

I think we have been prepared to spend time hearing each other's point of view, trying to understand what is important to each other, not expecting one person to always provide the answer. Early on in the relationship, I used to think that if we had a serious difference of views on something, it meant that Michael didn't love me anymore and would leave me. Over time I learned that it was safe to disagree and that we could talk our way through problems. If we have a minor "crabby" time now . . . I am instantly aware that it isn't important. If there is a pattern to solving disagreements, I suppose it is to back off, think about our own part in the problem and what exactly the problem really is, then get back together to talk it through some more. I've never believed in couples who claim to have been together for years and years without quarreling but Michael and I have had very few serious disagreements. There have been very few problems with the "us" bit of our life. Maybe we have always managed to talk our way through a problem before it became a big problem. The couple side of our life has always been important—sneaking a few hours together, going away for a night or two without the children, walking the dog together.

Physical affection is important to us both. If we have been crabby with each other, or if life is fine or very stressful, we touch often: hugs, holding hands when we're out, cuddling up together on the sofa. We'd both miss this so much if it wasn't happening and notice something wrong; it helps keep us in tune with each other.

In my first marriage my husband and I both had other sexual partners. This was largely his choice but I was fairly easy to convince that sexual fidelity wasn't important, as I enjoyed sex, wanted it frequently, and had little—(as in none)—experience before my relationship with my first husband.

However, I quickly found that it didn't work for me—I couldn't have a sexual relationship without becoming emotionally involved and I could also see that, for all his words, my husband didn't like my having other men in my life. I knew he had had sexual relationships with several women, but when we divorced I discovered that he had always been unfaithful—before we were married, within weeks of the wedding, throughout the whole marriage. Throughout the marriage I had struggled to see this from his point of view and recognized that I did enjoy sex with other people in spite of us having an active sex life together, but felt the risks were too great. Ultimately what happened was predictable. We were having a really rough time, he was seeing another woman and decided that she was the love of his life.

When Michael and I married, I don't remember consciously deciding that fidelity was important. I certainly didn't plan to have a relationship with anyone else but was cautious about thinking any infidelity would herald the end of the marriage. Since being with Michael I haven't ever felt I could possibly have a relationship with anyone else—it would be unthinkable and no fun if I couldn't tell Michael about it! There hasn't been a decision, as such, to be faithful to him, it just hasn't been an issue.

Children have always been central to our relationship . . . Michael was always prepared to challenge me about the upbringing of my sons if he thought there was a better way to handle a situation. This led to times when we had to have long discussions about an issue or situation, but produced solutions that we were both willing to try. My previous husband had always wanted to just say that I was doing a wonderful job and knew best, which really meant, "I can't be bothered; I don't care. Leave me out of this and just get on with it." I valued Michael's involvement even if sometimes I had to compromise because I knew parenting was as important to him as it was to me.

Having our daughter was an incredible time. A shared child was very precious. A girl seemed amazing. Most of all, though, I remember Michael's

involvement. He cared for the boys when I was suffering through the
pregnancy. He was interested in the birth process, and took such good care of
me while she was very small—taking the boys to school before he went to
work, coming home early, doing loads of household stuff so that I had time
to care for her and establish a feeding schedule for her. After the awfulness
I'd experienced when my other children had been born, including a stillbirth,
it was really healing to have such a happy experience. And we both loved her
so much. It was tough, though, at times. Our daughter slept really badly for
three years, and through that time we had one of Michael's sons living with
us, so we were a big family and there was a lot to do, but we both got stuck in
and enjoyed it. Most of the time. Michael's sons weren't living with us for
the worst of their adolescent stuff, although one of them caused a few
problems. My sons, however, really caused life to be difficult when they were
teenagers . . . Michael and I stayed united through this, though—talking it
through . . . trying to find solutions, and just going out together for an
evening when all else failed. How anyone copes with teenagers on their own
or within a relationship that isn't strong amazes me.

I notice that I'm referring to "his" sons and "my" sons and I realized that I
do this in my everyday life too. It sounds as if it's neatly split or separated,
but it isn't. I think I use the terms to clarify which sons I'm referring to,
rather than who has "ownership" of them.

It has always seemed important to me that the family relationships are
"open"—no pretence that we're all one straightforward family but clearly
acknowledging the complexities of having parents and stepparents, with each
of whom different relationships have to be worked out, so that, for example,
a "good" stepfather doesn't replace or isn't better than a "bad" father. Both
people have their own role to play and it's the energy and commitment they
put into that relationship that is ultimately important.

I never parented Michael's sons when they were very young. I have been
their stepmother since I married their dad, but the relationship I have with
them is based on the time, energy, and commitment I have been willing to
invest in them. I don't feel like I am their mother or the same as I feel about
my sons, but the relationship is just as strong and just as significant for all its
differences . . . I cannot imagine loving any grandchildren my sons may

produce any more than I already love the grandchildren that Michael's sons have given us.

But through the years there have been heartbreaks with our children too, which have also bound us together, because they are ours, and we give them our energy, time, and investment. One weekend my son came home from university and was really weird. He was abusive, verbally aggressive, and we were both frightened he would become physically aggressive too. I had some knowledge of mental health problems through my work in social work but still felt really unprepared to deal with what was happening. Michael had less knowledge and was equally thrown, upset and frightened by my son's behavior.

We were able to help each other—Michael could listen and accept the value but also the limits of the knowledge I had of mental health problems . . . I listened to his point of view . . . [we were] both crying, feeling completely helpless.

[We have lasted as a couple by] Sharing time together, listening to each other, respecting each other, being generous and willing to give the other "time out" but willing to drop what we're doing to support the other, and also—part of that—having a flexible, relaxed approach to who does what and when; never trying to score points off each other, except in jest; and having similar interests, but also able to do alone those things the other has no interest in; and valuing each other as parents and enjoying life as part of a big, complex, extended family.

Michael Jones:

My own parents were unhappy and I always wished they would separate, although I was never able to vocalize this to them. Ironically, they stayed together for my sake. They seemed to be in competition with each other, each trying to gain the higher moral ground; however, they both always tried to be kind to me, although the kindest act to me would have been for them to be kind to each other.

In my first marriage, we married young. It started well but then my wife began to suffer a mental condition. After therapy we agreed, me reluctantly, she should have a baby. She became pregnant and two sons followed and everything became much better and a very supportive and creative relationship followed. The big drawback was that my work as a television news editor took me away from home for longish periods, which she hated. There was a second main problem, which was that sex was never very satisfactory as it seemed to physically hurt my wife, and I remained an unskilled novice for a long time. My wife started accusing me of having affairs when away, which was untrue for a long time, but then became true, although I never admitted this. But in retrospect I'm sure she knew because my sexual technique had improved, although she still suffered physical pain, which made it very difficult. She had a very, very jealous nature. Eventually, when our children were seven and nine years old, while I was abroad, she started an affair with a neighbor, and when I returned, I left home. They married, and are still together . . .

When I met Marianne I had been sharing a house with another girlfriend, although we were no longer a couple. We met at a party. She was trying out a "Big Bold Stare" that she'd read about in a woman's magazine. I felt enormously flattered as she told me she'd seen me regularly walking my English sheepdog past her window on the way to the park. I was immediately attracted and we quickly established our availability credentials. We talked easily and I walked her home, where we kissed and cuddled on her sofa. We both admitted long afterwards that each was in fact quite a different personality from the person we each thought the other was at that party, but we were completely happy with that . . .

Our sex life was and is passionate and mostly fulfilling. Much of our humor is based on wordplay, banter, and attempted snappy dialogue, and it's a continuing delight for me that my wife will invariably laugh at my jokes—not stories, but usually ripostes, or one-liners—even if she's heard them many times before. After one passionate sexual encounter she exclaimed, "That was really, really nice," and my reactive reply came: "Makes up for all the rubbish ones!" Which, of course, now has become our enduring phrase: "Another rubbish one?" "Yeah." "Sorry!" Anyway, we think it's funny . . .

I am eleven years older than she. As I've grown older I've been unable to complete sex when I expect to, and I do have a benign prostate complaint.

This has led me to ration the number of times I'm willing to initiate. Marianne, after twenty years, is still much more highly sexed than my previous partners ever were, and she is completely frank about her sexual appetite. There have been times, particularly on hot days, when she's gone to the bedroom on her own to masturbate or told me she's done so after the event. We continue to have sex about once a week, sometimes not for a couple of weeks, sometimes, when we're relaxed and particularly on holidays, three or more times a week—not probably more than three as I don't think I could manage more. I do think she probably has the capacity to enjoy lesbian sex, and I have speculated with her that this might occur when I can no longer deliver, or if I die first. When we married I knew she had a strong sexual appetite, as did I, and she told me she had had at least one threesome during her first marriage—something I'd never experienced. I was sexually excited about the same happening for us, but Marianne eventually said I wouldn't like it afterwards—it would hurt me. I somewhat reluctantly accepted this, and in retrospect I think this is one of the many wise avenues of guidance that have flowed from her and her honesty.

We have shared so many great pleasures and remarkable events, including the birth of our daughter, and also two waterbirths, at home, of our two grandchildren . . . but also real sadness, difficulty, and tragedy. In 1998 another grandson was born . . . In 1999 he was rushed into hospital with pneumonia . . . He was stabilized but continued to have tests and we discovered he had an inherited condition which meant that he wouldn't live beyond twelve months. When Marianne was admitted to the hospital for routine gallstone keyhole surgery, our grandson died the day after she was discharged. At the highly emotive funeral the following week she was taken ill . . . and ironically put to bed in my ex-wife's bed—my son lived near her—eventually being readmitted to the hospital with pancreatitis. After a worrisome time she recovered well, although we remained deeply concerned for my son and his partner as they sank into depression. They do have a new baby, who is well, and life has started again for them.

Moreover, my stepson, then aged twenty, at university, started to suffer from what we suspected was a psychotic illness not unlike schizophrenia. We tried to get him treatment in his university town and eventually he was admitted—persuaded by his brother and the university GP—as a voluntary but aggressive patient in a mental ward. He wouldn't agree to see us. He had to leave his course early in the second year, but refused to have anything to do with us. He discharged himself from the hospital and with his father's connivance spent his remaining degree loan on a holiday to Thailand. We tried to stop this happening by involving anyone we could, as we were scared he'd kill himself. However, he returned and lived with his father for a very short time. His father refused to accept he had a mental illness and my wife and I had rows with his father. My stepson was then made to leave his father's house by his stepmother and ended up in various bedsits in a town near us but he still wouldn't talk to us; he was evicted from at least one for aggressive behavior—we were getting news from his contemporaries who were exceedingly worried for him.

During this long time Marianne was beside herself with grief, crying a great deal, and life was the pits; our daughter had chronic fatigue syndrome, and our relationship with her school was exceedingly difficult—we believe the deputy head was obstructing ways for her to progress.

A year later my stepson phoned us in a pitiful state: he'd walked into a doctor's surgery and asked for an appointment and was by then being prescribed antipsychotic drugs and wanted to come home. He came home, became a changed person, and returned to university last year. He is still being treated, has had some relapses, but has generally become a much more adult and aware person, and lovable.

It sounds ridiculous but the last time Marianne and I had a row was about nineteen years ago, and we eventually agreed we were both out of order, or maybe I forgot to admit I was out of order. We are acutely aware of some of the sniping and point scoring that goes on in some of our friends' marriages and we tend to joke and mimic pointless rows: "So how much longer were you intending to keep the cat locked in the bedroom?" "That's for me to know and you to find out." Or, "Shouldn't you have turned left back there?" "I'm going the scenic route."

I do simply adore my wife. She is a social worker, though, and I sometimes suspect that she is successfully using her learned, and natural, techniques on me! We give each other a veto on anything, but equally we allow each other most things, although Marianne is generally unselfish. Although she did insist, from the start, on adequate holidays—about which I was not at all bothered and almost against them. I learned to really enjoy holidays, though I'm always readier than her to return home. She demonstrates her love—tells me she loves me frequently—and continues to touch me in a very tactile way, and we hold hands. We enjoy being in each other's company and she is exceedingly kind—to my own children and their partners and children and much loved by them.

4

The Emotional Life of Love:
Sustaining Intimacy

MARTIN CURTIS and DENNIS GORDON

LOVE IS PRACTICALLY deified, often spoken of as something separate, in and of itself, visited ethereally upon us, but if this is so, it can just as likely leave. If we speak of love as suddenly alive, then suddenly dead, it seems as if love has nothing to do with our actions, willing, witting, or otherwise. But this is an illusion. Love is better thought of as a fabric of emotions and experiences, rather than a static, discrete entity, or even an unchanging, disembodied state. Love is both a state and a quality of interaction; it describes both what goes on and has gone on within a relationship. Actions—the things you do, often wholly mundane—keep love "alive" or make it "die." Indeed, as one interviewee reported discovering after giving up her "affair of the heart," love can be reborn. It can spring back to life, even when it has seemed nearly dead, by things you and your partner do, just as what you have done may have nearly, apparently, killed it. Mutual support, intimate and everyday communication, and to what degree you stay emotionally in tune can sustain the life of love.

Indeed, the narratives here suggest that relationships are always about little acts of will, both conscious and unconscious. You can choose to go down roads that wreck relationships, or down ones that can keep them going. How people interact can both produce and encourage intimacy (ie., physical and emotional closeness and comfort) and support (i.e., practical and emotional help and assistance). How they do these things can be seen in how couples communicate (i.e., verbal and nonverbal listening and responding).

> We don't push ourselves when there is stress: we take care of ourselves and patiently ride it out. We communicate very well with each other: discuss the "hard" things with respect and kindness, and are realistic in our expectations of each other.—**Karen Bell, 48**

Couples derive both comfort and pleasure from intimacy. "Intimacy," as it is used here, refers to how well understood a person feels; how free or safe he or she is to disclose personal, private matters (in whatever way these are defined, as people classify different things as private or personal); how intertwined their routines and habits are; how intense, private, meaningful, and profound the feelings and information, on the one hand, and the types of activities, on the other, that are routinely exchanged; and also how close, relaxed, and comfortable couples are with each other's bodies, words, and gestures. Intimacy can be assessed as an overarching aspect of a relationship—how deep and reliable is it for any given couple—or as something episodic. The start of romantic relationships has episodes of intimacy, often intense for both partners, but it may not build into a sense that intimacy can be sustained or stretched into varied areas of life with that person. Boundaries around too many domains as well as lopsided revelation and exposure can close down the development of intimacy. Happy couples here report that they have managed to expand these domains and that they are relatively equitable across the couple. They have also established for each other both trust and reliability that intimate moments or episodes can arise again and again. When this sort of trust, reliability, and continuing intimacy becomes sustained, it acts as a fulcrum around which enduring couples find security, acceptance, and a base from which to create additional pleasure.

> We have developed a saying in our house that ". . . no one gets punished for telling the truth." She understands and helps explain me to myself. The squeeze of her hand in mine reassures me. I tease her

sometimes saying that God has a garden in heaven waiting for her.—
Geoffrey Campbell, 58

Intimacy can come from language—(revelation of difficult, often-shame-
ful, or deeply private things) or physical expression (becoming naked, having
sex, stroking each other). But it can also arise from the comfort of routine—
that is, from knowing each other so well that language itself is not needed.

As couples talk about moments when a sense of intimacy and connection
is ruptured, it becomes clear that the capacity to have episodes of intimacy is
also linked to patient understanding, as well as to the ability to reflect and
learn from those points of rupture. The ability to learn from them
contributes to the important "past-present-future" balance in happy relationships. It affords the requisite longer-range perspective; having that perspective can help restore belief in the partner and so the potential for further
intimacy. For example, Debbie Gold, in chapter 2, complains about the
medical practice her husband joined and his partners who constantly take
advantage of him with the result that he is too often away from home. It is an
ongoing conflict, which, nonetheless, viewed within her relationship as a
whole, she remains upbeat about: "We come out of our arguments feeling
somewhat satisfied afterward. The same argument, again and again, about
this partner and the practice, and it feels like we've done a little bit of work
on it each time . . . I see us as a bond. I see us as being a permanent bond. I
see nothing breaking that permanent bond."

Intimacy is also linked to the ability to rely on your partner for emotional
or practical support and a willingness to be supportive in return. Support and
intimacy both breed and rely on trust. Furthermore, intimacy breeds courage
to request support; support breeds courage to disclose. It is a two-sided
equation. And while what men and women classify as "support" can look
different, as research has found, the stories told by the heterosexual couples
here suggest that they have crossed the gender divide and are able to read the
respective gestures of support, whether they be mainly verbal (women) or
practical (men), and also that they have learned to adapt to what each partner
needs, so that sometimes men get better at talking and women better at being
quiet, for instance. Moreover, "support" also refers to being able to, on the

one hand, read and understand what your partner needs, and on the other, to ask for what can be reasonably expected, given your partner's strengths, weaknesses, talents, and preferences.

Good communication (its underside is "communication breakdown") underlies the flow of intimacy and support. It is often cited as key to keeping relationships alive, but my heart sinks when I hear the word "communication" used by itself as a measure of a relationship, because, by itself, it is meaningless. All signs read between people, whether verbal or nonverbal, direct or indirect, clear or masked, are forms of communication. What is meaningful, research shows, is the following: (a) listening well (i.e., being attentive and getting the intended meaning); (b) keeping each other up-to-date with information that is integral to the running and doing of intertwined lives; (c) telling your deep and meaningful thoughts and feelings; (d) being clear; (e) being direct; and (f) being appropriate (i.e., being the appropriate bearer of information and doing so in the appropriate feeling and style). All are equal sides of the kind of communication that breeds emotional intimacy. Good communication does not consist solely in discussing difficult matters. Nor does it mean frequency or fluency in conversation. But it does refer to a flexible, comfortable style that allows for discussion of difficult topics when ready and if necessary. Like intimacy and support, good communication depends on making time and then focusing on each other. Moreover, feelings of emotional and physical intimacy and feeling supportive and supported are relational states: they must be communicated from one person to another and vice versa. Research on hardy, healthy families shows that clear, direct, open communication, in which people feel understood is paramount to their good functioning; indeed, it is a recipe for health in any relationship.[11]

Another key feeling underlying love is empathy, or the ability partners have to tune in to each other emotionally, as mothers are attuned to their babies. Empathy fosters a protective stance in a relationship, which in another book[12] I have argued is pivotal to successful relationships, and which other research, calling it by different names, agrees is central: each partner is equally vulnerable to the other, and each holds a responsibility, once tuned into this vulnerability, to be the other's singular ally. Over time successful partners flip in and out of being caretakers and care-receivers, sometimes in small ways within the course of a day, other times in greater depth over long periods.

> We have both experienced illnesses, one each, that were serious. My husband had an operation for removing a stone when we were living in Paris in 1963, and suffered a postoperative infection. In my turn I was ill with a fracture of the spine in 1990 and was in bed for a month. My husband cared for me and the family. In both cases the experiences cemented our relationship further. We are both empathetic with each other's ailments and enjoy the role of carer.—**Suzanne Brightman, 58**

Empathy denotes the feeling that your sentiments are understood, valued, and recognized. It is impossible to keep it alive without devoting time to each other, and in that time, focusing on each other. This means making an economic choice: how do you apportion time, energy, and focus to each other amid busy lives and other loyalties? Over and over again couples mention that they "make time for each other," often very consciously keeping days or evenings together sacred, assigning time for each other. Without this investment, you lose touch, you lose focus, you lose alertness to each other's interests and feelings, and in consequence, you lose the quickness to empathy.

Empathy is also fostered when it is reciprocated, when a difficult experience for one partner is appreciated as such by the other, even transforming a difficulty into something else.

> My wife suffers from a lack of self-confidence that causes her, at times, to be withdrawn. This has caused me to try to put myself in her shoes to try to help her out of this situation. It is an ongoing condition that we are slowly winning together . . . I have all the time for my wife that she needs. I never feel that her feelings are less important than mine. I appreciate her, and all she does for me and our relationship. I let her know, many times a day, that I love her, and encourage her to be herself as well as my wife.—**Matt Crowe, 49**

When conflict and difference arise, empathy is tested. It is fairly easy to feel attuned when not challenged. What augurs well for relationships is the capacity couples develop to take feelings on board after rows, friction, or in demanding times. The need for empathy when hurt or stressed is primitive. When small children skin knees they cry until their distress is registered, despite pain subsiding: first mothers must "kiss it better." Since saliva may actually do harm to an open wound, we know it is not the kiss itself that heals, but what it symbolizes: tenderness toward distress. Only then does the child jump back up and resume play. If the person who supposedly loves you better than others refuses to acknowledge your feelings, then it is hard to believe you are loved. At least, on balance; the occasional breach in empathy is expected between lovers, just as it is between mothers and children. Indeed, British psychiatrist Donald W. Winnicott let generations of mothers off the hook by positing that mothers have to be only "good enough," rather than perfect, to produce well-adjusted children.[13] In consequence (or retaliation) you might stop trying to do things that maintain love. Listening empathically and being heard in return, especially when doing so is problematic, are critical to sustaining and nurturing the original loving feelings. Marianne Jones, for instance, admits in chapter 3, "Early on in the relationship, I used to think that if we had a serious difference of views on something, it meant that Michael didn't love me anymore and would leave me. Over time I learned that it was safe to disagree and that we could talk our way through problems . . . We spend time hearing each other's point of view, trying to understand what is important to each other, not expecting one person to always provide the answer."

From reciprocal empathy grow other qualities: the ability to stand back and respect your partner, to feel loyal, to want to protect and support him or her. These are instincts generated by love, much like those the mother feels toward the baby to whom she is uniquely attuned. But they are instincts that can close down if not nurtured by reciprocity and habit. The small acts of will to remember respect and loyalty in the face of resentment and letdown can themselves lead to the renewal of caring. Finally, through empathic tuning in, one takes singular pleasure—the glow of love—in the person you have understood, and who has understood you in return, for empathy tends to breed an empathic connection.

The sense of loyalty and of focus, parts of empathy, that you are the chosen one above all others—"across a crowded room"; moreover, across a crowded room and your lover "only has eyes for you"—is easy to achieve in the beginning, harder when other demands pull focus away and other loyalties lay claim.

Judith S. Wallerstein and Sandra Blakeslee, in their study of enduring happiness in couples, *The Good Marriage*, talk about focusing on the couple, *qua* couple, as one "task" a couple needs to tackle successfully in order to reach a happy state.[14] In discussing normative development over the life cycle in Western societies, various theorists and researchers point to replacing the family of origin with the new partner and consequent new family at the center of emotional life and loyalty.[15] It is almost never a neat exchange and normally is continually tested. But if others—parents, children, a job, other friends, hobbies—are mostly chosen over the partner, what is being shown is the flip side of "across a crowded room," and the partner as the "one and only." At that point the partner is both let down and unprotected: disloyalty hurts. So does not being preferred. The not-chosen becomes the not-partner.

Once again, an underpinning of the emotional life of love is getting the economics of time and energy right. If couples don't choose to spend time and energy on each other, loyalty and respect remain undemonstrated. Some couples mark out times during the day (an evening walk or a glass of wine over dinner, undisturbed by children or phone calls), or vacations or weekends together, without children or friends, or activities, like gardening or listening to music together, as sacrosanct and privileged. For Sue and Bob Fox it was Thursday evenings. "We would have a sitter. And the two of us would take off. We used to spend a lot of time at a bar-restaurant in town where there would be these local colorful characters. Sometimes we would go to a movie, sometimes we'd just drive," Bob recalls.

Others remember events in which their partners (or in which they themselves) have made hard choices in favor of the relationship, sometimes alienating parents or close friends in the process.

Married life began with us living with my mum and gran. Mum was a very dominating person and ruled the roost. Many times, when Tom and I would be having an argument, Mum would step in and take over . . . It was a struggle. There were always two more people to consider, first, in our relationship . . . I became very depressed and soon lost my job. I felt I had reached the end. I knew I needed freedom. I eventually told my mum and explained everything to her. We cuddled each other and cried. It was such a relief. At last Tom, Mum, and I agreed on something: space was needed between us! That June we were offered a flat by the council. At last, our own front door! My mum saw us settled in and was happy for us . . . Three years have passed since her death. We feel stronger, relaxed, and more in love than ever. My mum's influence is still with me, but in the background, rather than the foreground.—**Justine Shelley, 33**

Closely allied to loyalty is respect. All relationships begin with an exalted respect for each other: delicacy for the other's feelings and a sense of awe for the other's gifts and talents predominate. Without the attention and privileges bestowed by your partner, such respect can fade: the opposite of both loyalty and respect is being taken for granted. Respect for each other is reflected in the decisions couples make, in large and small ways, as they live together, and take note (or not, as in the case of couples who are not happy together) of the differences between them.

One long (and telling) disagreement was that I desperately wanted to have a fourth child. Oliver did not, saying we couldn't afford it. We did try for one month, with no result. Finally Oliver said we'd continue trying and he would work even harder to earn more money . . . And that was the end of my wanting a fourth child: I at once knew I didn't want to shorten his life!—**Anna Tyler, 78**

Anna's experience is a rather dramatic example of the way in which both loyalty and respect can represent both loss (not having a fourth child) and also gain (not risking both a partner's health and goodwill) within a couple. The ensuing feeling of respect Oliver gained from Anna presumably strengthened and deepened their bond. Smaller, barely detectable instances of respect and loyalty bind these couples continually, as they report, from cooking meals specially tailored to the partner's tastes to pursuing private interests in moderation and in time slots that preserve time for the other.

The life of love depends on stoking these elements of the emotional connections between partners. In turn, these elements—focus, loyalty, respect, empathy, support, intimacy, and the style and modes of communication—depend on the choices couples make of time, energy, and attention for each other, and the perspective that says they are in this for the long term, in a singular alliance.

Martin Curtis and Dennis Gordon

Martin Curtis and Dennis Gordon live in Chicago in a comfortable sun-filled apartment, overlooking the lake. They have been together for thirty years. Martin, fifty-eight, was raised in rural Ohio; Dennis, sixty-three, in Wisconsin. They met as postgraduate students in Chicago in the mid-1960s. At that time Martin was married and a philosophy student, while Dennis, never married, was doing work on French history. Dennis had been a high school teacher after college. During this period he was in a heterosexual relationship, which ended when he moved to Chicago to work on his Ph.D.

Martin and Dennis were friends initially, meeting when they were students connected by a mutual interest in the seething campus politics of the turbulent 1960s. It turned out that not only the times were turbulent; so were their personal lives. Falling in love with each other changed the course of their individual trajectories, personally and professionally, from early in their relationship. But adaptations in smaller ways have been required over time, as while the two have common histories and interests, as Dennis observed, in some ways they could not be more different. The story of how they have forged a happy partnership is one of how a couple manage to remain emotionally connected, supportive, and respectful with tremendous grace.

Martin Curtis:

I came from a Protestant background, from stoic, undemonstrative, un-complaining types, who don't nag or do guilt trips and who, when they worry, they worry quietly. My father was the town postmaster, who suffered from ulcers, and at one point, when I was also ill at home for a long period, he was home with hepatitis. As a child, I was sickly, taught at home for long periods, long periods of frustration and boredom—I had a little school desk up against my bedroom wall. I remember trying to learn long division and screaming and kicking the wall because I couldn't get through it. Though I grew up in rural Ohio, my parents weren't unsophisticated—they'd both been to college. They'd come from ministers on one side, and farmers on the other. I was born during the war and my mother went back to be with her family in Ohio while my father was overseas. When he came back, they just stayed in Ohio.

Before high school I was very much involved with church—Sunday school and youth group. I was top of the class at school. So when I reached high school, I went to a better high school, in the big town, and lived with my aunt. I did very well there. My family was quite poor, and focused on saving and putting me and my sisters through college. I don't think I realized the extent of this—I remember wanting a European car, a Mercedes. Because in high school I was chosen as an exchange student and went to Norway one summer with American Friends Society [a Quaker international educational exchange organization] and that sort of Europeanized me. In high school I had friends who were sort of the nonathletic but smart—even nerdy—sort.

Then I went on to college—to Oberlin College, a small liberal arts school in the Midwest. It was a magical time for me. I got involved in music there—playing the trumpet and singing in the choir. I had my own classical music radio program. I thought I was going to be a lawyer, but instead I got interested in German history. So instead of law school I went to the University of Chicago to do a Ph.D., right in the middle of the '60s, finally finishing in 1973. It was the Cuban missile crisis while I was in college, then Vietnam—it was an exciting period to be studying international theories and history. In fact, I went through a conversion experience over Vietnam: my family had always been Republican and I became a Democrat and I think in a way my family went through a similar change.

During that time, when I first got to graduate school, there was something called the Student Homophile League. That was the first time I had ever encountered open homosexuality. I was married at the time. I had gay friends—people who worked in the library—before I got married, though they weren't frank about it. They were in the Homophile League. So I was sort of aware of that going on, and I was a little frightened by it.

I got married in 1967—and by then I was already in denial, frightened by these things. But that was the way it was done . . . There wasn't any question. Homosexuality wasn't a thing then. It was simply I was sexually aroused by some things connected with guys and the thought of it, and I wasn't particularly aroused by *Playboy* . . . I had known that pretty much since high school and there were a couple of situations in college even when I—well, one guy I kind of flirted with but we never did anything. Not that I labeled it as flirting. Even though I was conscious that I did want to be near this person, even to have sex with him. I'd experimented at age twelve to fourteen or so with some neighbor kids, but certainly didn't label it "homosexual" then. I remember looking up the word in the dictionary and I remember reading Krafft-Ebbing and it was kind of like pornography: there was a section there on homosexuality. So, sure I was aware, but the label didn't really exist in my mind . . . I felt my feelings were more in the sense of "traditional, European culture": that it was something people did, but it wasn't a lifestyle . . . Certainly it wasn't being gay as a birthright, a sort of genetic predisposition and therefore your God-given right, as it has become now. I just thought of myself as someone who would date girls and get married.

I had three or four girlfriends, but no sex until I met the woman, Gwen, I eventually married. When we got married neither or us wanted children then—we were both in graduate school at that point. I never really understood what love was until I met Dennis. I thought at that point that I loved Gwen, but it certainly wasn't a deep infatuation, more a kind of companionship, really. We parted, in the end, civilly . . . Leading up to that, we'd both had affairs, and she had become very involved with her supervisor

. . . Two years before we finally parted I went to Germany on a fellowship and she came along, trying to write up some of her research. By then there was a lot of tension and fighting. We were young, inexperienced, and in Germany, where she had less reason to be than I. But I don't think either of us thought we were going to split up. Then just before we left, we went to visit Norway, to revisit my AFS friends and family. While we were there, on an endless Norwegian summer evening, at a pretty wild party, she slept with someone, and so did I, of a sort—an unconsummated sexual relationship with a man.

When we came back she began to do research for the guy she had the affair with, and I had another sexual encounter—a one-off—with a man. It was the first time it was consummated, and it was very disturbing—the risk, the pain, the lack of emotional connection. And I couldn't talk about it with Gwen, so it was part of the breakdown, part of beginning to conceal things. Soon afterward I found out about her and her boss, through her carelessness. She swore off him, and then I found out she was considering being with him again, so I just walked out. As we were about to move and had just found another apartment, in that sense it was fortunate. She moved into the new one, and I just stayed. And that was the end—February 1972.

I knew Dennis at that point, through mutual friends, though I wasn't particularly friendly with him. I think he frightened me a bit. I mean he feels an obligation to talk with strangers! He'll speak to people in the elevator! He's open—he's much more aggressively social than I am. There was something about him that frightened me, and I don't think—I've asked myself this question—was it a potential attraction? But I don't think it was because I wasn't attracted to him physically then. It was later—not till 1972—when I guess I was really in trouble with Gwen, that I started to really get to know him and talk to him.

We used to see each other around campus and we started to have lunch together, talk about various things. So I started to talk about Gwen. He wasn't in any relationship. My understanding—he'll tell you his own story—is that he didn't think of himself as gay at all then. He'd had some girlfriends and had had sex with one. But he was very much into cerebral things—academics and religion. I think religion for him was—well, he got off on the deep end of Catholicism, though he was High Anglican. He was in the process of resigning himself to celibacy.

When I got to spend time with him, I got hooked on his wisdom. He was much more skillful than I—more experienced than I—in personal relations. And he's a good talker, free with advice. I'm not so good—I would stumble out a sentence or two and then he would be off, and that was comforting. I've always been a sucker for bright people—con artists, even—and that's what really attracted me to him.

So when I left Gwen I moved in with Dennis. I called him and said, "Listen, I have to go somewhere"—we hadn't sorted out the new apartment quite then—and he said, "Well, you can sleep on the couch for a couple of nights." So I went and stayed with him. It was two weeks before we actually became lovers. Over that period when I was getting to know him better, I became very affectionately attached to him. I just wanted to be with him, though I hadn't yet labeled that as a sexual feeling.

I didn't think he was doing that either. But he certainly had become a very good friend to me, and in those days . . . he was a serious cook and introduced me to a lot of things. He used to cook suppers for me—you know, the way to a man's heart . . . And we just enjoyed spending time together. I didn't think at that point that cooking for me was a seductive act at all, though. I think he recognized to some extent what was possible but denied it because of his cerebral nature and ideal—he fully expected it to be a platonic friendship of the type he had had with other friends in earlier places and times in his life.

During that period in which I stayed with him, it was very emotional. We did smoke pot in those days, and one night, about two weeks after I was staying there, he'd made me dinner and we smoked pot—and then we made love. I was the aggressor in this, but he was willing. I remember it being overwhelming. It was like a physical illness in the morning—the psychological impact of it was enormous. I just couldn't get out of bed. I recognized even then that it wasn't just a hangover. That this had been an important step.

I finally dragged myself out and we went to the movies—we saw *Klute*. I remember I cried on the way over there. The movie was good, though.

Dennis was remarkably strong. He was very comforting. His strength came out then—I didn't have it at that point. It was just as momentous, maybe, for him. But maybe not; these things take time. It wasn't a lifelong relationship at the first moment. I think he perhaps had some reservations about—or doubts—he wasn't just jumping in.

It's odd. I think for me, this was the revelation, in the real sense of the word, about my sexuality. Up to then I wasn't able to accept the fact that I fell into that category. And then, I welcomed the category. It made sense to me.

I knew . . . that it was love, that I wanted to be with him, and very soon. Within the next week. I think he was worried—of course I was very needy and emotional at that time. But I'm ornery in my own way . . . At one point he proposed we break it off. He went away on vacation and when he came back he was ready to break it off—that was the following summer. He was reacting to my willfulness, or partly just his being uncomfortable with being in the relationship. He hadn't imagined he was going to have one. Once or twice in the first year I might have felt really frustrated but never to doubt being with him. But Dennis did think, "Do I really want to be in this?" in that first year. He'd gone back to his family for the summer break and gone traveling and came back saying he wanted to break up. I begged him. And he gave in. I don't think he'd realized how much I'd really wanted *him* till then . . .

We didn't "come out"—it wasn't really a thing so much that you did in those days. We gradually introduced each other to our families, as you know, friends. It wasn't till fairly recently that I mentioned to my mother that we were having an anniversary. Our strategy was to make it clear that we were very attached to each other, and when we moved in completely together in 1978—because it was then that I moved back from Wisconsin after I left a job there—it became pretty obvious. So we did everything except call it by its name, which has been our strategy at work and otherwise. Dennis's mother died in 1989. When she was ill, she said something about being glad that Dennis had found me, and that she hoped we would take care of each other. It was really sweet.

Then I finished my Ph.D. and accepted my first academic job—with the logic of a graduate student at the time I felt there was no choice. Dennis already had a job, at a college in Chicago. It meant that I moved to Wisconsin, a few hours away, and we couldn't live together . . . We had rationalizations: it's only for four or five years; we'll have weekends; I'll come down to Chicago for summers, or he'll come to Wisconsin for vacations . . . I left after five years, without tenure. I didn't put my heart into competing for it. It was partly, no largely, because I finally wanted to live with Dennis. It didn't work being apart so much.

During that time I wasn't faithful, yet I think that both of us are not the kind of people for whom casual sex is very meaningful. I did have sex that wasn't really casual, you know, with people I liked and respected, bright and amusing, who probably had hopes regarding me that I didn't want to reciprocate. And I think Dennis had a few encounters, sort of tit for tat, as he knew I was going to be fooling around. We don't do one-night stands very well. But that hasn't happened for at least fifteen years. None tested our commitment to each other.

Once I decided I was leaving Wisconsin and returning to Dennis, it was wonderful. It definitely meant we were moving in together. We got an apartment together. It was a romantic step. There weren't really any academic jobs available in Chicago for me in my field, so instead I thought I'd try something else—law school, maybe, finance. Instead, I got a job with an international educational consultancy, and now I'm the head of it, and I've done very well by it.

Finally getting our own place together was great. We've always enjoyed sleeping together. We both like cooking, and eating out, and travel, and music, and theater. And there's the nearby church—it's Episcopal—and it is a central point of the gay community here. He got involved first and then I did. So we share the church, as well. Some people share the theater, some have a house in the country. With us I think it's mainly three things: the church, travel, and food. We also have a lot intellectually in common. We're both pretty Europeanized: Dennis speaks fluent French and I speak German and we're both learning Italian, as we love Italy. We're unhappy about a lot of aspects of American culture and styles; the materialism, the religious right, a lot of politics. Maybe the grass is always greener.

Church has been very important to both of us. I've always felt good about going to church, and till then I'd gone from time to time but felt bad about not going. I made the conscious decision to go to our present church not for religious but for social reasons. That is, I needed a community, something to do that wasn't work. We don't really socialize with people from the church—we do that mostly with the friends Dennis has built up over the years at his college. But the church and its activities still form a community for us . . . Some of the gay people at our church were recently talking and they said the nice thing is that it's not a place that "tolerates" homosexuality—it's increasingly a place where a lot of families and children go but somehow everything seems to work out—it's integrated.

In the early days we'd spend fairly long periods of time being intimate, having sex. I miss that. We don't do that anymore. We have sex not infrequently but not five times a week. Probably every two weeks or something like that. The variety, duration, amount, and foreplay, and so forth have declined sharply partly because of the physical energy that's required, and partly because of the time that's required. We tend to have sex in the morning and there's always then something to get up for, whether it's work, or chores on the weekend, or church, or whatever it is. So that—that's sort of disappointing, but at the same time it's not. I don't obsess about it. I'm grateful for what we have. I love sex and, for me, it's like peanuts—it's never enough! Sexual intimacy carried over a whole evening or an afternoon just doesn't seem to be possible anymore. But I will say that as an act of pleasuring each other—maybe partly *because* it's become rarer—it's probably more important.

I'm still a fairly pushy person with him. That was and has been an issue. I think for me a turning point was when we were out celebrating New Year's Eve—1973–1974—that I came to the realization that I was not always going to get my own way in this relationship. And we kind of made a symbolic declaration about that, which was that I loved him so much that if he felt strongly about something, I would let him have his way.

On the whole that's been the case since then, though I should say that I'm still stubborn and willful and I do quite often get my way, because I get in there faster, and quite often I cut off other courses . . . We've been together thirty years and even in the last five years I've been fighting this battle with myself to an extent. In fact the worst row we've had in the last few years is over window treatments. I mean—you'd think, as gay guys, we'd have no problem with what goes on a window! As I said, I'm faster, so as soon as we moved in, I declared I wanted nothing on the windows because I liked the light—just the venetian blinds, which come with the territory. So that's the way it was, but he has always said he wished we'd had drapes. The subject never really went away, so it came up again five years ago, years after we'd moved in. So I said, "Okay, let's look into it." But then I didn't give in; I said, "You only want drapes because your mother had drapes." To which he replied, "It's cold in here and they keep out the cold in winter." I said, "How can they possibly keep out the cold in the winter if the wind's going to blow right under them?" He said, "The glare in here off the floor off the water is terrible—we live with a view onto water—and we need drapes of some kind because it's blinding in here and it gets very hot with the sun reflecting in here." So I said, "Well, you can't very well have drapes because the air conditioner's in the window" . . . We let that go too far. I still have my way. We never got drapes. But I lost something, I have to say, because I didn't give in and because we didn't do drapes just *because* it would make him feel more comfortable, and I'm sorry about that. Because his response was to say, "Well, I guess we just can't talk about that anymore." I feel now he's sort of punishing me a little bit, of course . . .

There are only really small things that keep cropping up that are sort of disuniting . . . like I walk too fast: I like to make exercise out of it. But for him, it's a time for conversation. I need to be doing something all the time. He's much more interested in turning himself off: the computer off and the television on, while I do the opposite. It's only an issue because we live together in a not very large space. And I'm Felix and he's Oscar: he's got no awareness of things being out of order—he can walk right by something and not see it, while I'm constantly picking things up and resenting the fact that he hasn't. So I nag him! The dark side of it is that I can get feeling morally superior. So he reigns me in and tells me I'm making him feel "like I'm not worth anything." And I feel terrible. So I've taught myself a little game: I say, "If I were living here alone, would I cook this meal? Would I clean up this mess?" and of course I would. It's my choice. It doesn't make a difference him being here, for that, really. And he's taken on projects, like cleaning up his study. We both recognize the syndrome. We both make our gestures, even though it keeps cropping up. I learn to try to control myself, but it still happens. In fact, sometimes Dennis can get so angry he can almost tell me to pack my bags and get out, and then—this is to his credit—twenty-four hours later we've patched it up. When I become pushy or ornery or whatever, he's learned to say, "You know, this is your weakness, not mine!" And sometimes I laugh. Because it's such a syndrome! No matter how much we say we won't go through this, we do, over and over again!

I never ever feel I just want to get out, though. I absolutely never think it's going to end. I always recognize that this is a bad patch and that, you know, in a day or so we're going back to normal . . . there's so much good that we have. And we really need each other. In every way: physically, emotionally, materially. I always know we're going to get over this.

I think there's a Christian dimension to my understanding of our relationship. My theology's not too good, but basically, I think there are a couple of points. One is that nobody's perfect; you have to live with people's faults. And the other is what you hear from the pulpit frequently: "God's love is unconditional"—that there are transcending values: to be accepting, to live with someone despite his faults. That there is something that transcends the faults, transcends the problems, that transcends the moment, whatever that may be—the ego, the whims, the infidelities—that there's something there. I'm certainly not a Bible-thumping Christian, but I think the best, the closest I can come to a theology in my life, is a sense of grace, of providence that good things have happened to me, including and most especially my relationship with Dennis, that I absolutely did not deserve. As I come to the realization of the grace and happiness that it has brought me, completely undeserved, I'm constantly thankful for it.

From time to time I do say this to Dennis or we show each other how special we are to each other. Every year we have this tradition of celebrating our relationship at New Year's. We don't generally go out with other people—or if we do, he doesn't like it. We'd rather go out together. And then there's our anniversary, which comes soon afterward, in February.

We've talked about my sense of thankfulness. Well, you know, our church serves the gay community, and there have been a lot of deaths, and AIDS has been quite a part of this community. So, in the '80s, when it was so much the dominant thing, I used to say to Dennis—and I still think about it, though I don't say it as often as I used to—if I hadn't had Dennis, I would be dead. Because if I were alone, I would have certainly been promiscuous, and you didn't have to have been very promiscuous in the '80s to be dead. And that's another example of the devoutness I feel about our relationship.

I do think that being conscious of gratitude is very important. Just after supper when we're sitting there having finished, we hold hands a little bit, and quite often say something very explicit, like "thank you," or, "Dennis, what would my life be without you?" And he does the same to me. And it's good it should happen frequently.

Dennis said yesterday, when we were talking about participating in this study, you know, we think of ourselves as quite normal, a normal couple, like so many other normal couples. But every now and then someone says something to one or both of us about how much they admire how long we've been together, or how we are together, and of course, this makes us very proud and very humble. We're living our lives and are grateful for how well it's worked out.

Dennis Gordon:

The first thing to say about me is that I was an only child. I bring that into the relationship. I was never in any kind of real relationship before Martin—I mean, outside of friendships. I'd dated some women. But it was never living together or anything like that. I did feel something like love for some—but I was very cagey about anything developing. Consciously I thought that was because I had plans and fitting a relationship with any commitment into them didn't work. I wanted to study and I knew that would take a period of time, in which I didn't want to get bogged down. In fact I took five years after college— I taught in a high school during that time—to decide what exactly I wanted to study in graduate school . . . I wasn't sure if it would be history or literature.

During my time as a high school teacher I did have a relationship with a woman. We became quite close and we did a lot of things together. It was sexual but I didn't find it very passionate. She wanted to get married. She also wanted to have a child. But I had these other plans, so nothing came of it. I chose to leave—I'd been teaching in Madison, Wisconsin, and got a place to do a Ph.D. at the University of Chicago, so I did leave, for Chicago, and that was the end of it. It was a sort of loose relationship: we enjoyed each other's company, she'd cook me birthday dinners, but we always had our own places. I knew it wasn't going to work out long term, and I was excited about starting something new, a new life for myself in a new city.

I'd grown up in a smallish town in Wisconsin, near which both my parents' families had settled in the nineteenth century—I'm half Italian and half Austrian on one side and half English and half French on the other. When I was three, my father, who was only thirty-two at the time, died in a freakish medical accident. He'd had a bad tonsil infection; he'd run away when his parents were taking him and his siblings to have their tonsils out when he was a child so he'd never had them removed. He'd also developed a hyperthyroid problem, and in those days (the end of the '30s) they treated this with iodine. When the surgeon opened him up for the tonsillectomy, they found the thyroid gland had shredded and was all wrapped around his windpipe. He died on the operating table. I think it may have actually been a botched surgery.

I don't remember it, but it was a shock for my mother. She was really quite strong, from what people tell me. And she had a very supportive kinship network. That was my family. I had good, warm familial relationships, cousins who were like brothers and sisters to me; we exchanged holiday gifts and visits, and it was a lively, musical family in which there was culture and that kind of thing.

I was an only child, but I wasn't lonely. But now that I look back on it, I was something of a loner, in the sense that I enjoyed playing with neighbors' kids, but I also kind of liked doing things by myself. I was fairly independent, a reader—I remember myself as a little kid reading things in the backyard. I'd get lost in it. I still do that—read to escape. I was kind of a brainy kid, I guess you'd say, and I got quite a bit out of succeeding in school. In high school in particular I got kind of intellectually alive. I went to Amherst College and took a number of languages and placed, in French, into the literature level, so that was the beginning of my serious study of French literature, at the start of college. I loved the history and drama of studying French too, which was why I was torn between doing either history or French literature for a Ph.D.

At Amherst we went to chapel—or we could go to church in town. But you had to sign in; there was an honor code. I wasn't really a churchgoer then—only now and then. That came later. I liked going to the Episcopal church, which is the one I'm still in, but it didn't make a lot of demands on me. I was, in fact, a very independent, opinionated person in college. I had a lot of good friendships then, supportive intellectually and emotionally too, but not in a sexual sense or anything like that. I must have been remarkably repressed then.

Sexuality was not something I thought about a lot . . . even though there was a certain amount of experimenting and dating with women and all. When I heard about people living celibate lives—it wasn't something I considered for myself—in the course of my study, I didn't think it was a particularly big deal. You know, you choose this, or you choose that . . .

I went to the University of Chicago in 1963. Two years later Martin came, just out of college. We had a class together; I remember that he was going off to do something in eastern Europe, for his research, and I thought that was really interesting and exciting. That was back in cold war days and I'd never known anyone who'd gone behind the iron curtain. He and his wife were going to go. This would by then have been near 1969 or so. Meanwhile I'd gotten my job at the college, where I've remained ever since, and was finishing my Ph.D. I was very lucky to have gotten that job, and I moved into a very nice apartment belonging to the university. It was in that period that Martin came back from eastern Europe. I saw him and I was really interested in his experiences. I'm kind of a gregarious person despite not minding being alone and so I suggested we have lunch or something. He told me later that he was afraid of me—or words to that effect. And that he saw my friendliness as somehow or other sexual, or predatory, or maybe just kind of interested in him personally. I disabused him of that! I wasn't at all aware of that element. I had a number of friends who'd studied and researched abroad, especially in exotic, unusual places—and I was just fascinated by this stuff!

So, finally we got together for lunch and we talked and from then on I would see him once in a while for lunch. Then he began going to the university gym, and I worked out at the gym, and sometimes we would run together; and we would use the swimming pool at the same time, and he would begin talking to me. From that point he began talking more about himself. Little by little—actually it made me kind of uncomfortable to hear about it—he seemed to be having some kind of trouble in his marriage. I've always felt a little squeamish about listening to people's personal stories. I'm kind of warm and all, and I like others, but I like to keep my distance, boundaries. I didn't at that point think my boundary issues with Martin were about sexuality. They may have been, but that wasn't what I was conscious of.

This was at the end of the sixties, early seventies. My entire world was exploding. I was supporting the Vietnam War at the beginning. Not gung-ho, but it seemed very important, having to do with the cold war and stopping Communism, and I can remember very well the huge turnaround. It was really revolutionary for me with some of my friends in graduate school—this was when Johnson was president—to see that this was a horrible mistake, this war. It was bleeding the country and it was horribly brutal. I'm kind of by nature a conservative fellow, in a nonpolitical sense, but I began to have some serious doubts about things I'd taken for granted. And at the same time, this whole sexual explosion was going on too, the beginning of sexual liberation of every kind, including gay liberation. The church was moving to have women priests . . . In the midst of all this, within this context, I got talking more to Martin about his personal difficulties, because that was another part of it: it became a good thing to be self-revelatory, that was part of the sea change too.

Little by little he told me more about himself and his own sexual interests. This came on very slowly, over a period of months. I think I was really surprised to hear of his sexual interests and his sexual history. At least, I, in those innocent days, took it for granted that if someone was married, then they were married. At any rate I tried to be as supportive as I could. But then

I found myself, as we got more emotionally intimate, that I could understand more about what he was saying . . . I realized that I was feeling closer and closer to him and had, really, feelings that I hadn't experienced before with any other of my male friends . . . It wasn't initially, though, when I think about it anyway, a physical thing . . . But I began to look forward to seeing him. He'd gotten under my skin. I think as I look back now that it was a very happy coincidence of things.

I still was thinking about doing my usual "cutting out" . . . When I came back in the fall I found it was not possible to act on my decision to cut out— I couldn't just cut him out. I felt kind of filled with a feeling that I should reach out to him and stick with him. It just kind of came to me like that. That this really wasn't right just to treat him as any other person I knew. Because I realized I had very, very strong feelings towards him. Not of responsibility but fondness, and that it was kind of like something I should do if I was really going to be true to something in myself. An ethical thing, you know.

[Being physically intimate] was a totally new experience for me. And frightening, confusing . . .

When things finally really fell apart in his home, he just had to get out— they had personal trouble that had nothing to do with me. I offered him a place to stay. He stayed with me for several weeks. And it was during that period that we became intimate—February of '73. I was kind of frightened by it. I didn't know what he expected and I certainly didn't know what to expect. It must have been something like an opera buffa or something. But there was real respect for each other. We were taking each other very seriously. I knew that after we'd been intimate for the first time that this would be embedded within a relationship.

I don't know that I called it "love" then, but yes, sure, it was that. I did feel that I was in love with this man and I felt that he reciprocated. But I also saw signs that he wanted a certain amount of independence. I think he didn't want to go from one tie to another tie.

About a year and a half later he took his job in Wisconsin. We did a lot of things together before that. He loved sailing and we flew out east, rented a sailboat, picked it up on the coast, and sailed to Martha's Vineyard. It was kind of funny and a little traumatic too: he was like the captain of the ship and I don't like to take orders! We joke about it now and tell stories about that trip because actually I can't imagine two people who are more dissimilar than we are.

He and I are in almost every way, in terms of personality traits, different. He is rather northern, phlegmatic, a man of not too many words. As you see, I am the opposite! One of his childhood heroes is that man Taylor who was the efficiency expert. "Efficiency" is Martin's middle name and we joke about it a lot. He will tell me in the kitchen when I'm making the coffee in the morning or something that there's a more efficient way of taking this out of the refrigerator! His idea is at breakfast you make the coffee, you sit down, you have your breakfast, and you get on with things. And I—I stretch it out if I'm not going anywhere; I'll read the paper . . . So we're quite different.

We have just observed our thirtieth anniversary if we count that February as our first encounter, which we do. I think more significant is the twenty-five years living here, in this apartment, which we're celebrating too. Because that's the first time in my entire adult life I've actually shared a roof with somebody. And it was not easy for me at the beginning. We found it together and put stuff into it together and everything. But I somehow kept thinking— I never admitted this to him—that this was really like my place and he was sharing it with me!

No one close to us in our families has ever been anything but supportive of us being together. We're both from—though they're very different families—like New England families in the sense of letting people have their space, be themselves, and you don't pry. They would have had to have been brain dead not to understand that we have a life together because we talk about our life together.

But otherwise, I'm just not someone who goes around talking to people who don't matter to me about these things. My colleagues at the college know. One of my colleagues was chair of the department for several years and knew Martin. Actually, Martin taught as an adjunct at the college for a few years before we got together. So some people knew him and later on I said, "Martin and I are living together," and they were interested and glad to hear it.

We never—it may be something to do with our generation, I don't know—at any particular moment made this big declaration: "Oh, by the way, we're gay, and we're partners." The whole thing developed very organically. And nobody made any comments about it. Basically, my feelings have always been that it's a natural thing, so you act naturally about it. And if anyone asks you a question, directly, you tell them.

Martin is a very strong, steady person. Very steady. And I think very patient and persevering, in everything he does, not just a relationship. He is a very dependable person. As a matter of fact, it's very interesting: I mean, my mother knew we had this living-together relationship though we never had a talk about it. Just before she died, I was visiting her in the hospital and she said words to the effect that, "You really should stay with Martin because he's a very good man." Basically she saw his steadiness. So that was very important. He is very steady and I think he basically kept me from locking the bolt a great deal.

Our differences have always been around. When Martin sees me being inefficient he criticizes me. If he does it with a smile on his face then, you know, I answer him in kind. If he's serious about it, then I just tell him, as they say in the old country, to sod off! He's learned, as I've learned, to find the amount of seriousness in something. I've learned, for instance, that if Martin's under a lot of pressure at work, then I recognize that he will express that in ways of pushing the efficiency thing more, or something. So I will give him more leeway: we try to read the meaning behind something, not just the literal words. I take comfort from knowing, from understanding "this is the way his mind and emotional system work."

There are some things, because of his efficiency, he does superbly well. He's become the chef of the family. He loves it. It's a kind of a sensual thing for him and he finds it relaxing. When he comes back home from work, he loves to prepare a meal. There's a ritual to it. As long as I do the shopping, he'll do this. He's also very good at presentation. And of course I'll clean up afterwards, so it works out all right. But I have to tell you, it's wonderful to have somebody cook your meals in the evening, you know—it's really nice! Before we both did the cooking.

I'm the gregarious one. I do tend to be more of the ideas person, for who we're going to call and what we're going to do, what movies to see, what vacations to take.

He's an active person—Saturday mornings he just goes and does his gardening and other projects, while I like to sit and read mysteries, for example. I can do that—take a day off and read mysteries. But he wants to do serious things. He wants to do volunteer work when he retires—especially with the church, which he's become very involved with. He has so many responsibilities there. It's a big part of my life too, but not in quite the same way. For the last ten years he's been a member of the vestry—the governing board of the parish. The priest in charge depends on him a great deal because he really is good at this. In a sense I introduced him to the church and now I find myself, I'm like a parish widow in a sense!

I have a lot of intellectual interests to do with history and politics and religion that I would like to have discussions about. Martin is not a discusser. I can't imagine two people who are so close as we are and trust each other so well—our lives are totally combined—who simply don't sit regularly and talk about these issues.

I do know we agree, though, because we talk about it to some degree. I know, for example, that he's a Democrat and I'm a Democrat, and you know, that he thinks Bush is a jackass and I think Bush is a jackass. But then, in talking about details of policy, generally he doesn't want to talk about these things. Basically he thinks three, four, five minutes is long enough time to talk about these things.

Early in our relationship, when we weren't living together, we each had sexual experiences with others. It wasn't really relationships. I think that it was a function of several things. First of all, the newness for me of this kind of sexual experience: the sense that I really needed to experiment, to find out things about myself. And also, I think, a way of dealing with the thought that Martin isn't here, we're not married, after all, and I don't really want to be cut short. And so I really needed to grow a little in this regard. We did not talk about it. We developed a kind of an understanding. I mean, we did have a major difficulty when he was in Wisconsin because of an involvement he had there. Not a one-nighter. It was with a friend. It wasn't a relationship as far as he described it. And there was other experimenting as well. And Martin, unlike me, really wanted to be honest about this. And I didn't take it well at all. I think I felt very insecure because of my lack of experience and I was really quite angry and quite ready to call if off. Just kind of run away from it. But that was a momentary thing. And Martin was also very persistent. He just pulled me back.

He insisted, and we never talked about it afterwards. We decided that no matter what happened in the area of sexual experiences, don't ask and don't tell. I don't want to know about it. And I don't want you to know about it. And I think—I don't know how that's served him—but I think it's served me for that period of time. Because I didn't have to go into confessional mode with him and then afterwards, when we were building a life together here and taking on all these other things, that phase became history. I feel that both of us are faithful, I suppose. But I would put it even, I think, more honestly, not cynically: whether objectively faithful or not, I think, given what I know about my psychological and emotional makeup, I don't want to know what I don't want to know about. And there are other things that are very important. So in terms of finances and professional worries or health or whatever, obviously we want to be as open as possible. But in terms of sexual experimentation or peccadilloes or whatever, that, I think, is, for me, best not to go into. But also I think it's clear that if real relationships developed, you would eventually know, anyway. So I think at that point—well, that's the challenge, that's what I'd feel was a betrayal.

We haven't talked about it in twenty years but I think that Martin saw sexual expression as at times a natural part of friendship. And I never did. I couldn't imagine having a sexual experience with a friend. I wouldn't pontificate that everybody should be like this. People are wired differently about these things. I know there are a lot of gay and straight people with open relationships and all that . . . I can balance a lot of things but I don't think I can balance those kinds of things.

His moving to Chicago was the watershed for us. If he'd gone on to another academic job elsewhere, or stayed and gotten tenure in Wisconsin— 99 percent of people in our profession do that; they wouldn't think of not doing it—and we would have continued being apart, I don't know, but I doubt if this relationship would have developed.

Most of our friends are ones we know through my college who have become good friends of Martin's as well. He has some really good, close, wonderful continuing friends from his childhood, but they don't live close by. Except for the woman who's the chair of his board of trustees, we don't socialize with Martin's work friends. She's a fascinating woman, a collector of art, and when we go to eastern Europe, where she has a house, we see her, and when she's here, we take her out to dinner because she's so good to us. We also have close friends—older people he met through the parish and are now retired—that we spend every Thanksgiving with. He's a musician and she is a teacher. We now know their married children too. And Martin made friends from his work in eastern Europe and we stay in touch with them and they've become friends of mine too.

And wine, and food, and travel are things we share and love together too. Martin's told me he never knew about taking vacations till he met me. He always traveled before because he had to, traveled for some "reason." So I introduced Martin to that.

Some of the things I remember most vividly of shared experiences are venues—being in certain places that have been important to us. Like the first trip we took together to Italy, we stopped at a place on Lake Maggiore and it seemed like a very magical place to us.

Also, we marked our twenty-fifth anniversary together by going to Naples and the Amalfi coast. I can just close my eyes and I can see the gardens we were in and all that kind of thing. I don't know if this is the case with Martin—he's certainly very visual and does lots of photography—but I can simply kind of close my eyes, or try to center myself, if I want to relax or something, and bring one of these places into my mind. It's not simply that the places themselves are physically beautiful, it's the association, the sharing with one another.

We were very pragmatic, seat-of-the pants, experimental in deciding who does what—obviously, there's no gender bias to drive things. I remember that first year we'd moved in together Martin was looking for work. He'd basically left his job there and decided he didn't want another academic career, and that he wanted to come to Chicago to live with me, which always moves me when I think about it. Before he got a job, he was getting himself organized here so he had more time around here. So he'd do certain errands and things like that. But once he began working, he got really busy. And so then what kicked in was the difference in our schedules. I took responsibility for a lot of the meals in those early years. I would kind of figure out what we'd have and then shop for it and prepare something. But again his efficiency would come into play and he would suggest that maybe it's a good idea to make some things ahead of time so we could have more than one meal instead of these . . . And he began—it took a long time—he began doing some of his first regular cooking.

We share all the expenses. We have a common checking account for household things and we have a common MasterCard and common American Express, which we use for all of our household things. But we also maintain two very separate individual accounts for our checking and whatnot. I had to spend a lot of the '80s responsible for the finances of my aunts and then later on my mother. I kept their accounts and Martin said he would help out by keeping track of the bills here, he took all of that on and he's been doing it ever since. He's very good at it—he's a good manager. I'm really bad with figures, really bad. I did it before because I had to. It didn't come naturally to me. I'm good at some things but I'm not good at arithmetic. Again, like cooking, Martin seems to like fiddling with figures. So he gradually took over.

One can look at this in a negative sense too. It can be charming and smart but it can mean that you can then become rather more self-indulgent and say, "I don't have to do this. Isn't it nicer to sit up with a Scotch watching the news while he's in the kitchen?" Sometimes he says, "Well, you like to sit there and think great thoughts."

But I worry a little bit about it, to tell the truth. Because I'm thinking about, talking about, gender-defined roles, and I must say that, we've never had any particular concerns about gender roles of any kind, either in terms of our sexual relations, or social, or anything else. Some people do—I just don't understand this among gay people—but there's role playing and everything. But I do know a lot of women who lose their husbands and their husbands did everything—you know, the books and everything else—and they just don't know what to do afterwards. I remember talking to Martin's mother when his dad was dying of cancer. Martin was away and I called her to see how things were going. She said, "Okay. I'm trying to balance a check book; you know, John has always done this. It's not so easy to do."

Even though I'm soon going to retire and Martin's looking toward it in a few years, we seem to have less time to relax together now then when we were graduate students or when we were just starting out. I don't know what the answer is to that. I think it has to do with patterns; we got into the tradition, or habit, of making love or having sex in the morning, waking up. That seemed to be the time which seemed most natural. And this is certainly true during the last half of our time together. I mean, sometimes we would like to have an intimate hour or two in the afternoon when we had afternoons free, certainly at night during our first years together, but even then we liked the morning. We're both fairly early-morning people, not night-owlers. I mean Martin really kind of likes to get to bed and sleep fairly early on. Monday through Friday, there's the workday thing—the alarm goes off at six thirty and Martin's off, an efficient breakfast and so on. Or sometimes it would be me, when I had to get up to go to the college. So that leaves weekends. Sundays are a problem because of church. That leaves Saturday. So Saturday—you know, it's like in a sense when you have to be that attentive to the calendar, it's like what Roman Catholics complain about with the rhythm method: you have the calendar out. And also Martin likes to go to the gym on Saturdays—I do too.

So we basically don't anywhere near pay the attention to each other physically that we both feel we want and should do. It's not like it's been a problem but I think it might be something we want to work on more when we both have more time, or when I have more time, when I've stopped going out to the college. I sometimes think "why can't we—" but I don't act on this—"why don't we then have a quiet, intimate 'let's see where it leads' time at the end of the workday?"

I do think sex is better in a couple of ways, though. There's less urgency . . . I mean, in the first years there was, in fact, a certain amount of figuring out about roles. "Who takes the initiative" sort of thing. Once you become really familiar with the other person, not only emotionally but also physically, then it's more comfortable. It's not so much exploratory and in that sense the trust—familiarity, of course, can breed contempt, but I'm talking about trust and knowing what the other person enjoys and not having to figure it out—is good. And also it's kind of a little more—how should I say?—a little more relaxed, a little bit less quick in that sense.

The physical passion, the lust part, I think, certainly does come in even if the urgency is less. The physical reactions are there. And the losing yourself—the thing about sex more than anything else that's there, it's unique in this regard, is that you really get lost in it. And there's a certain point where other things are resolved. And that's why it's important too. Martin has always thought that, you know, having it regularly was very important and I think he still does. My sense is that he is really disappointed that he and I can't find more time to pay attention to each other in this way. And I feel that way too.

Sometimes the lack of frequency has to do with physical problems . . . I guess when you get to be past fifty—well past fifty—there may very well be, I'm sure a mathematician could figure out the probabilities, that where one person doesn't have an ache or a pain, the other person does. And so that kind of is a turnoff.

But here's how I feel about it: I still find Martin's body physically very attractive, very much a turn-on. But the idea of other old male bodies I find a turnoff. It's funny but I guess it's partly because I don't think of us as as old as we are. But it's more. I think that people—you have images of you and your partner, that's what history does, a history together does. So when you touch—this is my theory anyway—when you touch someone you've known for twenty or thirty years, you're touching that person who was once twenty-five, who's now fifty. It's the same person. If you could open somebody's head, I think you see multiple images, you see this person just as you see yourself in that same sort of way. If you look in the mirror you don't see yourself all the time as the same age you are now. If a relationship has really deepened over the years and grown, then there is a nonchronological aspect to this . . .

I remember a woman telling me that she was at a wedding and she went into the ladies' room and when she opened the door, there was a mirror there that she didn't realize was there and the first thing she said was, "Oh, excuse me!" because she thought it was some old woman that looked familiar to her. I don't think you do see yourself as your age when you get older. And I think that happens with the way you think about the other person.

Martin and I have been thinking a lot over the years that we have been incredibly lucky in a lot of ways. Things just seem to have worked out very naturally—getting along with our differences, different ways of dealing with the world, with people. We have a very privileged life, in a material sense, in a social, and a cultural sense. We're really lucky.

5

Can There Be Romance? Enjoying Love and the Art of Appreciation

LOUISE and DANNY BERNSTEIN

IN *THE GODFATHER*, Michael Corleone is struck by a "thunderbolt" on meeting his first, Sicilian wife. While the drama of falling in love has always been mythologized, that particular word, with its expectations, has entered our lexicon of love. We expect to feel struck, bowled over, the moment we meet a lover. In contrast, and unsung, other love stories, just as durable, powerful, and legitimate, can and do start more quietly. No matter how they start, though, they all share that singular moment of illumination, that punctuation point, when the love story begins. In the film *When Harry Met Sally*, Harry and Sally fall in love after years of off-again-on-again friendship. Absent fireworks, there is a moment of transformation when it feels as if they have seen each other for the first time, and then the love story proper starts, as the movie ends. Each couple's love story begins when romance enters. They love to tell it; their friends and children love to hear it.

I saw my wife first in 1960, who, like all Fairy Princesses, has remained young and beautiful to this day, as I sat a hotel bar, young, assured, devil-may-care, smoking a cigarette and nursing a beer, while flirting with a blonde at one side and a redhead on the other—when suddenly the hubbub of voices stilled, the lights dimmed, and there, across the room, bathed in golden light, was this apparition of radiant beauty, suffused with vibrant energy. Somehow I saw that she had a boyfriend, but what chance did he stand? This woman was mine!—**Geoffrey Campbell, 58**

Sometimes the initial feelings of romance are not shared. More typically, the love story begins simultaneously. Fueled by physical attraction, the happy story begins to unfold, as it did for Michael Corleone, at legendary first sight. If a couple is lucky, this magical moment spins into a future because the two match and blend in other ways, as well. All couples who have remained in love can point with some precision to when the romance in which they are stars began. As Louise Bernstein recalls in this chapter, "It was a beautiful day and we were driving somewhere in the suburbs and I was just driving with him and I wasn't even looking at him, and I was in the car, and then at that moment it was 'Eureka!' . . . I looked at him and I just saw him differently, as if a light went on and he looked different in it . . . and at that point we started developing a romantic, a sexual relationship."

I was taken with her red hair, as well as her all-round good looks and bright, intelligent personality, and then I found out she was going out with another member of the club. So, in effect, I stole her away from him. I was quite amazed at being so bold. She, of course, was willing to be rescued.—**Mark Morrison, 49**

Past the "how we met," the romantic tale, with its obvious scaling of heights of heady discovery, of, against all probability, finding this particular hero or heroine and then settling into the fabled "happily ever after" of domesticity, also relates tribulations the couple have overcome or faced together. Sharing these triumphs, over time, increases romance and the heroism of love. So even if Hollywood's version of those dizzying love-at-first-sight feelings becomes more muted, romance still remains key to the enduring story.

This is, in part, why happy couples tend to bring into their stories times when feelings of romance, passion, or gratitude are recaptured—whether describing how their partners have sustained them through poor health, or noticing that they have caught a glimpse of the younger person they fell in love with through the mask of older age. These feelings keep the heroes and heroines of the romance alive. It keeps their stories "love" stories.

> I gave Tim my heart, my life, and my dreams . . . And I still see the young boy I married.—**Sharon Oberland, 45**

Love stories begin with mystery, novelty, drama, a heightened sense of being within something elevated as well as a continually renewed sense that you have found your counterpart. This state of bliss does come with inevitable questions, though. Will the uniqueness be sustained? Will the drama die? Where will this story take me? The suspense of new love is integral to its continuation. If you know the ending and can always predict what happens next, the story loses its drive, and interest and attention flag. Keeping the romance of love alive is not only about sustaining the thrills of early passion. It is functional for love's continuation: romance keeps a couple interested.

A lifetime of love now can mean an awfully long time. Do couples sustain the original intensity? If so, how, as routine takes over and pulls attention and energy back to other matters? A main theme seems to be that they manage to renew their feelings in part through enjoying each other. From sharing books (sometimes across different tastes), to theater, to music, to travel, to sport and gardening, to mutual friends, these couples convey a sense that a good proportion of their lives contains finding fun and pleasure together. Over-ridingly, a shared sense of humor, built up over common shared experiences, is a chief facet of this pleasure. As Sue Fox describes it, "the same things strike us as funny . . . and we tend to be struck the same way by the same kinds of things." The private jokes and funny things shared are episodes within happy stories. More, these experiences and customs become the stuff itself of love. "My sense of humor" becomes "our sense of humor."

> I believe that our success in our years together has been almost entirely due to our love and mutual respect for each other, our firm commit-ment to the vows made at the wedding ceremony—and our sense of

humor. If you can laugh at your mistakes and foibles, then all is well.—
David Gascoigne, 56

Part of enjoying each other's company is being comfortable and intimate enough to see each other with unwashed hair and blemishes, with all pretense and artifice gone, and to feel easy enough with each other to luxuriate in friendship. Another phrase repeated over and over by the couples in the study is "he [or she] is my best friend." "I'll be your best friend" is a child's prime inducement, offered like gold, when she wants something. She'll sell her soul: her friendship. For children, having a best friend means relying on that friend to pick them across a crowded playing field. It means they will not be left on the edges, picked last for a team. It means someone will pal around with you on the playground, be a bulwark against bullies. With a best friend you create private games with unique rules that only two can play. You share in-jokes, giggling while others look blank. Your best friend agrees when you find siblings deeply pesty, parents unfair, teachers wicked, and feels your glow when the class heartthrob smiles and nods hello. The reliability, safe harbor, and comfort of a best friend, the person with whom there are private and special habits, play, and pleasure, with an acute and sympathetic ear, is what people report about their partners.

Our love is as deep as ever—he is my soul mate and my best friend. I think we complement each other perfectly. He is quiet and compassionate, whereby I tend to be headstrong and determined. He definitely brings out the best in me and has supported me throughout every episode of our lives.—**Noreen Reilly, 72**

Even the very best of friends can be fickle or insensitive, failing to rise to the inevitable downs. In marriages the downs can be severely testing: money crises, bouts of depression, illness, jealousy, or even a sudden act of violence. How can the stories focus on positives and not be diverted by negatives? Prior research suggests that one important factor is showing each other care, respect, and trust. The operative word is "show."

Couples who have sustained love know how to show pleasure in and appreciation of each other. This can be through a steady drip of phrases ("you look great tonight," "thanks for the supper," "what a good job you've done with the bookcases") or gestures (kisses on greeting and parting, hugs or warm smiles when pleased). But gratitude can appear in other guises, punctuating daily routines with surprising, romantic bursts (the bunch of flowers to celebrate an achievement or the ending of a quarrel, the waiting drinks and proffered massage at the end of a difficult day, the perfectly judged present, planning a special event for your partner).

> My partnership is special because my husband tells me he loves me every day and what I mean to him . . . When I cook him a meal, even if it's only beans on toast, he thanks me for it . . . I may be fifty-five but to him I will be forever young; I have no fear in growing old with him. He gives me the greatest respect and he is so gentle.—**Maxine Crowe, 55**

My prior research shows that couples cite "gratitude" as one of the key things they value in keeping their romantic relationships alive.[16] Gratitude is what we all need from a partner: it can be the salve that makes pain bearable, reinforcing one's sense of uniqueness, or the "only you" quality of romantic love. The old complaint, "My husband doesn't appreciate me" or "my wife takes me for granted" points to what happens when gratitude is not expressed often enough. When it is, however—that is, when a loving gesture, an encouraging word, or a gentle demonstration of romance is offered—it tells your partner that you notice and appreciate the effort he or she puts into living together. Voicing how much you value your partner, or how happy you are that she or he is in your life, or how much you note her or his efforts for you can lengthen a memory foreshortened by irritation or momentary alienation. Noting "there is a history here that includes good times" can wave away a storm of angry words, cancel a spiral into despair, and turn a potential story of disaffection into one of appreciation.

Couples do, of course, vary on how that gratitude, or appreciation, is expressed. Francesca Cancian, in an important study of love in the 1980s, called *Love in America: Gender and Self-Development,*[17] in common with Barbara

Ehrenreich and her coauthors, in their seminal book, *Remaking Love: The Feminization of Sex*,[18] have independently made points about how "love" has been colonized by women as its experts: we look for overt, direct signs, that is, emotional connection through conversation, and outright declarations. In contrast, men often feel they are performing loving acts by making repairs, working hard at their jobs to pay for things couples jointly enjoy or need, or taking care of safety. They think they are repaying their spouses' loving words with loving gestures. Unfortunately, they often feel these go un-recognized and, as has been documented particularly by Cancian, they are often correct.

From the research I have done, corroborated by the accounts given for the present study, it is apparently not enough to feel that you care or to maintain an idea in your head that you value your partner. Couples who maintain love show or do things. This seems, indeed, to deepen the original passion by further layers. Action and affirmation apparently do more than heighten self-esteem. They actively help to restoke the original passion.

> I spent the first two and a half years pretty much in bed, unable to do much. My husband became mom, dad, housecleaner, cook, etc., as well as taking care of me and going to work. There have been many tears, depressions, anger, and fear expressed over the years . . . We didn't know if or when I would ever be okay. It has been very slow. I think I am now up to about 80 percent. My husband has been a cheerleader, supporter, and comforter to me. He kept me connected to the family, the kids, and to life during the most difficult of times for me. He has always made me feel special, important, and loved, even when I was in deep depression or just feeling and acting bitchy—**Janet Kramer, 49**

Expressing gratitude, doing things that feel caring, supportive, and romantic, is impossible to sustain continuously. Clearly, from accounts gathered for this book and from other research on hardy couples, many couples experience a great deal of discord. Happy, enduring relationship stories are those marked by feeling pleasure and comfort more of the time than not, rather than being free of either discord or conflict.[19] For a relationship to continue to feel happy, the balance of good or positive feelings, over time, outweighs the negative ones. Too much unpleasantness, again, rather than the absence of it, is what describes unhappy couples. Expressions of appreciation, verbal, physical, or symbolic through gesture or gift, all help to deliver such balance.

Louise and Danny Bernstein

Louise and Danny Bernstein live in southern Maryland; one of their two sons, now both grown, lives in Philadelphia, the other abroad. Louise, fifty-seven, runs a community arts program and grew up in Baltimore. Danny, fifty-eight, grew up in the same part of Maryland in which they now live. Both are Jewish, second-generation Americans who went to Ivy League colleges. Louise had had a few relationships before she met Danny; Danny had one serious one spanning his college years. Danny is a political consultant. The eldest and most professionally and personally successful of five children, he studied for a postgraduate degree in political science and worked as a political organizer and adviser, first in Boston and then in the Washington-Maryland area. He had recently returned to this area when he met Louise. Louise, a well-loved child, happier than her siblings, who were more complicated in their dispositions and desires, was close to her parents. After college Louise went to Yale Graduate School for a Ph.D. in Italian, during which time she spent a year researching in Italy. There she had a relationship with a man recently separated from his wife; the relationship ended and she returned to New Haven. She then abandoned her doctoral work. Unsure where she was going to go or what she would do next, she returned to Baltimore, then moved on to Washington, where she'd landed a job she reports she loved, with an international cultural-exchange organization. They met in D.C. in 1968.

Danny and Louise Bernstein's stories contain examples of poor health, distress, and discordant loyalties scattered across their independent accounts of overriding appreciation, pleasure, and respect, all of which have been clearly demonstrated to each other in the many years they have shared.

Louise Bernstein:

Our kids know the whole story of our courtship, and how I was sitting in the car and I fell in love with him, and how I said, "Are you going to ask me to marry you?" And they always laugh at the story, the story that we have always told them, year after year. But to this day, more and more now than before, I say to Danny, "It's true: I am so lucky that I met you." Because I have the life that I wanted, and I could only have had that kind of life with a man like him.

. . . When I was a small child, I was very happy. I remember—and I was a very responsible kid, but I always wanted to have fun—I wanted to be happy, and I knew my life would be happy, and I would be. I did have a sunny disposition. I would sort of, I would *avoid* unhappy situations and would be drawn to situations that made me happy, and I had to fight to work at it, but I thought it was important to have a happy life: I was only going to have one time!

My roommate's friend was a friend of Danny's. My roommate was fixed up with Danny and I with his friend, Dave, who actually became his business partner eventually. Danny knew from that moment that I—not my room-mate, his date, remember—was going to be the woman he would marry. He told Dave, on the way home, "Don't go out with her again. I'm going to marry her." So of course, Dave asked me out the next day. And so did Danny. I did go out with Dave again and we had an awful experience, but we're all friends now . . . At that point I was not at all interested in Danny. I thought he was very nice. I thought he'd make someone a very nice husband—that he'd be president of the temple, that sort, and not for me. He was persistent, but not pesty. I did tell him not to bother. And he just said, "Let me be the judge of that."

And I let him. I think that I was open to it just because he was very different from anyone I had been dating. I'd gone out with some real highfliers: one who became head of a college, another who was high profile at the time, who was married and kept pursuing me, which really annoyed me because I didn't want anything to do with him. The man I'd been going out with in Italy was separated from his wife and he pursued me hotly, and we had a very intense relationship. I think Danny was a contrast. He was ready to go at my pace. It felt comfortable to me.

He is a good listener and at this time I was so torn leaving graduate school. He's a tremendous listener, and to this day I talk a lot and he listens, and he knows what to screen out and what—always knows what—to hear. And sometimes I say, "Don't listen to me, I'm just chatting," but he knows—he knows when it's important, what to hone in on. I always feel he's attentive.

And I knew he was a "fine" person: he was politically committed, of high moral character, almost gentle. And the men of that age were not particularly gentle, well-mannered, well-spoken. And very interested . . . to have a good time, go to the theater, go out to eat, talk about books, all the things that had been important to us, thoughout our lives. From the beginning we had fun. As I said, I knew from a young age that I was going to have a happy life. And I felt that it was in my power to enhance my happiness by avoiding things that were painful and by being attracted to things that were good for me . . . And, not that I haven't had knocks, as everyone does, but I feel that I am very buoyant, and my relationships with men—I knew that sometimes the relationships with the most exciting men would have a short, well, you know, that the half-life would be shorter, and that . . . a long-term relationship would really require something more than that charisma, that sexual charge, that's there at first.

And I had never had a relationship where I had been friendly and *then* become intensely sexually attracted. That is what happened. And that was the first time that that had ever happened. That's the opposite of my parents. My father at the age of twenty-four saw my mother at the age of fourteen and decided he was going to marry her, but waited till she was twenty. So *that's* the love story that I'd grown up with!

So one day we were going out to see Tom Stoppard's play *Eureka!* I actually remember what I was wearing and I am not usually conscious of that kind of thing. I was dressed up—more than I ever get dressed up now, with stockings and heels and the whole thing—and we went to see that play and it was a lot of fun; it was about a vacuum cleaner and we laughed and laughed afterwards . . . This was in the late spring of 1968 and it was a beautiful day and we were driving somewhere in the suburbs and I was just driving with him and I wasn't even looking at him, and I was in the car, and then at that moment it was "Eureka!" This was after we'd seen the play. I was thinking, "*This* might be it; this *is* it; and *I want to be with him.*" I looked at him and I just saw him differently, as if a light went on and he looked different in it. And I am sure he knew that it turned at that point, and at that point we started developing a romantic, a sexual relationship. And it felt perfectly natural, with as much urgency—we were just primed and ready at that point and it moved very quickly.

That was in June and we got married in September.

At that time he was living near his parents, having just moved back to Maryland—he'd just gotten his job. I met his parents and I liked them, but I felt the one thing that would be really rough was that I was not an observant Jew and they were. And that was an issue in one way or another for a while. They figured out quickly that I wasn't religious, though they hoped I'd be a traditional Jewish daughter-in-law. It was clear that I was not; I am not a pushover and my mother-in-law was a very strong person who wanted things done in a certain way. It took my mother-in-law and me ten years to negotiate a peace.

So I moved to Maryland, and I started taking courses and Danny had this job tailor-made for him, with an office here and eventually in Washington, and we had an almost completely unproblematic, simple time. Except when his parents felt like they could just come without calling, just expect us to do things with them and their way. I think that was the one thing: establishing those boundaries, and I think since my own parents understood boundaries implicitly, or mine, anyway, as they'd grown up with me—I mean my mother-in-law, she didn't work, apart from for the temple, and was a very bright woman. But still she had a hard time understanding. I had a hard time getting her to understand that we had boundaries. Danny didn't stand up to her. He had a hard time confronting his mother, a very hard time, and that was at times frustrating to me. He didn't want to take care of it, though I asked him, "please." He just couldn't do it. From the beginning they were angry about my standing up to them, and they ruined our wedding. The night before it she wanted me to spend the night with her and a couple of her friends and I was with my family, and didn't want to. So they came to our wedding really angry. But Danny did not get resentful at me for this. He was just embarrassed. I was pissed off. I just stood my ground. With this whole issue with his parents he was glad I was taking care of it . . . He let me get on with it. It was hard for him to confront his parents and he didn't and I was sometimes a little annoyed, but I just figured, "Well, one of us has to do it, and I guess it will be me." I resented him sometimes for it, but it didn't interfere with our relationship, and the other thing was he really appreciated that I did it. I know that because he told me.

I think they expected because he was going out with someone who was Jewish and was marrying her, we'd just join the temple and slip into their lives and all—and you know, my parents didn't even belong to a temple, and we had to find a rabbi to marry us. Danny was the firstborn of five children and his parents cared a lot about what people in their community thought of him. My parents didn't give a shit. His parents belonged to a country club and they were hoping that we'd have this huge wedding. I went to college on a scholarship, graduate school on a scholarship. My father earned a decent living—we had everything that we thought was important to have but we didn't belong to clubs. I wanted to get married at home, and that was the first thing: "I can't dance at my son's wedding?" And my mother said to me, "I will give you the wedding that you want. Tell us what you want and if we can do it, we'll do it." Well, we wanted to get married with only thirty people. Actually, Danny wanted only six people.

They wanted us to join their temple. When our son was born, they wanted to hold a briss for him. They wanted to drop in and out of our house whenever. I did, eventually, win and set the boundaries. One day they came to see us, without calling, and I said when they came to the door, "I'm happy to see you, but in the future you are going to have to call before you come." And they were pissed off; they were really mad at me. My mother-in-law lost her own mother when she was young, and was raised by one relative after another; she wanted to hold on to Danny and her family. I understood what motivated her and I empathized with her, but I still set the boundaries.

We've had difficult things like that but never anything that has remotely challenged either our love for each other or our marriage in any way. Ever.

Before kids—we had our first child three years after we got married—we had lots of fun, lots of enjoyment, and that continued. When our older son was born, he weaned himself at seven months and we went away for twelve days on our own. We had a great time. And the baby survived! So we continued and I think we did that every year, including again when our younger son was born and he weaned himself at six months. We often went away on our own without them. We always had family dinners, every night—I love to cook—and we are very close with our children, and we all began to go away on wonderful vacations together too, but we always had one night a week when Danny and I went out alone. When we were both working, we'd take the kids out for dinner one night a week. We all have a lot in common—common interests, common sense of humor, ability and interest in talking together about family issues, politics, music, books, theater. Both kids now are writers.

You know, my own parents had a happy marriage, not the kind of marriage I wanted: my mother was very, very intelligent, and she left college three months before she graduated, even though my father wanted her to wait: she decided she wanted to get married and she didn't want to finish college, and so she didn't. And so she didn't have her degree but she loved to read, she was very intelligent, and she was bored at home.

. . . My father's parents were born in the Ukraine, and my mother's mother was born in Poland and her father in the Austro-Hungarian Empire. And she was absolutely exquisite. My father, I mean he was eighty-five years old and talking about how beautiful she was. My mother would come down to go out, let's say, and my father would say to me, "Doesn't she look beautiful," and he meant it, and he'd look at her longingly. And my mother was very ill for the last fifteen years of her life and my father, though he was ten years older, took care of her by himself . . . She died three years before him and he died when he was ninety.

Her own mother thought that her daughter should have married a doctor, someone with a lot of prestige, and my mother married for love. My father had a great life. If she'd married a professional, she probably would have had an easier life professionally but she was in love with my father till the day she died: it was a *love* relationship . . . And he was so proud of her, very proud of her. Actually my husband is similar in that way, you know. No matter what I would want to do, he would encourage me.

When she did go to work after she'd stayed at home till I was a teenager, she opened the first paperback bookstore in the area, and then she wasn't home all the time. It was great—I could read anything I wanted, and I was very autonomous at that time. I had my own friends—they all became musicians, writers, academics. We all went off to college, and it was, like, a great sort of platform, this group in high school, to take off and meet other people.

After we got married I was taking courses to get my teaching certificate; we only had one car and I hitchhiked to classes. And then three years later our son was born. I didn't work then. But Danny was working all hours . . . I went back to work part-time eventually, when the children were still little. I loved being a mother but staying at home wasn't enough and I did volunteer work at first. It was actually Danny who said, "You don't have to wait so long! Just do it: you got a babysitter. You can get day care!" I wasn't really sure what I wanted to do, but I have always been very lucky: things have come up, and one of Danny's partner's wives was just starting up an ad agency at home and we began to do it together. We did that for years together and had a great time. And I did that kind of work for a while and had a ball till I just started thinking, "I really have to be doing something that feeds me a little bit more," and that's when I began to do the community arts center things.

So I was managing an agency and I had two little children and that was tough—not that it challenged our marriage—but it was very stressful to have two young children and be working and I developed a very bad back problem. It happened at a time when I was investing a lot in my work, working very, very hard. In fact I remember a couple of weeks before it happened, I was out with a client and I had to call my day care person to say that I was going to be late and I couldn't remember my own telephone number. And shortly after that my back went out. I needed help for everything. I ended up in bed with this back for about a year—well, in bed, without getting out of bed, for four months.

When I was in bed with my back, I was giving 10 percent to our life together, and Danny 90 percent. And then I had the chance to do the same thing for him when he needed me—I'll let him tell you about that. But he basically collapsed, after his father died, and after he'd been working all hours. He collapsed in front of us, as he came up the driveway, home from work. I thought he'd had a heart attack. He was in his thirties; the kids were small. He had palpitations, got very claustrophic, couldn't drive.

He'd really struck out on his own when he'd left home for college—it was like he was born when he left his family. It wasn't until after he met me and we'd settled near them that they tried to suck him in again. And I think with his father's death—his father wanted him to be professional, and a success, which he was, and his father bragged about him so much it became a burden to him. He worked very hard, was very determined, was a great father, great husband, and we had a ball. But he was burdened, and he kept things inside, and didn't talk much. I think during those years, after his "crash," he really came to understand deeply what it meant to listen and understand. I mean, he always listened—but then to understand, and to see more of the dynamics and how important it was for him to express himself, not keep it inside. I know when he is unhappy, intuitively. I just bug him until he tells me and now he can. He loves it now when I do it, but he didn't love it at first. We talk a lot. We talk, we back off, you know, we tinker a lot.

I think he has gotten angry with me maybe about five times in our whole marriage, and I don't get angry, I just keep talking. I had to learn to get angry because, not that I would stew, but sometimes I would kind of let things go and then when I was really upset it would seem that I was acting a little more forcefully than the situation warranted, so I had to learn to kind of let the steam out gradually. My moods are much more apparent; Danny is quieter. But he is less reflective about his moods. I've got a million moods and he may have them too, but he doesn't even know it. Or maybe he doesn't have to have them. But I sort of live my life a little impressionistically: I observe things, but they're part, you know, of the larger—they're details in the larger—picture and I don't get bogged down in the details so I don't get so easily upset.

So, for instance, I was working with some people in a gallery at work and we were sitting around having lunch and one of the women was making some comment about her husband and how she wanted to punch him out, and one of the other women said, "Oh God, that happens to me too." And I was just silent, so she turned to me and said, "Doesn't that happen to you?" and I said, "No, it really doesn't." I said we have had to negotiate, over the years, but I can't say that I've felt like striking him.

But I got angry with him once. I got really angry and I threw a chicken potpie in the kitchen. I think it was because he was always working so late. He wasn't spending enough time with us. He was working very hard and he had forgotten that he kind of has to have some boundaries, like "Come home!" you know. This was during the early years when I was mostly at home with the kids.

And, probably as in most marriages, our children at times have been a challenge and I would say that we have—I consider our children to be two amazing people that I am proud to know and be related to, and we get along very well—but we had a stressful time when our younger son was thirteen and my mother, who by then was very sick, began behaving very horribly to him. He was a bit overweight, as some kids are in puberty, and she gave him scales for his birthday! And she just denigrated him. I think she had expectations of him and also—and this is just my interpretation—I think she felt that everything had been taken from her: she'd had a mastectomy, her health had deteriorated a lot, my siblings' marriages hadn't worked out. And in my thirties, which is the time we're talking about, my mother became jealous of me. She saw me having a "perfect" life. On my best day I will never be as beautiful as my mother was, but I think, she just thought life was passing her by. And she took it out on him—and she thought we were too permissive with both kids anyway. She kept being very abusive, and during that time she kept getting more ill. I finally had to remove myself, after one thing after another. I couldn't allow her to be with us, with our children. We both tried—Danny and I—to confront her. Even my father. But she just couldn't see what she was doing. I had been very, very close with my mother. It was very, very painful . . .

Danny and I still talk a lot. Actually, Danny listens more, still. He doesn't answer right away, he processes it, and things change. I mean it's not "I win, you lose." We both come to a point where we understand that this is the best, and it doesn't mean that we agree 100 percent. In fact, he has helped me so much in letting go and letting things evolve. I mean, I was so upset with my mother and our son and what was happening there, and he would say, "You just have to maybe leave her and him alone, leave him in his room; he'll come out and talk some day." I have faith in Danny. And if it doesn't work, we'd try something else.

You know, when a bad thing happens, sometimes it opens a window and lets in some good. For Danny it happened when he collapsed on the driveway a year—almost a year to the day—after his father died. And for me, when I hurt my back. But when these challenging events happen and you have to cope, it either brings you together and you learn from it, or . . . For me it was the best thing that ever happened when I hurt my back. I realized that I couldn't drive myself, try to do everything, please my mother, and all those kinds of things. And when Danny collapsed that was one time where— actually it is probably the only time—that I said to him, "If you don't go for help, I am giving up on you." I didn't mean it but I had to stress to him that he had to start exploring what was causing this problem.

Our sex life—from that time when the light went on in the car—has been great. It's gone up and down. I had a hysterectomy when I was forty-two, and you know you don't come home from the hospital and start having sex, but this wasn't a problem. This is a guy who—well, we just waited. We've had a very healthy sex life, a very fulfilling one.

I'm going through menopause now because I went off HRT [hormone replacement therapy]. I think he is amazing. I can't tell you how many times during the night I take off my nightgown and throw off the covers, then I'm freezing, and he just laughs. And I have fluctuations in sexual desire—I've talked to women who've had hysterectomies and they've said it has affected their libido. But it's only occasionally. My gynecologist said to me, "I'm removing your uterus and ovaries, not your libido—that's all up here, in your head." Most, not all, of it is. But, I mean, I wish I hadn't had to have *had* a hysterectomy. But whatever consequences there are, we work around. Danny knows the change in desire in me, but he says, "we try other things." And other things work. You know, we've always had a very active, and healthy, and happy sex life and I think that is part of why we are both so happy too. It's mutual.

We had to consciously make time when the kids were around. We moved from a kind of a *Leave It to Beaver* sort of house when the kids were nine and twelve to a house that had a bedroom—ours—on the first floor and theirs on the second. And we'd go away and have our one night a week apart from them. So I'd have to say that we never let our children intrude on our sex life. When they were younger it would have been less frequent anyway because we'd be too tired . . .

I've never looked at anyone else and said, "Oh, they are so lucky!" and I've never looked at another man. And I don't think Danny has looked at another woman. He is still the person I want to be with. I mean, now our children aren't around, we have lots of friends, but we enjoy each other's company. I like to be with him.

I have never lost sight of why I'm in this relationship. Not once. Never. He is my best friend, from that moment in the car until today he is my best friend. There is nothing I wouldn't tell him. There's no competitor for best friend, but we do share other best friends—another couple, for example, who are also very close and we are both very close with them. And though we share some passions, we have separate passions. For instance, Danny likes to garden. I just like to pick. I like fiction, he likes nonfiction. He likes early opera, I like later opera. He is much more open now to trying things—I push him a bit—he'd never thought he'd be trying. There are many things I like to do by myself, and don't want him to be with me, like walking because it was the time I cleared my head, a sort of meditative . . . thing. He'd say, "Can I walk with you?" and I'd say, "I kind of like to walk by myself." Now sometimes we walk together because now I've got plenty of time to meditate when no one else is around.

Our older son is abroad now, a correspondent for a paper. When I told him we were being interviewed for this he said, "You guys should write the book. I've never seen two people who loved each other as much after so long."

Danny Bernstein:

I like to start our story with the moment I first saw her. I was fixed up with her roommate by a friend of a mutual friend. I remember arriving at the door—the third floor of a building in Washington. I had this sinking feeling that this very short person in front of me was the one I was going to spend the evening with—and then I saw Louise, and it's funny, but I said to myself, "I am going to marry this woman."

To this day I have no idea why I knew that then. I'm not a terribly instinctive person, and it shocked me. I was definitely not prepared for that feeling. I was not looking to get married. I was twenty-seven, and I was certainly thinking about it, but . . . I mean it was overwhelming, absolutely overwhelming.

I did have an idea of the kind of person I was going to marry: Audrey Hepburn! Well, Louise was small and dark . . . I tell Louise she looked like Audrey in those days—her hair was a little more gamine looking then. I don't know. She must have been sending out something, or I was—actually, if I was, she just wasn't getting it . . . But that's how we met . . . And probably six weeks after that I asked her to marry me . . . She, uh, "declined."

I was disappointed but I wasn't deterred. I mean, I just felt this absolute, single-minded determination to marry this woman. And she said, "No, I will be your friend," and I said to myself, "Sure." I decided not to be put off. I went away—I let six weeks go by and didn't say anything else about it. I stayed close. I saw her every weekend. I was pretty determined that it was going to happen, like a quest, you know. It was a more determined quest than any other in my life prior or afterward. It was not at all characteristic of me, either. I can be pigheadedly determined about things sometimes, and sometimes there is a kind of arrogance, but I wasn't arrogant about it. I wasn't saying to her, "You are making a mistake"—or anything of the sort. I just sort of backed off and decided that I was willing to take the risk of being rejected . . . I would have felt terrible. By the time I asked her to marry me, six weeks after meeting her, I had really fallen in love.

And this was with no sexual relationship, no indication of any sexual interest on her part at all. It really is one of the strangest things I have ever done. Probably the strangest.

But we were both enjoying each other's company, both having a good time. I knew she was. I did think that her backing off was to some degree about her uncertainty about where she was going at that moment; she'd just left graduate school and all. It was just too much: asking her that quickly. I mean, I also asked her to come to Europe, where I was about to go skiing, with me after just three weeks! So I went without her and wrote her postcards all the time. Which she threw out! Hah! To this day she says she wishes she'd kept them. I'm sure they were nice postcards, written from lovely places.

I can tell you exactly when it changed for her. We'd seen a little-known work by Tom Stoppard: *Eureka!* It was a really good piece. In fact, I've never been able to find it on a list of his works. A one-act play, very funny—about a vacuum cleaner! He might well reject having any connection to it. But anyway, we were driving back from the theater and going out for Chinese food somewhere in the suburbs. And it was just pretty clear to me that if I'd asked her to marry me that night she would have said yes. I think I waited till the next week—I think it was on a tennis court or something. I think I am pretty good—or by then had gotten pretty good—at dealing with instincts and intuition. I had thought about it a lot. So I just could tell. And we began a sexual relationship. And that was when it became fairly clear. Casual sex wouldn't have been something she would have been interested in, nor I— certainly not with her. So once it turned, it turned.

I grew up here, in this part of Maryland, and went to an Ivy League college in New England. I took a job back here, with a political agency, a perfect job for me, so I came back—part of President Johnson's War on Poverty program. I'd been involved, in Boston, in community-development work, working in poor communities. I didn't want to come back here, but I couldn't pass up this job. I was twenty-seven years old and I had become director of the agency. I guess in some ways I was ready to settle down. Soon afterward I moved on to something bigger and then with a partner we set up a consultancy. I was really enjoying living here, surprisingly.

When my grandparents, who came from eastern Europe around the turn of the last century, came to this country, they ended up in this area. So both my parents were brought up here. I was the eldest of all the grandchildren and there were a lot—and at one time the whole clan were in this area. One aunt went off to New York—she was being suffocated—and never came back. And one of my great-uncles went off to work for the gangster Meyer Lansky, so he spent an awful lot of time in Havana when the Mob had lots of interests there. Seriously! There were a lot of Jewish gangsters! My great-grandmother had come and settled here too, and she was 104 when she died. I found it all rather suffocating, which is why I was happy to leave and uncertain about coming back—it was the job that got me.

I was the firstborn, and the firstborn male, so there were a lot of expectations on my shoulders. My father never fulfilled his own. My father would have liked to have taught or been a lawyer. He was orphaned, essentially—his mother was institutionalized—and he was raised by the clan, the extended family. No one talked about what happened to my grandmother. My father didn't talk about how he suffered from this. I'd say he suffered, certainly: from a lack of discretion. He was charming, very bright, would have gotten into Harvard, as he graduated at the top of his class, but instead he didn't have money, so he went to University of Maryland, when it was primarily an agricultural college, and he dropped out. He had to make a living. He was in the retail hardware business, a terrific salesman. And like so many salesmen he began to believe his own stories . . . He eventually went bankrupt, as they lived higher than they should have. Living high wasn't necessarily what my mother wanted. She was also orphaned, brought up by two aunts. She's still alive, but has dementia . . . She lived on the edge of fear with him because of his financial excesses. He was doing it for himself, not for her: it was important for him. And these times were shameful and kept secret from us children. I only found out after my sister's wedding, when my father had far overextended himself, and they were back in that state again. I realized my mother was getting creditor calls. You know, those phone calls.

This tension was going on while I was a child but I was off being a Boy Scout. All the time. I was camping and hiking and part of it had to do with the fact that there was at times a lot of tension in the house, a fair amount of screaming, and not a pleasant place to be, so I chose to distance myself from it all through my childhood. It was mostly my mother and I was petrified of her. Though my father was devoted to my mother—he was very affectionate.

They were Jewish, but my father wasn't very observant—my mother was more. He felt very strongly about family and my mother was a great believer in tradition. So rather than being religious, they were synagogue-goers. The concept of the Jewish tradition was very important and my mother became head of the temple sisterhood. During childhood I went to temple and enjoyed the ritual of it. By the time I was ten, I was, to borrow Christopher Hitchens's phrase, an anti-theist, rather than an atheist. I didn't believe in God.

I don't have Louise's happy disposition but I do have a sense of humor, a bit bizarre at times. She has a much lighter disposition and is kind of zany, with a lot of energy. But we share that when I was a child, like her, if I found a point of resistance in something, I'd go in another direction. I knew how to enjoy myself. Had lots of friends; my difficult time was in college, when from having been first in my class, and finding high school very easy, but from a smallish and relatively sleepy area, I was suddenly with all these high-fliers. I entered the back of one class and I heard one guy speaking Latin. I'd never heard anyone speaking Latin. I thought, "My God! What am I doing here? This is a different world!" Which became my world, but that first year was very hard.

Growing up, and later, I was disappointed in my father. His expectations of me were a real burden. I didn't want that, didn't want him living his life through me . . . I didn't want to have to rescue him . . . I went to graduate school mostly because it was better than going to Vietnam, which was my choice at the time. But when I began to work, that early job was very rewarding, and I did a lot of good things personally. I prospered, I supported my family—all those good and important things. Making money wasn't a pressure. By the time our sons were born, it was clear to me that I wasn't going to have a fortune but I would have enough to support my family . . . So I was doing a lot of what he wanted. I had not worked that out before he died. It took me five years of therapy afterward, and it was very hard.

Before we had children, things were not complicated—we didn't have children as additional issues, and we played a lot. Whatever we did, it was a lot simpler. We'd go to films, had lots of friends; it was simple. And really quite lovely. We decided to have kids about three years after we got married and we had them, no complications. But I was a motion machine then. I was always active, like my mother. Louise did most of the articulating of what was going on and setting the agenda with my parents. I just reacted. But it seemed right. Her judgments were good. Which was something I knew about her from the beginning, from listening to her. I knew from that first time—the date that wasn't a date with her—that she was very smart and had common sense and a very strong sense of who she was at that point even though she was disappointed about grad school and all.

Louise always talked more easily, tried to get me to open up, and that had felt like pressure. I dealt with it by shutting down and she knew that, which produced a tension. The areas of tension then were related to the relationship with my family, which were a source of problems for her. And she didn't feel that I gave her the support she needed when dealing mostly with my mother, a real challenge to her. It could come up between us maybe once a week. And it would happen because my mother would decide that she wanted to just drop in—we lived so close by . . . My mother had expectations of what we'd do with the kids . . . joining the temple, education. In fact, we did eventually join a temple. As I said a number of years ago in a somewhat flip remark, "I'll give [the kids] the same opportunity to reject it that was given to me." They have a strong sense of Jewish identity now. They are politically left-leaning and are very concerned by current events . . .

Louise expected me to say something to my parents and I wouldn't. I knew I wouldn't so I never said I would. I just ducked it. I hoped that Louise would do it. My mother would be angry at me, and at Louise too. My father was less aggressive in this, but I didn't want to have to disappoint him as well. I knew he'd understand better than my mother. But I couldn't deal with it. Till the day he died. That issue did get easier. Because my wife put her foot down. She dealt with it. I did feel guilty about not doing it . . . And the way I dealt with work—working all the time—it might have been symptomatic of how I dealt with other pressures and stresses.

Louise and I had been married about eight or nine years, and our kids were six and three, and I was building my consultancy practice and I was working, maybe, eighty, ninety hours, sometimes one hundred hours a week for about a two-year period before my father's death. The fact is, the work was there, and I kept doing it. Home was not something I tried to avoid—it was never difficult. It only got difficult when it came to dealing with my parents. Louise wasn't working then, and at the time it was okay with me—when she did go back, it was a challenge for me. But I was racing along, working fiercely, and then my father died. I took about a week break, didn't really stop, and then a year after that I passed out. I was taken to a hospital. I thought at the time I was having a heart attack, though I hadn't had any symptoms beforehand. It happened right in front of my house. Police came and brought me to the hospital. I spent the night. I was checked out. And then I started having panic attacks. I became unstuck. The panic attacks lasted about a year, on and off. Not with any specific regularity. I couldn't ride in the car. I was able to do short distances, though, so I could get to work. I felt claustrophobic. A few months afterward we went to New York one weekend and I couldn't sit in the theater. Luckily the play was just awful . . . In any event, a bit of medication and talking, you know, to a psychiatrist helped. It took me a long time to open up to Louise.

Eventually I talked to her, but not in that first year. It was too hard—the things that were coming out were too embarrassing—I couldn't bring myself to utter them to her. Things about my father that wouldn't embarrass me today, but then were secrets. Finally, I'd heard myself say those things often enough in therapy that they didn't seem so awful. During that time I would sometimes be able to let Louise comfort me, but when she got too close to the subject of my parents, I shut down. In many ways during that time I acted just like my father, with secret thoughts, not sharing things, not sharing fears or concerns with her, like my father with my mother. I realized that, though we'd talked before, after this point Louise and I were able to talk about anything. I'd been such a single-minded, determined kind of person, I was hardly self-reflective. In my major relationship before Louise I'd not been self-disclosing. I wasn't capable of it. When I met Louise, I became more so, but not to the extent I could be after this therapy.

By two years later, which is when Louise was bedridden with her back problem, I was talking, functioning, much happier. I felt much better. But when Louise had her back problem—it was a ruptured disk—she lay down in bed for three or four months. That was to see if it would heal without an operation, and after getting out of bed, after living in this bedroom for three months, apart from having all her muscles atrophy, she was claustrophobic. It was terrible. So we tore down the ceiling and put in a skylight. Finally, we sold the house two years later. After that experience and the recuperation she was unhappy, crying . . . It wasn't unlike what had happened to me. I didn't run away during that time. I don't think I ever would have, but the difference was I could talk to her at that point. It would have been harder to do that pretherapy. Even though it was uncomfortable for me to talk about demons, I could do it. During that time the kids were certainly aware I'd been in the hospital, and that Louise had been bedridden, and that scared them. We spent a lot of time together then—I made dinner every night. No more eighty-hour weeks.

By that time my mother had realized that her daughter-in-law was tough and determined and the stuff with her had died down. And she'd come to appreciate her more, and started relying on her. In fact, Louise got along with her better than I ever did. But by this time her own mother was ill with a series of illnesses and then she became very difficult with our younger son, completely intolerant of any kind of resistance to her expectations that he be obeisant and doting. Which was not his style—he's not emotive like Louise or his older brother. Around adolescence it got worse and my mother-in-law became overly critical. She was smart and interesting, but she was—she wasn't a happy person. Louise felt she had to make a choice for our son. We agreed on that—we said it to her mother overtly, with my poor father-in-law, a good guy but somewhat passive, there. We told her that we wouldn't tolerate this sort of behavior and if she was going to have any kind of relationship with her grandson, she would have to change. She didn't know what we meant. She wouldn't accept any of it. Take the fact she gave him scales for his birthday: she thought he ought to have been grateful . . . There was no resolution. We just saw her infrequently, or less frequently, after that. It was never healed, and my mother-in-law took it to the grave with her. I'd had lots of affection for her, but after that I kept my distance. Louise was just tormented by it.

We talked about it all the time. By that time I had no difficulty talking about anything. After 1980, when I'd had my crash and had therapy, and I began to talk, our relationship began to feel different and feels different today. It is much deeper than it ever was. It had a second life, one where I almost started acting like an adult . . . Some things are hard.

We have always been demonstrative, physically affectionate. We touch a lot, hold hands. There's a lot of physical contact. For the most part, sex has been good—certainly satisfying for me. There have been ups and downs—you know, physical well-being has had its effect. But we feel intimate and that gets expressed in both sex and in our touching a lot. I can't say I haven't fantasized about other women—because the day I stop doing that, oh, God—my wife's sex life will stop too!

When I crashed in 1978—it was a nervous breakdown: an old-fashioned word and I guess it would be called "stress" now—I wanted to flee. Not to leave Louise, though that would have been the logical extension of that feeling. Just to get out of the pressure of living a life that I couldn't manage. But I have never felt that I didn't want to be with *her*. The initial attraction has matured. We've matured. We've spent a lot of time together.

I don't like to be away from her. I've been away—sometimes two days. But we are best friends. We have a great time together. I don't spend time alone with other people but Louise does. I like her friends. I don't begrudge her time with them. We have a lot of mutual friends. We share a love of theater, of food, lots of things. I have other dear friends, but she is my best friend.

6

Inside and Outside the Bedroom:
Having Sex and the Question of Fidelity

IONA BIDDLE and JAMIE HARRIS
WILLIAM and DIANA PATTON

WE ARE SHAPED by an eroticized public imagery that fills our lives with sexual visions, notions, and expectations. How do these get lived out within long-term relationships? Most of those public sexual images concern the first flush of sex, or imply only the first encounter, when straightforward lust uncomplicatedly explodes into orgasm, or so we are led to believe. The urgency of early sex, like that of early love, each informing the other, is easy, even if the sex itself needs improvement. It is infused with novelty. It is pushed by a primal anxiety—how acceptable am I now that I have bared all? How much can I depend on this new, exciting connection—will it be gone tomorrow, replaced by someone better? During this phase, each time desire is satiated, it is refreshed, springing up anew, until dailiness, comfort, and security settle anxiety, until novelty subsides into deeper knowledge of bodies and tastes. Is having wonderful sex, or even sex that simply satisfies each partner, fundamental to a happy love story? Can you have such a story with no sex at all? The answer to both questions is a hazy "yes" and "no."

There is no cultural blueprint for good sex beyond this, for sex between middle-age, lumpy bodies, never mind old, wrinkled ones with bad hips and penile dysfunction. Yet even the older couples, often saddled with both sags and conditions that impede penetrative sex, say they have found ways to feel pleasure together, to stay sexually connected, to stay happy. They express wonder that love and physical gratification can still be mined together so many years later.

Just as the daily intensity of first love diminishes over time, so, commonly, does that of sex. The thrills of novelty, conquest, and triumph, the urgency that sends couples coupling at every opportunity (and in as many places as is possible) fade even within successful partnerships. While many rue losing the rampant spontaneity of pressing lust, couples typically weather the loss rather painlessly. Instead, the original passion and frequency of sex are replaced by wisdom and even relief at not being dominated ("sexually driven," as one interviewee put it) by such imperatives. What they often call "more depth"—the freedom to explore in security and comfort, the continued affirmation of desire and desirability, the expression of increasing appreciation and affirmation, the weaving of history into the present through sex— seems a fair exchange.

That is not to say couples do not welcome moments, even whole periods, in which urgency and intensity temporarily resurface—for example, when away on holiday, or when they've reunited after a rift or difficulty.

> If we have had a big row I can't stand it and want to make up right away. But I've learned I have to leave him alone to calm down . . . and actually, the separation can work wonders: because we miss each other, when we meet up it's romantic. Sex can help here, too, because it reminds us of why we are special to one another, and also makes us close. So does laughter: breaking a sulk with laughter is fantastic!—
> **Joanne Long, 40**

One myth propagated by current sexual folklore is certainly exploded by the stories the couples tell here: you do not necessarily continue as you start and sex does not necessarily become more boring or routine. Sex, even attractiveness to each other, can both decline and improve over the years. Moreover, the mechanics of sex can become more satisfying and better over time, with knowledge and trust breeding the ability to be honest and sensitive and for partners to be able to guide each other to greater satisfaction.

> We were both virgins but we'd read a helpful book. Henry's mother said she'd enjoyed sex. At first, of course, it was physically agony. Then fine, especially after about five years, when we discovered about an orgasm for me. Henry was always especially happy and confident the day after sex. It was two or three times a week when we were trying for our first baby. After that, about once a week, always at Henry's suggestion and through common consent.—**Geraldine Slocombe, 81**

Couples who have been together for a long time and have had good sex have banked years of continually rekindled sexual desire and gratification. In that sense it is no wonder that they will see each other sexually: it is the lens they have used for each other over and over. Sex has formed as a habit between them: they have been stimulated by notions of each other over and over again; thus, they can be keen to embark on sex again and again. Contrary to ideas that familiarity breeds contempt, clearly things can work the other way with sex: more sex, or, more good sex, leads to more and more good sex. Provided it remains genuine (the couple are both sensitive to and interested in each other) and stimulating, it can continue, on and on. So it is not surprising that couples who are happy together sexually say it gets better in many ways.

Sex and desire are varied themes threaded through these stories, and as the stories unfold, it is clear that, as one interviewee said, "[part of] the best kept secret is that sex is resilient." It changes, and physical appreciation, intimacy, and desire take different forms, over time and circumstances. As eighty-two-year-old Mary Watkins, married for almost sixty years and whose story appears in the epilogue, reports, sex went from being important "because of novelty" in the first few years, to less so "due to family and domestic duties," then important again after menopause "due to the fact that no pregnancy was possible," and then less so—though "still very pleasurable"—after the age of seventy.

The gender divide does exist, though, and within heterosexual relationships, most particularly, it can become problematic around sex. A major gender difference is the relative importance attached to sex in the relationship. Women more often talk about the fact that they know their partners find it important so they will "schedule" it in—not necessarily grudgingly, but because they are sensitive to their partners' feelings. They know the men will feel bad and interpret their lack of interest (most often incorrectly) as a rejection. This is an example of the genders making an empathic bridge to each other, in the same way that men have learned to moderate their approaches to their female partners, so that the "mood" is right and the women feel desirable and acceptable. (This is not to say that there are not exceptions to this: one man wrote in to say that sex was entirely overrated and it had never been important to him at all. His wife did not participate in the research, so we do not know if this was so for her too.) There are also variations in both desire and appetite within same-sex relationships, usually having to do with the vagaries of the individuals' lives as much as anything. As Dennis relates in chapter 4, between working, going to church, and making it to the gym, he and his partner sometimes do not pay the attention to each other physically that they both feel they want and should do. "It's like what Roman Catholics complain about with the rhythm method: you have the calendar out," he says.

What Queen Victoria asked about lesbians, we can ask about long-enduring couples: What do they do? How do they do it? What couples actually *do* when they're having sex also seems to vary. Many of the couples report that variety keeps them interested—as one interviewee comments, they vary the times (mostly not at night, more in the afternoons; sometimes spontaneous); the place (they go away; have sex in the woods; in the car); and what is done (they introduced sex toys after some years). The spirit of play also helps many of the couples reporting for this book. Cuddling, taking baths together, even shopping together can stoke desire.

We have fun! We play! We're like babies. We play in the bath; we go bike riding; we go to the beach. We're like playmates.—**Rena Morelli, 39**

There is also variety in the nature of the sex couples report having because sex can be for many things. It can be for connecting emotionally; for playing; a tension release; an expression and feeling of comfort and ease with each other; a way to disconnect from other things and feel yourself to be "sexual" rather than a mother, father, or career person; for expressing feelings of lust, desire, and affirmation as a man or woman again; for fun, whether raucous or light, or for an experience of brilliance; and for feeling the deepest love connection possible.

> Like any couple, sex is important for us. In the early periods it was experimental as we explored our own boundaries. Sex was at least daily. Within twelve months this became twice weekly . . . But sex has remained important, spontaneous, more often at night—often in the middle of the night (when I am rested and less stressed after a day's toil!). It varies considerably now. Sometimes several weeks can pass between us having sex, relying more heavily on petting and cuddling, which we both like. These gaps are sometimes broken by quite heavy sex, which often still stretches boundaries, new positions, anal—for example—but is always gentle and mutual.—**Rich Gibbins**

How is it possible for couples to keep having sex over many years, and still enjoy it? Variety is one part of the answer. Another is that they seem to make time for it. Time is an issue here in two major ways: (1) There has to *be* time in which to have sex. With competing demands on time, with diminishing energy—especially when there are children and jobs to focus on—and with diminished urgency as sex becomes nestled into a routine joint life, finding time becomes problematic. Sex needs time in which to happen and a time set aside to underscore its importance and for the couple to focus on each other and on their own pleasure. (2) The frequency of sex is another area of confusion, befuddlement, and concern for most enduring relationships: couples who tolerate fluctuations in frequency seem to be able to be happiest sexually. In other words, you do not have to be carrying on like bunnies, as many couples relate about the early phase of their relationship, to feel that you are having good sex. A quota of sex that equates with a good sex life does not exist. Contentment, or ease, over the question of frequency has much to do with creating a story that allows a long view of desire for each other and pleasure in each other—the past-present-future element of enduring love. If you have this perspective, fallow periods are allowed to occur; you do not feel a need to rewrite the story of a happy sex life if you find yourself in such a period. On the other hand, as one of the couples in this chapter has found, there is a danger in letting fallow sexual periods extend too long. Calibrating emotional and physical distance seems to be something these couples develop, reuniting after certain stretches without sex, and sometimes having periods of increased frequency.

It seems that, with age, frequency does decline, on the whole. Some people find it bittersweet to relinquish the image of themselves as robust, constant lovers but adjustments are made together, without losing desire for or interest in having sex with one another. Another loss for most of these long-term couples (but not all) is novelty in sexual partners. Sexually forsaking others is a complex matter, which we will discuss more fully when we talk about the relationship between happiness and fidelity, below. It is not a simple loss. This complexity is seen in the way the monogamous men in this study who note the desire to remain sexually attractive and alive to a multiplicity of sexual possibilities also say they remain committed to being "true" to their partners. Those who have forsaken others seem to find ways of rewriting this sacrifice as a loss that has gains: better sex with one person through constancy, concentration, and intimacy, and also an easier life—or, something better lived through fantasy, perhaps for another life.

> I've had two affairs, and I think Adrienne has had two as well. I think it's all right provided that it does not threaten the partnership. As you get older the interest in having affairs loses both its importance and its effect.—**Philip Silverman, 73**

Along with fluctuations in frequency come reports of fluctuations in desire, mostly from women. As women have noted, this is partly a hormonal phenomenon: after menopause and a hysterectomy, many women do feel less desire, apparently; but as Louise Bernstein, in chapter 5, says, a lot is in the head, and desire, while diminished, can be restarted, reengaged. Understanding partners do not seem to take their partners' declining desire as a reflection of their interest in or attraction to them, *per se*, but as a concomitant of feminine physical aging. One interviewee mentions that her partner still desires her, despite her discolored and misshapen breast after breast cancer, despite his advanced age, and despite the period, particularly during cancer treatment, when there was no sex at all.

In the same way, women partners seem to adjust, in even later years, to their male partners' problems with erections. While these couples may feel sad at losing something that was once so pleasurable and bonding, they report finding other ways to feel close physically and even at times to attain sexual satiation. In fact, couples report a certain sense of comfort and triumph in weathering old age and creating something new together. Thus, declining desire and frequency with age and the pressing demands of busy lives can get recast as a new way they have to adjust, together, as a committed couple, and so, another way they show love.

> About five years ago Henry had a prostatectomy. Then he could only function about once a month, with no ejaculation. It was very sad. He discovered this infrequency made it very painful for me, and very difficult for me to get an orgasm and so he stopped, saying that he refused to hurt me, although I protested that the pain was worth it. Since then, though, we thoroughly enjoy cuddling in bed, and this doesn't now seem to cause arousal in either of us. Occasionally it did to start with, but now it hardly ever does.—**Geraldine Slocombe, 81**

It is hard to talk about sex—even the couples in this book found it so. It could be addressed only after we had covered other intimate topics, such as feelings, tastes, and backgrounds, and then, only late in the interviews, when the subject of sex could be fitted into the context of the relationship they were describing. Most couples find it is not easy to put sex, a language commonly without words, into words, even with their intimate partners. And, like "love," the word, itself, "sex," has many connotations. Martin, in fact, almost always talks about sex with Dennis as "intimacy" rather than "sex," while, in chapter 7, Richard uses the word "fire" and describes Tina as emotionally "hot."

In John Donne's poetry, orgasm—when consciousness of time and space momentarily goes—is conflated with death. Having sex with someone does entail a symbolic potential surrender to a deathlike moment in the presence of another, who is doing the same with you. So, at bottom, it is an intense existential exposure, while at a material level you are exposing bodies, and in particular, your most intimate, usually concealed, parts. So, as Donne implies, sex is, in its very essence, a risky business: really and symbolically, you are exposed, and at the very least—in its final, orgasmic moments—intensely vulnerable to and defenseless against (since you have given over your consciousness) each other.

Clearly, people bypass this intense vulnerability and exposure during sex all the time. It is possible to make sex impersonal: you can blot out the other by taking him or her out of the equation—through imagining him into someone or something else, or by turning her into a cardboard figure, or cartoon ("objectifying"). But when sex is contextualized within a long-term, happy relationship, in which the partners do feel emotionally alive and loving to each other, this cannot happen. This does not mean that long-term happy couples do not have sex in which they can be "cartoonish" characters or can imagine others while making love. Rather, it is because of the very comfort, ease, and knowledge of each other that couples allow themselves this capacity. Because the relationship is one in which they are tuned in to each other outside of sex, sex can become a moment in which they are allowed to play, imaginatively, within it.

> In later years I have discovered that I get great sexual enjoyment from being caned, which she does often. It's nothing to do with domination. It's just mutual fun, just as she loves having her back scratched.—
> **Andrew Lovington, 73**

Paradoxically, sex is not an alienated state even if during sex people find themselves replacing their partners for moments with Marilyn Monroe or Brad Pitt. Sex is an interlude woven into the fabric of these couples' joined lives. Imagination may have been freed during sex, but in the end, it is the partner they have been with and with whom they continue. Some couples play sexual "games," sometimes with marital aids. Because they are so emotionally connected, the sexual play and imagination connect these games to the real people who are in them.

"What's love got to do with it?" Tina Turner asked. As far as sex goes, it's the comfort and security of knowing how acceptable and accepting you are of each other, that you are desired and desiring, and that the feelings associated with sex have the capacity to increase over the years. This is why the couples here almost always say that sex has "gotten better." With that as its baseline, these couples feel free to explore during sex, to surrender their insecurities about how "good in bed" they are (and in the majority of cases this is a discarded concept) or how acceptable their sexual proclivities and tastes may be. They also keep relocating and acting on their own feelings of desire and desirability, and this despite changes in their looks and the suppleness of their bodies.

What about fidelity? Not many people in this book report having affairs, and not many express regret about maintaining fidelity, even if there are wistful glances at other women (for it is mainly the men who report regret at all). Yet fidelity is not a necessity for happiness for some small proportion of couples. A few report periods (often early, or more occasionally, in the middle period of their relationships) in which there have been an affair or affairs (or some sort of extramarital sexual encounters). Happiness can remain unaffected or even be increased if these affairs remain unknown (as a few reports and prior research on the effects of affairs[20] have suggested) and/or have not contaminated feelings about the partner, or if they have added to appreciation or wisdom about the partnership. Some couples report a period of having an open marriage (typically occurring before the arrival of children), which has ended but, in retrospect, has not diminished happiness in the long run.

Research does suggest that, in general (not just in happy couples), there are more extra-partnership sexual relationships or encounters in male same-sex relationships than in female or heterosexual ones.[21] It also indicates that affairs are more likely to occur at certain periods during a relationship than others:[22] (1) early on, when there may be difficulties in intimacy, time together, and sex, particularly upon the arrival of children; (2) in the early child-rearing years (for similar reasons); (3) during middle age; and (4) in the more disengaged relationships, when the last child leaves home. These are all periods in which a couple's emotional closeness, shared time, and pleasure are most tested.

> When we first met we were attracted but our relationship was not, at first, exclusive . . . To my knowledge Philip has had one affair. This affair was never a threat to the marriage but it was part of an unhappy time. I've had three . . . Discretion was always crucial. But our marriage was always the prime relationship.—**Adrienne Silverman, 71**

Affairs themselves may not lead to marital dissolution directly (indeed, in some cases they can lead to restructuring and renewal in the relationship), but often can lead to it ultimately. Some relationships—particularly open marriages—thrive when there are other sexual partners, at least for a time. But, in general, for most people monogamy is what characterizes both the style and aim of their relationships throughout, or is what they settle into. Many couples remain open-minded about monogamy, in principle, while also recognizing that it could be a risky business even for the most stable couple.

> I don't feel that sexual constancy is absolutely essential to a successful partnership but I have to feel sufficiently secure in all the other bonds which tie us. In this I have absolute faith that any outside relationship would not affect his need for me. I think either of us could take a lover, but for me, I would rather not know.—**Anna Lovington, 61**

By and large, monogamy is the policy most have adopted. Some research suggests that monogamy may not be the chosen pattern for large swathes of married people. But it also indicates that at the time of an affair, a percentage (no reliable research exists on how large this is) of people embark on it because their partnership feels unsatisfactory in some way. In other words, there is typically a relationship between the reasons for and satisfaction from the affair and the partnership itself. A separate and related, but crucial, issue is the fact that most affairs are secret, making their discovery a critical point for the marriage. If a clandestine affair is discovered or revealed, the partnership is traumatized, and sometimes eventually breaks up (though sometimes it recovers and even improves); even though sometimes the breakup is not necessarily attributed to the affair.[32] 19 So while there is not a direct correlation between having affairs and couples' unhappiness, there is generally some connection between them.

> I think fidelity is important to our type of relationship as we love each other so much that it would be difficult to fancy anyone else. I have always been monogamous in my relationships and loyal to the partner at the time. For me, sex is to do with the personality and the strength of the relationship, etc., so I could only imagine infidelity would accompany a complete breakdown of the relationship.—**Katy Gibbins, 37**

However, while living monogamously, many men, in particular, voice the admission Jimmy Carter made—that he lusted for other women and had not stopped committing adultery in the mind, even if he had in the body—but without Carter's repentance for it. At the same time these men's partners do not, on the whole, seem to share this need. In a study of affairs, I found this gender difference alive too.[24]

For some, happiness lies in the freedom to be open to new sexual partners. However, as many of these testimonies report, typically, monogamy feels the clearest route to fostering and maintaining particular qualities governing long-term happiness: a sense of security; the surety that you are chosen above all; that there is equal committed energy and focus upon the relationship (and that resources important for the relationship are not doled out to someone else); that intimate pleasure between you is unique; and trust (for much infidelity is conducted in secrecy, so if discovered, it represents a betrayal of trust).

I had an "affair of the heart" that nearly destroyed my partner and our relationship . . . We've worked diligently on trust and continually redefine the meaning this event has had on both of our lives. I learned that if sexual interest wanes, that does not mean the end of a relationship. I learned that my sexuality was tied into a high, a fantasy about the person, and that never lasts . . . I also realized that my excitement about my partner waned in part because of anger that needed to be addressed, and I learned for the first time if feelings of sexual interest go out the window, they can also return!—**Patty Berg, 54**

Sex is one way beyond words and practicalities couples develop to sustain their connectedness together. What these long-enduring couples testify is that sex, just as anything between them, undergoes changes, including how it gets done and what it means. Sometimes it connects them to the lustiness of their first meeting, sometimes to the comfort of their shared routines and customs, sometimes to the delights of playfulness, sometimes to their deepest and most inadmissible fantasies, and sometimes just to the knowledge that there is someone next to them in bed who will be next to them the next day and the next, and sex expresses how important that is.

The two couples' stories that follow show the centrality of sex within their relationships in quite different ways. For one couple sex is their primary way of connecting, as they have often had troubling talking easily; its usual expression is deeply emotional. For the other, sex has a more variegated expression. Both couples have grappled with the problem of frequency. For one, fidelity became a pivotal problem. For the other, it is a nonissue, in part because of the role infidelity played in a previous marriage. Yet each couple's stories underscore both the renewability of their desire for each other and the hardiness of their sexual connection despite conflict and distress.

Iona Biddle and Jamie Harris

Iona Biddle, thirty-one, and Jamie Harris, thirty-nine, live in a suburb of Birmingham. Iona is an office manager for a small travel firm, and Jamie is an

IT specialist. They live in a small semidetached house off a busy road with Iona's twelve-year-old son, Ryan, from a former marriage, their daughter, Kylie, who is six, and two cats and a dog. It is a neat, bright, and lively house, clearly lovingly decorated and kept up. They have been together for ten years, and were planning to be married the week after our interview. Iona is a warm, pretty, sharp-witted woman, while Jamie is a quiet, good-looking man, seemingly much cooler-tempered, with a sweet and easy demeanor. They are vibrant together, if tired by busy lives, and, not surprisingly, each of them readily says that sex has been one of the single greatest bonds they share.

They met after having had previous sexual partners—in Jamie's case, quite a few, in Iona's, rather fewer. They are making a comparative judgement when each reports, separately, that no other sexual relationship has come close to delivering such huge emotional and physical satisfaction as what they experience with each other; sex, more than words, forms their deepest mode of connection. Like Diana and William Patton, whose stories follow, they connect after emotional distance and show their passion for each other through sex. Yet, despite this, Jamie found himself considering leaving after months of sexual disengagement and perceived rejection following a fallow sexual period that stretched beyond his tolerable boundaries, incumbent on five years of broken nights after their daughter's birth. Iona had grown greedier for sleep than sex, and—more reliant on words in the relationship than the more shy and reserved Jamie and, thus, happy as long as they were talking—she had remained undisturbed by the lack of sex. But Jamie, less immersed in the minutiae of their daughter's and his stepson's rearing, was left lost, feeling disconnected and unvalued, as one of the couple's most important and usual means of connection and affirmation became so attenuated. At work—and it is often at work close relationships can become dangerous in such circumstances—he grew closer to a female colleague. She declared her interest and Jamie found himself immersed in thoughts of leaving. This couple's story shows how even happy couples can totter on the brink, reconsider their criteria for happiness, reinvest, restructure their relationship, and once again feel happy together.

Iona Biddle:

I grew up not far from here. My mother was Spanish and my father English. She came over here to learn English and train as a nurse and they met, and she ended up staying. It was a very unhappy marriage. They split up when I was young. My father went off—he chased another woman to Australia. He eventually came back, without the woman, and then he moved back in with my grandmother, nearby.

I was with my mother and we'd go back to Spain on vacations to visit her family. She was very close to her mother, and did miss being there, but she had me and so she stayed here. Her own father had abandoned her and her mother and sister when she was very young. This was deeply shameful and scandalous for them . . . My mother had hopes and plans for me and I was a good girl and good at school. Until my teenage years.

I'm not good at math at all . . . that would be the thing at school that I didn't want to have to do, when I got to be a teenager in particular . . . That's not what I wanted then, spending all my weekends, while my friends were partying, with a private math tutor, which is what my mother was doing for me. So I resented her even more. Although now I appreciate it, at the time, all the little things she did—I ended up resenting my mother; I thought she didn't love me, that she enjoyed making me unhappy. It sounds awful now, but that's how I felt as a teenager.

My dad was quite a weak character. My mum's strong. He said, "Oh, don't make the girl study, she's at school all week." Of course, I'm hearing this. My dad's a soft touch. I wanted a dog, my mum says no, my dad gets me a dog.

One day I said, "I want to go live with my dad. I hate you!" I was fourteen. She wrote me a letter, said she'd never force anyone to stay with her. "No one will ever love you as much as me. I'm your mum. You may not realize this till you're older." The letter was pages, pages long. As a teenager I didn't appreciate the feeling that'd gone into it. She must have sat bawling her eyes out writing it.

I resented my mum for letting me go. If she hadn't let me go, I wouldn't have gotten into this, gotten pregnant, wouldn't have met that idiot, Ray, the father of Ryan . . . So, in a way, I resented her, when the problems came in: why didn't she make me stay with her? But I know why she didn't, with her background. Because people had left her. Her own father, her husband. I realized my dad didn't do my cooking, washing, ironing, cleaning. His mother, my nan, was horrible, hated my mother, resented my mother, because my mother was foreign. She was old-fashioned, 1900s: my dad should have married an English girl.

During my early childhood she wasn't a grandmother who showed me any love; she didn't come around to visit. She didn't relate to my mother at all. As soon as they divorced, it was only through my dad that I would see her. She didn't come round to help my mum out or anything like that. She was horrible really. In fact, when she died, I didn't shed a tear, or go to the funeral. Whereas my maternal grandmother was different. Though we couldn't really converse, there was a connection. My paternal grandmother was outraged that I should get pregnant at eighteen. My maternal grand-mother, although she was older, and Catholic, she gave me a hug and cuddle. She took Ryan in her arms and she cried, "My little grandson!" No mention of any sort of disgrace . . . She herself had gone through where she'd been an outcast when her husband abandoned her. We couldn't converse but she would speak to my mum and she would tell me, and some things you don't need to say. There's a way of communicating with somebody where you don't have to say anything. She would write letters to me and Mum would interpret and so I have a great deal of affection for her and was upset when she died.

I moved in with my dad and his mother. She treated him like a little boy, even though there were two brothers—my dad and my uncle—because my dad still lived with his mother, she was more of a fusspot over him. I saw her as a wicked, domineering woman. She was quite intelligent—she got a scholarship to a school, which was quite good for a girl in those days. She'd sit doing crosswords in the *Times* and she'd have no problem. To add insult to injury, not only did he live with her but also with her sister—a spinster, a virgin, never been with a man. Very religious and thought she was one of the chosen few.

From seeing my dad once a week and him taking me out to buy stickers at

W. H. Smith, to now living with him, his mother and auntie in a house, where . . . for six months, a year, my pride kept me from saying anything. Then I went to my mum and said, "I want to come back. I'm so sorry . . . I was wrong to leave." But by then she'd already sold her place over here and was planning to move back to Spain. Because, as she rightly said, the only thing keeping her in the country was me: my school, my friends, my connections here. I said to her and said to her since, when I became an adult myself, "Why did you not move to Spain after my dad had left and I was a babe in arms? Why did you stay here in this country, with no friends, no family, no support? Why didn't you go back to Spain to your mum and sister?" She said, "Because I refuse to bring another girl into this world who wouldn't know her father."

She made all those sacrifices for me so that I wouldn't feel so rejected as she had felt, but, you see, it's all backfired on her. He left her. Then I left her. So she knows now, she kicks herself, thinking, "Should've just said, 'Sod the father and up and left for Spain'" and, of course, I probably would have had a better life. So it broke her heart when I said I was leaving; she gave it a few months, and in the end I think she couldn't stand it anymore. She decided to go back to her own mum, who was elderly by then—eighty-five, eighty-six—and needed my mum. So she said to me, "You can come back with me, but you'll have to live in Spain because I've sold the house now." Of course I didn't want to. As bad as it was at my dad's, the choice of uprooting all my life . . . they're so important, friends, at that age. God knows why, because they're so fickle, but to me at that time, they were. So I continued to stay with my father . . . I do remember feeling suicidal at times, not suicidal like I would slit my wrists, but depressed and alone and sad, and not having a mum, and trapped.

I stayed in school but I had met this boyfriend at fourteen—Ray, who is Ryan's dad. And I guess I saw that as an escape. The relationship continued because my mum had gone and I saw him as a way out of living with my dad. And so we just stayed together. Teenagers. Silly. He's got a bit of a drink problem . . . it's escalated over time. But he was romantic. He wasn't particularly nice and sensitive. But what it was, and I think about it now, his mum and dad were really homely—had a real home. So I don't think it was actually Ray that I wanted to stay with, it was his mum and dad, a couple that were together, still together after thirty years. They had a nice house, sat at home together . . . that's why I stayed.

Then I got pregnant at seventeen and had Ryan at eighteen. I got married when I was eight months pregnant . . . When I found out I was pregnant, I didn't even really think about things . . . not that the pregnancy was planned, but I was quite erratic in my pill taking, and I wonder whether or not that deep down, I thought to myself, well, to get pregnant would be good. I had a friend that had a little girl too. I thought, great, brilliant. I didn't think for one moment that, you know, it was bad and my life was over. To the contrary. I thought I'd have someone to love.

I didn't tell my mum till I was six months pregnant. I knew she would be so disappointed. Because she lived in Spain and didn't see me, she didn't have to know. She didn't feel it was a disgrace, more a waste of my life. She just wanted me to have choices. And she always said, "You can't really rely on a man. You've got to keep yourself academic, you've got to look after yourself as a woman." So I knew that by having a baby, I hadn't really got so much of a choice, so I wouldn't be going on to college or university or all these aspirations she had. Therefore I didn't tell her. But I wasn't disappointed.

My father was disappointed but not in the same way as my mum. But his mum—it was awful. It was a disgrace: not to the family name or anything. Just to have sex—having sex before you're twenty-four . . . it was so dramatic and she'd be moaning at my dad and I could hear. It was a three-bedroom house and I had a room upstairs and I would come in from school and lock myself in my room. I saw her as a witch. I remember once—and this must have affected me because I remember it clearly—the only time she showed me affection was once when I fell down the stairs at home and I really hurt myself and she came out of the room to see and said, "What's that noise, and are you okay?" and when she looked at my face, it was as if she cared. And I started crying. I wasn't crying because of the fall. I was crying because maybe this woman does care about me . . . I'm sure she didn't hate me and despise me. But she certainly didn't love me the way little granny is supposed to love granddaughter.

At this point I was working in a bank . . . I met this woman there and told her about the traumas I was having at home and she said, "Why don't you come live with us? You can get on the council waiting list for housing. If you come live with us, you'll have to sleep on the couch, and when they come and look at you, they'll see this pregnant woman who can't possibly sleep on the couch!" So at that time I thought it was a brilliant idea and I moved in with them. Eight weeks. It didn't last long. Because this woman lived with her man, and had this really weird relationship—not in a sexual sense . . . It was just that, she was a really large lady and he was a really slim man . . . Then she said that he was in love with me and he'd always wanted children and she couldn't have children or something . . . Anyway, I moved out, pronto, and back in with my dad.

I think we decided to get married because Ray's parents thought it was a good idea. But we had nowhere to live and it was so absurd. Ray moved in with us . . . After Ryan was about two or three months, I knew this was so awful—what had I got this man for? He wasn't providing accommodation or food. Although Ray was working—a milkman or something corny at the time—his money was his own money. He really didn't do me any favors and I thought, "What's the point of having this guy around?" I'd already got people around me I hate . . .

One day he threatened me with a knife—not in a really violent way. I don't want to come across dramatic: we were having a row or something and he was drinking, and of course, I never really felt threatened in a way that I felt scared, because we were in my dad's house and my dad was downstairs—I only had to shout for him. We had a row and he said, "Oh, you dago!" You know that saying . . . it's very offensive, especially from your husband. He had a penknife, and I saw right away that he was temperamental, scary—not scary: weird. Crazy. Crazy. So I thought, "How am I going to get rid of this man?" I knew the marriage was over. I knew it was a farce. I knew at that point that, although I had a child, my life wasn't over. You can still meet somebody with a baby. I wasn't going to end up stuck with a man like that . . .

So I set up some cock-and-bull story—now it's quite funny—that we were going to move to Scotland. We couldn't afford to buy around here on his wage; we could only afford to buy in Scotland. So I rang up Barratt

Homes to see what they were building up there. I had no intention of moving. But I planted the seed and idea that we would move to Scotland. I made it that, "Don't lose hope, Ray, we're going to stay together as a marriage, and we'll be in Scotland together once we've got the house, but we need to split up for a while; you need to move back to your parents, as it's clear it's not working with all of us here with my dad and gran. We're going to go to Scotland, we're going to look at a house, we're going to put a deposit, we're going to do all the things—but in the meantime, let's do this—it's too much pressure staying in this house together." Because he wouldn't have let me go otherwise. He was too possessive.

So he swallowed that; he moved back in with his parents. I think I got out of finally going to Scotland because I just created arguments every time we got together, which was typical of being with Ray anyway. Then things happened: my dad put a deposit down! Eight hundred pounds for this newly built complex in Scotland! He got it back—I only let him put it down because I knew he'd get it back. I made sure it was refundable. Crazy. But everyone believed me.

I didn't tell any of my friends that I was marrying Ray. I knew I shouldn't be marrying him; I didn't feel too proud I was doing it. I don't tell anyone that I've been married. If people say to me, "You were a single mother; you had Ryan at eighteen," I say yes, so nobody knows.

After he was back at his parents I went to a solicitor and said I wanted to start divorce proceedings. The first he knew the marriage was ending was when he got a solicitor's letter. Then he went and committed a crime—a burglary—and ended up in prison. This was after we divorced, but his parents then cut me off, blaming me, saying that if I hadn't left him, he wouldn't have been traumatized and he wouldn't have committed it. Ryan's still got a relationship with him. Since Kylie was born that's been stronger . . .

I had a few boyfriends in the period—a few years—till I met Jamie. I went to a friend's work party once with her and met a guy, Stephen, who's still a friend now. I met him and I think I thought I was in love with him. We had sex once. I got pregnant. It was a complete nightmare. I told him and he was quite callous and cold and said, "You're not the first, and not the last for this to happen. Get rid of it." I couldn't tell my dad. I was disappointed in myself as well. So I had a termination. That traumatized me . . . I thought I was in love with this man. The fact that I was in love with him and he didn't seem to care traumatized me more than the actual termination, to be quite honest.

I went on holiday to try to get over it. Then he rang me to say, "You weren't really pregnant, were you? You were just winding me up, weren't you?" You know, you try to analyze things—why people's behavior is what it is. He's twenty-three and he's met this girl, with a baby, and he dates me a few times, and we sleep together. He's thinking, "I've known her a month, and she sleeps with me: how many others?" . . . I can see it from his point of view. You have to take that on. That's why we're still friends. Because over time he's explained it. He knows he was out of order. Now he's got no children. "It's just," he said, "you were the one for me! I shouldn't have treated you that way!" Isn't it ironic? But there was no going back for me.

Then I went to work at the airport and I met a man, but he was married— but I didn't know he was married. I know. It sounds like an old cliché. I was twenty-one . . . I felt so guilty. But I haven't had any contact with him since . . . I never knew his address—that should have planted suspicion in me. That should have told me, but I didn't know him that long. We'd just meet up for a meal, or after work we'd go to the pictures. That sort of thing.

I love Jamie, and he's the one for me, definitely. But there's an element of, I have to know that Stephen's available as a friend. It isn't like, "Oh I want to go to bed with you." Since we stopped—and we were only in a relationship for a short while—we've been friends. There's always this thing, can men and women be friends? Maybe they can't because men are always thinking more about sex, but maybe it's because we already had sex . . . There have been times in my life when I've had disasters or problems and I've rung him up and he's always been there, and we'll talk to each other, and we'll meet up, and it's so innocent. Ryan will even come. Jamie knows about it and he's always been fine about it.

I met Jamie when he was teaching me computers. I went on a training course from work, and Jamie was my instructor.

I must admit I didn't meet him and think, "Oh, this is a potential" . . . he grew on me. He was very calm, quiet, and reserved, and came across as . . . older. He is older, by about eight years. I kind of thought, although I hadn't had loads of experience with men, but I thought, "It's hard to find a man half-decent." It was a breath of fresh air to find a man who was single, wasn't a divorcé, or [didn't have] three kids by different women, and he wasn't on drugs, and he didn't drink. He was a teetotaler. Things like that would come out in our lessons, in conversations, over coffee breaks, or afterwards in the pub. Things like that started to attract me. I thought, "He's got nice eyes. He's kind of cute."

He made the first move by sending me a birthday card, which was quite clever, really. And then I had to get in touch to thank him, and then we met for coffee, and that's how it started . . .

Jamie is very quiet and doesn't easily say what's on his mind. We're very different in that respect. We may not communicate in the same manner; I'm more "in your face." But we still communicate, somehow we still communicate. I know a lot about him and he does of me. Although I'm not trying to pretend I know everything about him and it's not wise to . . .

But because he doesn't speak out I didn't know that he was so upset by our not having sex very often—it could be a few months. It would be brilliant when we had it. I wasn't really counting or keeping track of things, but he must have been, and now I realize how alienated from me and rejected he felt. But I didn't at the time. It was because this woman . . . someone told me that she'd seen them having coffee or something together . . . And I guess it looked like more than that . . . I don't know. It was a shock. A real shock. And it was only when I confronted him with it that he said what had been happening and how he had been thinking, and then we could put things right.

Which we could—you know, I feel he's the one for me, the confirmation of that is through the way we have sex, the way we both feel through sex. It is like nothing I've had before. It is how we communicate most deeply. I think part of the appeal is that we do know each other, that we now have known each other for a long time and therefore I know a lot about him, and I want to know more about him. It's the niceness of knowing that you can learn more and more about somebody, and that people change, people progress, people grow with you, and their feelings and ideas and things change, and you can be part of their life to learn about that—and that is how I thought about things after things blew up about that woman. And I think because of that attitude the sex becomes better. Because you feel connection there. You feel a connection with someone mentally, and physically.

. . . I've never felt particularly as if I've had some kind of wonderful figure, and since I've had Kylie, I've not been as confident with my figure at all. When I first met Jamie, I'd just had Ryan. I wasn't overly confident, but I wasn't insecure; I didn't have hangups—my thighs, my bum, my boobs—you know, I was okay. Because I had one child and was still very young, childbirth hadn't really done that much damage to me. I'm a size ten and okay, but after time, after time and with age, and after Kylie I've widened and, you know, got flabbier, and that sort of thing. He still makes me feel as desirable as I was then—which is great, fantastic—if not more desirable. Because in a way I truly think that he finds me as attractive as before, but because he knows me, perhaps, or he knows what I like. And therefore that turns him on. I don't know—I can't really speak for him, but that's how it appears to me.

For me, it's got to be a mental thing: if we've just had a major row, I can't possibly go have passionate sex with him. It's not the way I am, although I know some couples do. So for me, it's more in my head, and if I'm relaxed and feeling happy, then that will come out in sex. So that must be why our sex life is so good, because we get on well. I don't know which comes first . . .

Kylie, our daughter, is six, and she is a handful. She doesn't sleep much, and till recently she would come in in the middle of the night. There have been very few nights since she was born when she's slept through the night. I was desperate for sleep.

We haven't had a conflict-free relationship, so the frequency of sex does vary in terms of how much conflict there is going on. And Kylie's driving us crazy and keeping us up, particularly me—sleeplessness was a big part of that. We are learning to manage conflict better. He used to leave, just not be there if there was conflict, or walk out if there was a row. I would feel abandoned. I understand it differently now—he's getting his head together, he's taking himself away from the heat, not getting hurt, all that, so I don't feel abandoned, and I just get on with something. I channel the energy and do the ironing or something instead of feeling upset. He tries to cool things down—I now recognize him doing that.

As a woman I read magazines and silly things that you shouldn't and you get the impression that men are all about sex, think about sex all the time, they should make the first move. I guess because Jamie doesn't, isn't really like that, if he feels rejected mentally as well, as he did during that whole period, he wouldn't come on to me. We could be lying next to one another on the bed and he wouldn't come on to me. Because he kind of would know we just had an argument, so therefore I wouldn't want to and he would feel "she would reject me, so therefore I won't do it." In a way, I respect him for that, but it has caused problems. I wanted him to make the first move, but then he doesn't, so I'm not going to . . . So this distance gets more out of hand and then there's no sex for months. It gets dangerous.

I don't make the first move a lot because I feel like a bit of a whore . . . not a whore, but if we're not connected mentally, then you kind of think I don't want to make the first move sexually because we're not getting on very well and it won't be good sex and I wouldn't want to spoil the great sex thing that we have. I feel we've got to sort out the problems we have first, but then it escalates. We're not really being that intimate and nice to each other because we're not having sex, and we're not having sex because we're not relating to each other. We get out of this problem—about who's going to initiate, and how are we going to start having sex again—by connecting emotionally first. We talk. Sometimes after an argument.

That's what happened with this other woman. It was a symptom of it.

I'd found out he'd had coffee with her or whatever because she told me, and he said he had. First I was silent for a day or two, imagining all sorts of things, and then I ended up with an outburst. I was pleased then because he turned around and said, "It's only you." And then of course that heals that barrier. Part of me thought he must have been having sex with someone because we hadn't had sex for maybe four months and this woman is, you know . . . I didn't think that at the time. No. To his peril, really, he's made me feel so safe and secure that I never, ever felt he'd go have sex with someone else.

So I thought, "Iona, this is a wake-up call! What are you doing! There are other women out there. Single women!" When I found that out, it's not as if I did what some women do, which is come on to their men . . . try to pretend

I didn't see it, that it's not there. Sort out the relationship so he'd forget about her—I had to confront that because I knew if I didn't, I could try and seduce him, try and have sex with him, but it'd be crap. What's the point of having crap sex?

I felt insecure, although he said to me that he hadn't slept with her and hadn't wanted to. It sounds a bit weird, but in a way, at that particular point if he'd have told me he'd slept with her, I don't think I would have split up with him over it. There'd have been lots of considerations in my mind. I wouldn't have kicked him out right then. Because the distance was my fault. I'd been quite horrible, very moody and confrontational as you get when you don't sleep and are overstressed. That makes him retreat. It had been a quite awkward situation. I was aware that it was bad.

If we'd have been getting on really well and he'd have done that, then, no question about it. He'd have betrayed the whole illusion of what our relationship was. And when he said he hadn't—he gave me her phone number, where she worked, said I could speak to her, he didn't seem to be shying away from me confronting the situation. So I had confirmation that he hadn't gone any further and didn't want to and the opportunity for me to confirm that. And then I said, "I still don't really know what to believe, and I still don't feel confident." And he said, "You know I'm not a great believer in marriage . . . but I want to get married."

We'd been together for nine years then and it was a kind of way to make me feel confident. We were both not great believers. Jamie had no romantic ideas about marriage, and had seen a not-good marriage with his parents. To me, marriage was something that had really terrible consequences. So many of my friends have spent thousands and thousands of pounds on the one day, then the marriage lasts a year and then divorce court. But we decided to get married to symbolically cement what we have. And that's how I felt when he said that. To me, that felt that he must really, really want to be with me and really love me, because he's suggesting something that he doesn't feel the need to do.

So marriage was a symbolic gesture that meant a lot and I really ought to shake that girl's hand—she's probably made us both accept and realize that, yes, let's do it. That's the way that's come about. It's a case of "why not now?" It wasn't romantic, he didn't get down on one knee, but I didn't need him to; it didn't matter. I'm cynical, but all that's nonsense. So many people, their men serenade them and then go out and have an affair.

He is the first person I think of when I'm distressed—that's what I mean by "happy in a couple." When I need a friend, it's him. I feel secure, I trust him; he brings out things in me which I admire and I didn't know were there at times. I mean sexually. Emotionally. I didn't know that I had the intensity that I have: I was sick with the feelings of jealousy. I'd never experienced that before. He's also a calming influence on me . . . We're very different characters, different people; we bring out the best in each other. Not all the time. "Opposites attract," in some ways, is a true saying. He's practical. I'm not as practical.

I find him attractive after all this time and that's it.

Jamie Harris:

I grew up in Leeds, happy, parents together, not a very intimate or talkative household, but I thought I was happy growing up. I went to Birmingham to university, to train to be a teacher, and I left home at eighteen for that . . . We didn't talk much after I left. I'd pop home for the weekend now and then. But it wasn't at all an intimate relationship.

I was shy and quiet as a child . . . When I left home, I was already playing music—guitar . . . and when I got to university, to do teacher training, I got involved with a band. I was singing and playing guitar and writing songs while I was a student. We were relatively successful. We didn't press records, as you did back then, but we did get on the local radio and stuff. This would have been from 1980 to around '83, '84. That was really what I was driven by rather than the work I was supposed to be doing at university. During university, in between part one and part two of the course, when there was a break, I had to have a serious operation on my leg. I was in a hospital bed for nine days; it was supposed to be an overnight operation but it went a bit wrong. I was under a district nurse for just over six months . . . because it kept bleeding, so she came to change the bandages. I did move back home to Leeds with my parents during that period. I came back down when my leg was better, but by then I'd sort of lost momentum. What I did was spend my student grant money on a guitar. Playing with the band became more serious then. Finally I made the decision to leave my university course. I didn't talk about it with my parents or anyone.

I was convinced I was going to be a famous musician—that's where all my energy and direction was. And then the band went their separate ways at the end of university . . . The keyboard player and I stayed in touch for a while and did a little bit of stuff together, but then they all got their separate lives and I didn't have the strength of character to continue it on a solo basis, although I do a little bit. I still play but I don't do it much. When Kylie was born, the guitar was sold . . . that had to be done. Different, change of, priorities. I grew up significantly then, when she came. But, yeah, I still dabble. It was very therapeutic for me, because I'm quite a quiet person anyway—I don't talk and open up easily. But I found I could do that through writing lyrics.

To an extent I had a social world through music . . . we were quite close, the four of us, and we did a little tour where we went off in a van and did various places all around the Midlands. I wouldn't have missed it—I think it was a very valuable experience.

I had my first girlfriend at university. There were three of us who all hung around together and we went down to the local chip shop and there were two girls there and they started chatting and following us and eventually they came back with us and had a cup of tea and it just went on from there: that was my first girlfriend, Eleanor. We got close—it was my first sexual relationship of any sort, and I was twenty-one. I saw her for about eight months or so, and then I rang up one day and said, "Can I speak to Eleanor, please?" and her mother said, "She's not here, she's in hospital." "Is she all right?" I said, and she said, "Yes, they're both doing fine." Mother and child! I thought, "Crikey!" And we hadn't even gone all the way!

So I go rushing off to the hospital and sure enough there she is with this baby next to her! She'd been pregnant while I'd been seeing her. She was quite a slim girl and it didn't really show very much. In retrospect, it probably did but I wasn't clever enough to spot it. The story was that she was pregnant when she met me but only just . . . I stayed with her for a while, I didn't just go, "Oh no!" I thought, "I think we'll have a go at this, family life—we'll have a play with that." But she was kind of—her mother was, I think, a single parent at first as well and she took a lot of that responsibility on board and helped her with the kid and everything . . . I saw her on and off for about eighteen months. That was in the early '80s.

I left university to concentrate on music but I hung around the area, where my friends still were. I did part-time work, in restaurants, and doing a little IT support work. I became a cleaner, a porter at the university, so I was cleaning the campus, which was quite amusing. I was living cheaply because I was staying on a friend's floor . . . all that kind of stuff you do when you're young. Then after about a year or so I had to knuckle down and get a proper job.

It was always in catering—the only kind of actual work experience that I had then, really, even though I had all the academic stuff. I'd apply for other jobs—I remember applying to a record company—and wherever I went it was always either "you haven't got the experience" or "you're overqualified." And I thought. "Overqualified? Hang on a minute—I just want to earn some money!"

And then this chain of American restaurants opened up here and they were advertising for catering assistant kind of people. So I went along to that and this very important person in my life—father figure, maybe—interviewed me. He was going to be the manager—an Irish bloke, Dan. Very strong character and a leader type. Kind of took me under his wing and I grew and matured as a person within that organization, becoming a manager, and then a trainer . . . the teacher thing came back in again. I became a regional training manager, ending up with a car. The organization grew fast. Then they realized they had to cut things, and that was middle management, which affected me. They wanted me to go back to the restaurants, and I said, "No thanks." At that time a friend of mine was working as an IT consultant, doing training, and he pushed me to join him and said, "You can do it." That was in 1990. That's how I met Iona—she was my pupil.

Working in that restaurant organization gave me responsibility and I've responded to that and I've even been sensible enough to stop and look back and think, "Blimey, I was washing dishes a few years ago and look where I am now." I think a lot of what I do now—it's an American company—the training they put us through to an extent is . . . you could argue it's brainwashing, but . . . I think even now . . . it was a very good training process . . . and I was given a lot of opportunities . . . The area manager created this position for me to grow into because he knew what my interests were. I'm very grateful for all of that . . . All the stuff that should have happened to me at university happened to me in that organization.

But I'm disappointed with myself because I've devoted myself to educating and training people and getting through qualifications, and I look at myself and think, "Hang on, you only got halfway through this." I also started an environmental health degree as well—this was after I'd met Iona. I only got halfway through that—financial reasons that time. I also only got halfway through a higher-education certificate in training and development. So yes, I got to a stage where I was sitting back, thinking, "Hang on a minute: Mr 50 percent here. What's going on?" I had something to prove to myself, which I've done. I completed that NVQ this year, and now I'm looking to go through the Open University to consolidate all the stuff I've done in a university degree or something. I only need a few more courses to attain that.

Before I met Iona, I'd lived with two other women. One I went to Yorkshire with to start up a restaurant, living in a hotel . . . We went through a lot together . . . but she was very jealous and I was very flirty. Toward the end there was another woman in the background . . . And then after that was the next woman I lived with. She was—we got on fabulously well and if I wasn't where I am now with Iona, I'd be thinking I should be with her. Because she was such a kind, very generous person. I couldn't fault her at all, really. I was stupid to let her go . . . But what happened was I was working as a trainer in computers and I met this girl I thought I felt something very strongly for. So much so that I had gone to my girlfriend and said, "I've met somebody who's made a big impression on me. I'm really sorry about this but I want to see if I can take it any further with her." I thought I loved her. I struggle with that word . . . what does it mean? So, I tried to do the right thing—I tried to finish, rather than see this other girl behind her back. I moved in with a male friend. It didn't work out with this new one . . . It wasn't serious for her at all . . . Then I went a bit mad for about a year, sowing my oats, making up for lost time; stuff I should have done when I was eighteen or nineteen.

Then I met Iona. In 1992. When I first saw her, I thought she was quite striking, but I immediately thought, "She's far too good for me—I'm not even going to try anything here; she's way above my league!" I thought she was stunningly attractive. I thought, "I can't go anywhere near that!" She was living with her father and her son at that point, in a two-bedroom flat. She was only twenty-odd. We had a normal instructor-pupil relationship, with a bit of banter, chitchat about this and that. And that must have gone on for a couple of months or so. I'd see her twice a week . . . Then suddenly one day Iona turns around and says, "Now this is the last lesson I'm coming to because I don't think I'm really getting anywhere with you." So I said, "Okay."

She's not really a confident person, at least in technology. She's actually making the right decisions—this is typical of her all over—but she's not confident that it's the right decision and she'll um and ah when she should have gone with her instinct in the first place. So, I thought, "fair enough." And at the end of that lesson she went away and I thought, "I'm not going to see her again." And it was then that it hit me that there was something more going on than perhaps I was aware of, that I had some sort of feelings toward her. It didn't strike me until then.

I had once been out with her after class for a drink and it had been a disaster because I was so shy. And that might have been part of why she decided to stop coming. So I went off and she went off. I was very depressed thinking I was never going to see her. I didn't understand what I was actually feeling. So I remember making some excuse to get some information about something she knew . . . I rang up and said, "Oh, I'm sorry to bother you, but have you heard of this thing." And then we started chatting again. I did some stupid romantic stuff. I happened to mention about the group and that I wrote songs, and she's quite interested in music, generally. So I purposely chose some songs, a bit-romanticky-type songs, ballads, and I put them on a tape and I stuffed it in her letter box, and ran away quickly . . . That was my attempt to communicate. And so she listens to all these lovely, romantic, deep feelings and obviously gets completely the wrong idea about me!

Because it's difficult—I can write these lyrics and poems and songs, with all these lovely feelings, but I can't do it, I can't show it . . . except that way. So she thinks, this man's great! He thinks all these lovely things! And I think it went on from there. I think we ended up going out to the pictures and one thing led to another and the rest is history.

I was still thinking, "Blimey! She's too good for me!" I took her to see *Indecent Proposal*, quite a romantic film, and then we went out for a meal afterward and I bumped into someone I knew. I remember thinking I felt good about the fact I was with this fantastic woman. But I was still very shy and wasn't talking much at all. I don't think at that stage and even now I've got the skills to talk one-to-one with a woman I find that attractive, in the beginning. I don't talk easily.

I mean, in the relationship with Iona, I'm okay one-to-one now. Maybe the communication processes are very different for her and me. I like to be very precise and think through everything very carefully before I say anything, whereas she'll just open her mouth and say the first thing that comes out, which is usually the wrong thing and she'll change her mind and say something else. She gets frustrated with me when she asks me a question and I don't reply immediately because I'm trying to think of exactly the right thing to say . . . and by the time I've thought of it she's asked me three other questions.

I think we've learned to tolerate each other. I think we understand that we think differently but it's one of those things which we always tend to argue about, that keeps coming up. It's always there. The content might change, but the process is the same, in terms of that lack of easy communication style. She's very good with people—her job roles have always been about that—so in terms of talking and dealing with people, she's fine. But when it comes to us, there isn't an easy active-listening process going on . . .

We've neither of us got brothers or sisters, and because of the family relationships we've got, we don't have a lot of help. There's always something going on that needs to be done; there's always practical considerations, this needs doing, that needs doing—the dog's crapped on the carpet so it needs washing, that sort of thing. Kylie's very—she's not hyper, but she's very demanding in terms of attention. I don't know why. She doesn't go to bed till around ten. By the time she goes to bed, Ryan's lucky if he gets an hour of anyone's time before he goes to bed, and then, we're in bed by midnight, both knackered! We have managed to go out on our own a few times in the past few years—not much, it has to be very carefully orchestrated—and we do as much as we can with Kylie and Ryan, like on short-break holidays . . . But it's been like this since the beginning, because she was a single parent with a tiny child when we met.

And it was difficult then. I mean, I wanted to be with her, and to an extent I wanted to help her out of the situation she was in . . . rescuing from her evil father! He's not my perception of a father. From my own dad, my idea of "dads" is great: they always help and they do this and they do that. He's not. He leeches out of you. He's a weak character. A very nice guy, very genuine, very generous, but very irritating, and Iona looked after him, rather than the other way around.

I wasn't aware really of falling in love with her. I've had this thing about not getting attached. I'm attached, though.

When she got pregnant with Kylie, we were in a particularly bad time. We had rows. In the right environment our differences actually complement each other nicely. But if there's stuff wrong, we can have conflict. It's mostly that I don't speak when Iona wants me to . . . and all that. So when she was pregnant, she produces a pregnancy test thing, which she's just done, and puts it down: "What do you think of that? Positive!" Rather than, "Oh, Jamie, we're having a baby!"

There was a big change in me then: I'm going to be a father. It was clear to me. She was considering an abortion and my answer was, "Well, we're going to have a baby."

This is going to sound a bit silly, but the nature of our physical relationship with each other is so amazing still, that it struck me that this was meant to be. Two people don't work together in this way so well without there being a physiological reason . . . This child was meant to be. That's what was going through my head.

And it's still that way, even after sleepless nights, and all that stress . . . absolutely! It's amazing! I've probably slept with maybe twenty women. All shapes and sizes, all different. And it's never been this perfect. The chemistry is just . . . meant to be. We keep desiring each other.

I did struggle with our relationship starting off with having a child in it. We got on quite well, Ryan and I, from the beginning. I could do things he was impressed with and I became in some way the father he never had. His real dad is a complete arsehole, he really is. That's not just me saying that because of the situation. He's thirty-odd, still lives with his mother and father. Skinhead. Alcoholic. Ex-convict. You name it. He's got nothing going for him . . . So I always have this other man in our life . . . And you know, I was watching a nature program a while ago—you know, you get these where they're looking at the psychology of animals, and lions; your male lion is strolling along and he meets a female who's got a cub by another male lion, and he eats it! And I can understand that! It's definitely a biological thing. I suppose as humans we can overcome that because we can rationalize things better. But there's an instinct—"that's not my genes so why should I invest so much in him?"—which might have been different if his father wasn't around at all. I do resent Ryan seeing his father . . . though they spend their time playing computer games, which they both like.

But I think Iona does understand that, and, like the talking differently, it comes up and we go over it . . .

With the talking, my solution is to disappear and do something else and come back when she's calmed down a bit. And that can work. It's not impossible, if you're tolerant and patient. And I think I've become more tolerant and patient, and she's learning to be too.

I also have become more knowledgeable about her cycle, as well. Hormonally, she can go from one extreme to another, and then, if I know, I have more strategies to deal with it. And now I'm invested—now I also have Kylie. And I couldn't leave. I am attached.

When we have conflicts, or arguments I will walk away—that's a way to cool off, a strategy, and then I think, "So who cares if I'm right or wrong?"

I will let her know I'm over it by making some sort of peace offering, like a cup of tea or something, or I'll go and see what she's up to, and I'll say, "Are you okay?" and a bit of a physical touch. I will sometimes say I'm sorry for something, though it's not easy. I often get told by her that I should have said "sorry," so I guess I don't say it as often as I should.

It's important to me to feel wanted and attractive. Especially as you get older, you get a bit worried about things like that. So I do flirt. Not with any malicious intent and often not even consciously . . . So I had a lot of attention from another woman more recently and I found that flattering. Iona found out about it. Basically Iona has forgiven my "indiscretion"— though it wasn't an affair. I stopped because I wanted to stop it. It was a conscious decision, and before she found out.

I possibly was anxious about how attractive I was to Iona . . . A long time no showing it, no sex that is the connection, the deepest one . . . the attachment . . . The insecurity is always there and it came to a head over this thing, and Iona fought for me, to get me back. So it's less likely that it's going to come up again. I thought, "Blimey! This person really does want me, and she's willing to fight for that!"

Since this, I feel my attachment to her has deepened. If the flirting thing happens—or if I see someone walking down the street and think, "Well! she's a bit of all right"—I'll think to myself, "So what? I've got so much more at home." My hormones will say, "Hey, let's go and spread some seed." But rationally I say, "Hang on a minute. That's going to be time and energy and effort, and it's probably not going to be anything like as good as what I've got waiting for me at home." That's quite a revelation to me. A difference between being younger and being more mature. Who was it who said, "There's no point going out for hamburgers when you've got steak at home?" Paul Newman? I can identify with that now. Twenty years ago I wouldn't have understood.

It would be wrong to say that the frequency of our sexual relationship hasn't flagged. Certainly when Kylie came along we were both very tired. She didn't sleep through for a long time; years really, and, like I said before, we didn't have any help in a practical sense, so it's been hard work, frustrating. We tried everything to get her to sleep, and sometimes she slept in our bed. That didn't help our sex life. So it would be wrong to say it's not waxed and waned—of course it has, with levels of energy and all the rest of it.

The level of communication in the bedroom—we don't talk, we don't speak. It's very nonvocal. It's touch, and neither of us will force ourselves upon the other: that doesn't happen. If there's no response, it doesn't happen. That's quite a trusting, understanding aspect of it. It's amazing, really—difficult to put into words. It's changed only in terms of peaks and troughs, but if anything, it's intensified, gradually, as we've become more comfortable with each other, and get to know each other better. It's not stagnated at all. I think as you get more comfortable with each other—I think it's very different for men and women, and if you understand that concept, and are adaptable to it with your partner, then you're well on your way. For most women—certainly for Iona—it's not a physical thing, but it's very emotional . . . she's got to be secure in a lot of senses. Free from distractions. Anything that's going on in here is going to get in the way. Understanding that is important.

It can be that when we've had conflict we won't make love because that means not feeling emotionally close . . . When we make love it's in the context of the emotional life, for me too.

It's easier now—sex—because we know each other better. We can hit the right buttons. But, I mean, that's not lessened the excitement. In the early days it's all about discovery and there's a thrill in the fact that you don't know what's going to happen. So that's changed—it's different now; to an extent you do know what's going to happen usually, but you're happy and thrilled that it is happening.

Even though it may feel familiar, it's not stale; it's not always the same, either. It's not predictable. I suppose there is still an element of the initial thrill there.

I think part of the excitement is that Iona and I are so different. When we first met, Iona had this idea that because I was so quiet, J would like her friend who was quiet. So she kind of set this thing up where I'd meet her friend . . . So she's brought her friend and her friend's all dolled up—curls and makeup and all that. And I was completely not interested . . . There was nothing, stagnant, with the girl who was supposed to be so like me. There's a more interesting and intriguing dynamic between opposites and I still feel that with her, so even if I don't find it easy to talk intimately, and she finds it hard to listen to me completely, I'm still interested in her.

There are other pleasures in our relationship too. We'll sit down and watch a film or TV. And the house is something very much of what we share. Right from the beginning. It's a never-ending project, isn't it?

At the moment things are much easier than they've ever been because Iona's mother is now back from Spain. She's decided to move back here. So she stayed with us for a few months, and now she's sharing a flat with a colleague down the road. She's fantastic! She'll see a pile of ironing and boom, she's there. We've had more help in the past few months than we've ever had before. And we're using it now as a way of getting out together.

Neither of us has very close friends, to be honest. Maybe that's an only-child thing. But very occasionally I might go out with some people from work or something and she'll go out and see her girlfriends.

What do I mean by saying, "we're a happy couple?" It's so hard to find words that mean anything when you're trying to define something that strong . . . It's very assuring. It makes me very content, very happy knowing that she's here; she'll always be here. There's nothing at all that she'll never be here—she'll be here for me to come home to. So, there's a security. I just cannot for one second stand that she would leave me, or she would not be here. Perhaps I'm being very selfish thinking that. But that's what I think. And I think that's quite important to me in terms of having somebody, knowing that there's someone there that knows yourself so well, and can read and understand you without you saying anything, can understand where you're at. Over time I've learned that.

And it's like all these significant events have put that to the test. And it's won through even stronger, you know. Over time it's developing, changing. A sense that whatever it is we've got together, there's no reason to lose this; this is important; we've got to keep this. And I think it's that force that pulls it back together, a memory of what we do have, that's so strong. And I'm also intrigued as to how it's going to get better. The underlying trend is, whatever those axes are on a graph—contentment, happiness, whatever—they're going up. How is it going to develop even more? I want to see how that works.

William and Diana Patton

William, fifty-two, and Diana, forty-three, live down a wooded lane, in a rambling house on a pond, amid the glorious moors of Yorkshire. Diana was born in London, but moved midway through her childhood when her parents decided to pursue a rural dream in the moors. After school she traveled around the world, settling for a time in New Zealand, where she lived for a few years with an Italian–New Zealander. They planned to marry after trying life together in the U.K., but he couldn't adapt to living there and she didn't want to leave; the relationship ended and Diana moved to live near her parents in Yorkshire. Working there for a marketing firm, she met William when she was twenty-five and he was thirty-two. William had divorced the year earlier. His two children were both at boarding school, but he shared care and control with their mother and saw them at holidays and on weekends. William had owned two thriving farms but sold them when he divorced. When he met Diana, he was still farming but was about to move into a small cottage, where he would eventually set up a business developing special-offers packages for company promotions. He and a partner built it up very successfully over the following fourteen years. A few years ago it was sold to a larger company based in Edinburgh, of which William is now a director. Diana has a small interior design business. They have two children, ages fifteen and thirteen.

William Patton:

I grew up very happily in an upper-middle-class home, extremely content. There were four of us: my sister, myself, and my parents, and we got on very well. My sister went to Bristol University and had just got her degree in psychology when she was, sadly, killed. She was coming back from a student delegation to India, a sort of "helping in the postcolonial trauma we'd left the Indian subcontinent with"—a lot of students went out there then, around 1968. Her bus hit a train. Nearly thirty were killed. That hit just when I was doing A-levels. I was going to go on to Durham University to read history, but I couldn't really think what the relevance of doing that was. I was also accepted by Sandhurst, the equivalent, I guess, of West Point—something that was in the family, as lots of relatives had been there. I'd been to an amazing school in the Scottish Highlands, which had been very like five years of Royal Marine Commando training, physically incredibly rigorous and wonderfully lacking in any form of petty authority . . . I was meant to go to Winchester, very serious and academic, and that just wouldn't have been me. My dad took me up to Scotland with my mum to see the school and . . . I said, "Dad, Mum, there's no choice. It's in a baronial castle overlooking the mountains, there's red deer, there's ptarmigan, it's on an eleven-mile-long rock where we can sail, I can mountain climb. This is my idea of heaven."

I was really sad when my sister was killed. We were very close. We were so different, we were completely noncompetitive . . . I feel it more now than then. I've talked to her all my life anyhow, even now—we were good friends. I don't believe in an afterlife or anything like that. I don't believe she'll come back, but she's inside me, absolutely. That provides me with a lot of wisdom I wouldn't have in myself . . . My father and mother were, of course, shattered with their own daughter killed.

In that period I decided not to do history at Durham but to go to Sandhurst. I was spurred on to it by my father's saying, "You're a long-haired lefty: they'll never have you!" I said to myself, "I'll show them." I'd just been trained to run a corps of soldiers at my school in Scotland. I was going to show them I could do it. So I went.

I was there for five days and someone came up to me and said, "We have singled you out for something very special. We want you to work for military intelligence. But to do so you will not be allowed to continue your course at Sandhurst. We process people at Sandhurst and you come out so obviously a soldier, because that's the whole purpose of two years of knocking you down and building you up, that we can't have you stay if you take on this work." The pitch they gave was extremely powerful. They'd singled me out, among all the people at Sandhurst, which had been highly competitive to get into in the first place. And the man who was doing the pitch could have been one of my great-uncles. That's what was really clever. I completely related to him. He was gentle and calm, and he ran me for five years. He was the epitome of the English gentleman.

I wasn't a spy. A spy is a trained man who goes out and joins the CIA or the SIS, is trained at their schools. I was doing special operations, special missions, undercover . . . I became a "sleeper." You find your own job in a place where they tell you to go. I had to find one in South Africa, and I found one in industry. They believed in the domino theory at the time and they were desperate to protect industry and the economy there. If southern Africa fell, then the U.K. and other Western economies were at risk, as there were Communist forces around, including from the north, and others. Or so went the belief. The ANC were considered the enemy at that time. Basically my role was to work in my end of the industry and just feed information back if I managed to pick up any. If there was a sudden panic, I had a quick way of contacting a contact out there if need be. I had to send reports in code. I met the person years later down in Hampshire who used to read them and he said they were the most insubordinate reports he'd ever seen! Ninety-nine percent of the time I was living a normal life out there.

My first wife came out to join me there. We'd grown up together. She never knew. I lived out there and did overland trips between South Africa and England. That involved going into French military establishments in the middle of the Sahara, but I did that without her knowledge.

And I proved very good at it. I came across information that the ANC were going to do a bombing. I was in an absolute panic and couldn't find my contact details—I hadn't taken it seriously enough to put it in a place where I could remember! Then I did find it and contacted him and to my amazement was picked up by the South African authorities and put under protection. I was naïve then and hadn't realized the full extent, the appalling time and extent of apartheid—the military people had been my friends. Of course, at that point I was exposed and I had to leave. So I was sent out of there to the Sudan, began working out there, and witnessed an appalling atrocity—a trial of chemical and biological weapons that was linked to our government—and that was it.

I wanted out. I'd witnessed something that was totally against everything I believed in. It was a trial and I wasn't meant to see it, but I did. I did and tried to get people out, to help them, to save them from the certain injuries they would have sustained.

. . . That was happening when I was twenty-one and the woman I would later marry had moved out to South Africa to be with me, and she knew nothing of this. I just said to her, "I'm going home. I'm going to change what I'm doing. I'm going to farm" . . . I got quite a big payout. She also had some family money. So we came home and got married, and then bought a farm in the wilds of Scotland, where I'd been so happy at school. The very basis of my first relationship was based on all this that had happened. Would I have married her anyway? I doubt it, you know. It was expedient and important at the time.

I think the only thing she really could have seen that was strikingly different in me was that I wasn't my normal ebullient self. And I had repeated nightmares. When we were separated, when the marriage was over, I said, "Look, I'm finding this is the time—for my catharsis. I am writing a book about this, and I'm going to try to get it published. I've got to ask your permission beforehand." So I explained it all to her for the first time and she said, "Thank God. That explains everything."

I did really want to marry when I said it, and I was very committed to the relationship. But I feel guilty because there was a massive deception that went on . . . I did slip up twice after we got married, though—I was committed, but I did have two flings. And I don't think that was about the loosening of my commitment to my first marriage. I think it was me coming out of myself.

We came back from Africa, got married, and went to Scotland. It was remote. That's what I needed, and looking after animals is a great Band-Aid. I farmed ethically. It was like a repair for what I'd been through. The whole lifestyle soothed me and I got very fit. Very shortly afterward we had two children—we both wanted them and there we were, farmers, with livestock, and kids. It fitted.

I loved farming, but I began to miss people. I love people—I'm not a cynic. People are basically decent. Farming didn't bring me into enough contact with others.

So I started developing my own small mail-order business, selling things to other farmers that I'd found helpful to me. And I began to deal in cattle and sheep. I was back doing what I was good at—building relationships with dealers, buying machinery and selling it, the kind of jobs I'd had in Africa. I'm a trader, really, at heart.

My first marriage was withering away and dying. My first wife hated being in Scotland. She was lonely and unhappy and disgruntled all the time and kept saying that she wanted us to leave. We weren't getting along. So we ran away from the inevitable and sold up in Scotland and came down to Yorkshire, where we bought another farm. I think I resented her for that. I wouldn't have left Scotland. But in the meantime I'd felt that I had unfinished business educationally: I'd never done a university degree. So when we moved down here, I took up a degree course. When we'd sold Scotland, we'd sold very well, having bought up the two neighboring farms and making a really good going concern of it, which meant we could buy one down here and build it up.

By then our relationship just wasn't working. We were well-off, with two lovely children—everything that you could ask for in many ways—but we didn't appreciate what we had, really. She asked for a trial separation, but I said there was no such thing: you either are committed or you leave. Maybe I was looking for an out by being so hard-line. Diana says I can sometimes be coldly final. I said, "Right. That's it. We've got enough money to build our own separate lives and go our own separate ways." At that point we agreed mutually that this was the way to go. Our children were young, and that was difficult.

It did get messy: my first wife didn't feel as confident as I. Her insecurity got focused on money. It got aggressive then, and blaming. I wanted to keep the farm we were in, if I could . . . But I lost all in the end. Maybe it was guilt money, including guilt about not having told her about what I'd been doing that had propelled me into the marriage. I handed her everything, in effect. I moved into a tiny cottage—a little two-up, two-down in a little village—I set up education funds for the kids for private education. And it was generous enough, in fact, so that when they went through university they had more than enough on top for spending money to help them through.

I met Diana about two years after I was separated . . . At that point I was living at the farm, and a completely wacky mate of mine whose wife had run off had moved in with me. He's a wonderful guy—looks like an American biker, bald on top, hair down his back. A wonderful friend. His wife had left him and he asked if he could spend the night. He ended up staying two years. We had quite a wild time . . . So it was in that phase when I first met Diana.

I'd seen her about and I'd met her mum and dad and I saw her and I thought, "Wow!" She has a great body, really good-looking—she's a statuesque blonde. And I had heard that she'd had a pretty wild life—traveled around the world, had a bunch of relationships, had just come back from New Zealand . . . Actually, she wasn't as she'd been advertised at all. Or how she'd advertised herself: "Oh, I'm going off to Canada next!" Absolute nonsense. She was looking for a mate, who would look after her and provide her with what she needed one way or the other. In fact, I found somebody who was desperate to settle down and very insecure.

At that point I had to be very open with her. I said, "Don't expect marriage or children." She's not manipulative. She adapted to my situation, and actually she slowly weaned me from this slightly bohemian bachelor life. I moved into the tiny cottage and she helped set it up and my wild mate went off to America, so his influence left my life. You pretend you're having a great time but in fact there's an element of shallowness in it, and even on occasions an element of loneliness in that sort of lifestyle. I didn't have a job, and was wondering what I was going to do for a career. I also didn't have much money. I was building up my tiny business, and with great fortune I bumped into someone who had a connection with a big American company who was interested in what I was doing. So we joined up . . . For fourteen years we built up . . . that business together and it was very successful. One thing that's really good about her: when we met, we had damn all financially and it was fine.

We moved in together eventually but we didn't marry for a long time. First we lived in separate cottages nearby, then we bought a house together. That was a very definite choice—a real landmark of a commitment. I still hadn't made the final one yet. When we did make that commitment to get married, it was when we were at the right stage of our lives to say "I am committed." She was there before me. When I made that commitment, it was for life . . . I made it in a clearheaded way. I did that, as a conscious decision, when our first child was born. I felt very bad that we couldn't get married in a church—just the registry office. I wanted that for Diana—she deserved it. But she was so lovely about it, and we had a wonderful, happy party. That was about nine months after our son was born.

I didn't have a moment where I thought clearly—at least then—"This is the one I want to be with." But, then, I've never had that sickness, madness, out-of-control feeling about love, the way people talk about "falling in love." I believe it must be wonderful and agony and all the rest, but I've never had that—perhaps that's a pity. Instead, with Diana it's been a much more gradual development. I'm more in love, more attracted to her now than I've ever been.

Diana was clear earlier than I that she wanted to get married. She got pregnant—we hadn't planned it and I wasn't necessarily ready then. And she had a miscarriage. That was three years into our relationship. I wasn't really emotionally, financially, ready after my failed marriage. I hate failure. I show myself as laid-back, but under it all, I hate failure. That was a big, classic failure—my first marriage. Doing that to my kids tore me apart. I'd see them at weekends, but Diana has never been entirely comfortable with the kids and the amount of time, and money, via their mother, that they have taken. So that has remained painful and problematic. At first, though, there wasn't a problem. Diana was my girlfriend, they were my children. But when she got pregnant, when we had our own kids, things changed and got less comfortable. Before the time I had come to want us to have a child, I don't even think then I was telling myself it was "love." I was completely sexually driven, and the relationship seemed primarily sexually driven. Because ours is not an easy relationship, and it wasn't then. She's got a foul temper—extreme—you know, slamming doors and dramas, and howling, especially then. Twice she said at that time, "I'm off" and I thought she was. But that was much earlier on; there was a gradual transition to the commitment. It developed to the point where I felt, "I don't want her to go off; I don't want to go off."

. . . I was very, very happy when Diana got pregnant again but still not talking about marriage. For me the watershed was that she had preeclampsia and very nearly died giving birth. The doctor in charge said, "If we have to make a decision between the child and your wife—(they thought we were married, and called me Mr. Hood, Diana's maiden name)—who will you choose?" It wasn't a question: I said, "my wife." When I thought she was going to die, I thought, "Shit, how will I live life without her?" That was the watershed. When I thought she was going to die when Jonathan was born and they both lived and it was absolutely fine and I saw him cesareaned out of her—and, without being soppy about it, as I've done lots of cesareans myself on animals—that was it, there was my commitment right there. And I didn't want this boy to carry anything other than my name. That was part of it. He was ours, and I proposed to Diana.

But it hasn't been clear sailing. The real casualty has been the time I spend with my older children. They are not so comfortable in our house. This is where Diana is difficult. And I could be seen as being weak. So what I do is take the line of least resistance. I keep in constant contact with them in the way that's most convenient so it doesn't impinge on our relationship. The two young ones—Diana's and mine—adore their siblings, and are always asking for them. There's no competition or rivalry because the age difference is so great. They feel like they're all full brothers and sisters. But that may be why Diana feels left out. She hates hearing anything about their mother, who was giving me still a very hard time when we met and that dominated a lot of the early years of our relationship, and Diana feels I was hard done by in the settlement. So I try not to mention if I've heard anything or been in any contact with their mother: why pick the scab? Diana doesn't like it, but she lives with it: she knows there's occasional contact. We both live with it, in our ways.

Diana's also very impatient and can nag a lot—both me and the kids. And she's still very insecure, in general, and hates any criticism. So she nags us—"You haven't folded the towel"—but I try never to bring certain things up. Like I'd keep our house much tidier than she does. One time she went away with a friend to the Caribbean and I took the week off work, in theory to look after the children, but I did a complete clean of the house like it's never been cleaned before. And she was furious. She wouldn't say, "Gosh, it's cleaner!" Because she would never admit it needed better cleaning. We don't live in squalor but there were certain things, like old dresses that had been in the wash basket for two years, which I flung out. If I ever told this story in her presence, she'd just storm out! She's quick to anger. I answer her back often, though I also don't bring a lot of things up—like the dresses in the wash basket. In the mix of life it's a very, very small thing to live with, her quickness to anger, her nagging, her sensitivity to criticism, amongst all the positives.

But if she flares up, I usually answer her back and we have a good row. Oh, we do row! It childishly escalates to banging doors and rushing off to sleep in the spare room! She's overly sensitive to criticism—she admits it, and it stems from a couple of bad relationships . . . If I keep out of the way, she'll recover quicker, but I'm not often good at that . . . So I'm left reflecting, after the doors have slammed or I'm left alone in the bedroom, "Oh, shit. I can't leave it this way"—especially when I have to go up to Edinburgh for a few days of work early in the morning! If I leave it a bit for her to calm down more—if I don't, I'll get another missile and it will take longer—then it gets healed. One of us will come back in and we'll be in each other's arms by the middle of the night one way or another. Then we get nestled in.

I gather she used to be a real sulker and hold a grudge for a long time. She doesn't with me. If you take the time, it settles down quite quickly and then we make up. The way it finishes is to be apart; that causes defusion and the recontact is a gentle one. An apology. If she's in the room it's just, you know, a little kiss on the shoulder, or something like that. Or saying, "I can't sleep, and it's miserable you being cross." So she'll come back in. She hates it when I'm cross with her. I don't stay cross. When her temper's down, I recover. One of us will say, "Look we've been childish," that sort of thing. Saying "sorry" later will stop things.

It makes me desperate when I'm really cross with her: I think, "How can I live with this when I'm older?" . . . But then suddenly I think, first, "I couldn't leave the children." Then I think, "I can't leave her." I think about her vulnerability. And it doesn't take long to get to that, and I feel connected to her again. Because I don't really have a temper—I mean, I don't sulk. It just dissolves in me. What happens with the anger with Diana, it dissolves, and then the stupidity of it hits me. A gentle flood comes and the anger just washes through. And then I can feel why I'm with her again. It didn't happen that way with my first wife, because I didn't love her. I love Diana.

What I realized in thinking about my first and second marriages is that, in the second, respect is the underlying tenet. I cared for my first wife but I never thought she was my equal. Diana totally is. I hate my own gender for the way it behaves sometimes to women—well, quite often. I loathe crude bias. And I do think Diana is completely my equal as an independent, thinking person. I need to respect my partner in life and I respect her deeply. She'd had experience and been around by the time we'd met—unlike my first wife. I knew that I was "chosen"—not out of ignorance or desperation. I'm strongly the provider financially but I know that, if need be, she could step in because when we first met she was earning as much as I was. I come to her intellectually absolutely as an equal. I admire her.

She has strong views—not necessarily mine. I mean I'm a wishy-washy liberal and she's conservative. She's a very kind person but we don't necessarily share the same politics and views on people. If she were prejudiced or had religious beliefs that I couldn't relate to, that would be a problem. Broad values—like kindness, decency, and fairness—are shared. She reads like mad, though we don't necessarily share the same tastes in books; I love that she reads like mad. I love buying her books and I often get it wrong. But that doesn't matter. She'll laugh, "William, you've just bought me the most appalling book! Absolutely appalling!"

We share a circle of friends and have lots of fun with them. We love to entertain. We have this lovely house in a lovely setting, and Diana loves it when she gets dressed up and feels really attractive, and she's a wonderful hostess. I love people's company. And when Diana's at her best, and dressed up and feeling like she looks great, she's stimulated, and I get stimulated. It's sexy. We like food and smells, and the house smells all wonderful then. So it's got all the ingredients to make us feel great. We don't do it a lot, but we have an annual large party which everyone expects us to have now. And Diana does it brilliantly.

Though we laugh at a lot of different things—we share a lot of humor. I love it when we're watching things on TV and she will suddenly roar with laughter and cackle away like an old hag—she's got a very funny cackle—I'll be laughing because she's laughing, not necessarily because I've found it funny . . . We spend a lot of time with our children and get lots of pleasure from them, and from our house. Our house always needs something doing to it, and we garden together. We're around together on weekends.

. . . She's a brilliant cook. The best. Cooks healthy food. And she likes her food herself. And there are a lot of simple aesthetic things we enjoy. When one of my uncles died, he left me a bit of money and I took us to Florence because I'd been there years ago and enjoyed it and she'd never been. It was her birthday—this was early in our relationship. I took her to the Uffizi and . . . there were Botticellis which she already knew and loved, and she just adored it. We were in Venice the other day and spent time at the Peggy Guggenheim Collection. We're not culture-vultures, but if we're in London or Paris, we'll try to go to whatever exhibition's on. As we've gotten older and more affluent, we can afford to do more of that.

And the sex side of things works fine. She's a lovely lover. More a taker than a giver, but my idea of a successful time together sexually is that she's satisfied. She's not selfish and I get complete satisfaction from what I manage to give her . . . She is as physically attractive, if not more so, to me than when I first met her. She isn't the shape that I would have thought I'd go for—but she's everything I desire. Her skin. She doesn't work out and is overweight a bit, but, you know, I don't mind at all. I don't mind if she has wrinkles—they're signs of character, though she does. I know her so well—I just love her. She's vain and would feel destroyed if she were badly scarred but I know I'd learn to love the scars. I think her body now contains the history of what she is and what we've been. When she comes in and is, say, wearing a short-sleeved T-shirt, she knows I'm going to stroke her arms, and sometimes she finds it a nuisance with me pawing at her. But she does lean across and knows I'll stroke her. If we're sitting on the sofa next to each other, she'd expect her arms to be stroked or scratched or whatever.

And that immediately stimulates me. I'm a pain in the ass. Actually we never make love before we go to sleep anymore, though we used to. We now mostly do it in the afternoons. Which is fine if I'm working at home . . . And on weekends we close the door and the kids have always known not to come in at that time—Mum and Dad are going in for a "lie-down."

I guess because I'm getting older, my sex drive is decreasing. Before I used to start getting difficult after four or five days. I don't know if it's maturity or age but now I can let it run for longer. She'll say she can see I'm getting ratty. What I adore is that she'll have the same thing. And I'll say, "Diana, you're getting ratty because you haven't had any" and she'll deny it. And then we do. And that's been the problem!

Occasionally she'll say, "Come on, William. Let's have a quickie!" I know it's not going to be the best, but I can't resist, and it does put me in a better mood. I guess it's physical and chemical. But I also feel more connected to her, and there's an urgency that's gone. It's definitely also that I'm stimulated by her. She's the only one who can make me not irritable. And after we've made love, I'm much more loving toward her. For most of our life together it was every two, three, or four days. Now the pattern's changed, at least over the past five years. There are now more ebb-and-flow periods—sometimes when we'll have a lot and then periods when we won't at all.

In fact, sex is now more spontaneous than it was for a while. Not when we were first together: we were at it then like a couple of rabbits! We're both pretty uninhibited, so it could happen if we went out for a walk . . . We do use sex toys . . . She's open, and I am, to variation in what we do . . . we don't get stuck into patterns. And we make sure we go away together to those nice places without the children.

She is lovely with the kids. It's all down to respect. I love her, I adore her. It's a thing that's grown and grown. We've been lucky too. We started with nothing and we're very proud of the fact that although I had lots before, it was a complete restart . . . When we've had money to spend in the past, and now we're having more, she's been very good. She's insisted we go on holiday as a family regularly; she makes me spend money which I might not spend on enjoyment of life together; both the family and just the two of us. We get on so well when there's just the two of us. We both miss our kids achingly when we're away but we're terrific on our own.

We've had to adapt to a different lifestyle with the job I'm doing now, which takes me up to Edinburgh for a few days at a time a few times a month. At first she didn't like it, but now she thinks it's great—she says she's not sure she'll want it to stop because she'll have to adapt to having me home all the time then. Finally, there's a trust. We know we can adapt to whatever we need to. Part of my reason for respecting her is that I do trust her totally. I'm not naïve—I know that anyone could have an affair if the circumstances are right . . . I would never say it couldn't happen to Diana or to me. But I think it's very unlikely that it would. I think it would ruin our lives if it did. I don't have the desire to. In my current business and job there are lots of opportunities, in theory. But I'm aware of the risks and what I have and what I'd be jeopardizing. It's just not worth it. I don't have the desire to stray, and if I did, I'd need my head examined. The boundaries are there in my relationships outside of my marriage. I choose them to be there.

Diana Patton:

I was born in London—well, just outside of London—where my father owned a business fixing racing cars. He was a rally driver himself. My parents married young—around twenty-one—and had three kids while they were still young: me, a younger sister, and an older brother. I'm very close with my parents—particularly my mother. My mum was an art student and she became a potter, and did pottery while we were kids. They were each other's first love. Amazingly enough they were both virgins until they got married. They were very much in love, and I saw them as in love while I was growing up. They were very passionate, I think, then. My mother especially. They did have terrible rows—but then William and I do too. I think possibly our relationship is quite similar to theirs, apart from the fact that we were older when we got married. And also my father was much more happy to let Mum take the dominant role—I look at them now and I think he's really quite passive, even though he was a rally driver and a bit exciting. In those days he was away quite a lot, so that left my mum very much at home, doing the suburban thing, and she really was quite ambitious and got bored doing all that.

So eventually they decided to do something together—something that wasn't going to take him away all the time and that would get them out of the suburbs. They packed up that business and went up to the Yorkshire moors. Very naïvely they bought a hotel on the moor. They knew nothing about catering, apart from the fact that my mother was a very good cook. But it was something to do together. They did very well.

We were there in the hotel for about three years and then they went into farming—and they did that very well too. Even so, we never had any money.

There's no money in either thing. I remember that if we fell over and ripped the knees of our jeans, that was always a big deal—sort of "How could you do that? I can't afford to buy you another pair!" Ultimately that pressure trickled down to us in terms of our education . . . At the point at which we would have gone to university, it became clear that money was going to be a problem, so I did a secretarial course instead of what I should have done— what I wanted to do—which would have been a B.A. in English. I still regret that I didn't. I was keen by that time to get out of the countryside and go to London anyway. Which is where I did my course, and lived there for three years. Beyond that I'd wanted to travel. So that's what I did instead: lived in London and then traveled.

I have an aunt who lives in New Zealand, who'd invited me out there, so I went over. I was twenty-one . . . The flats and houses you could get there then! I'd been living in this grotty place in west London, just horrible—you know, no central heating, no garden, freezing all the time—and then I got this flat right near the beach! Frangipani blossoms above me on the way to work! The smell! Why would you want to live anywhere else, really?

I ended up staying as long as I did—three years—because I got involved with this Italian–New Zealander chap, as one does, who was lovely. He was lovely but he was very—I don't know. He was very Kiwi. But then as soon as he got with his Italian parents, he'd become Italian. His parents didn't speak English and didn't like me. I wasn't going to look after him properly, his mother said, "because English girls don't." So, in the end that relationship fell apart. But first he came over to England, to Yorkshire, and stayed with me and my parents for a while . . . He actually liked that, but it was clear that he wasn't going to settle down in Yorkshire, and I realized I wasn't going to be the right kind of Italian wife for him in New Zealand. And that I really didn't want to settle down there anyway. So I went back and made plans to return. I was too English, really. And New Zealand's too far away. I came home. To Yorkshire and the farm.

I lived at home for a bit then got a job and flat in York. I did the same sort of thing I'd been doing—in marketing, PR, promotions. I had a great job. But I did something very naughty: I began to have an affair with my boss, who was married. I sort of went home at weekends because I couldn't see him then. This went on for a few years—going nowhere. So by the time I was twenty-five, I was still seeing him and one day when I was home for a weekend, my sister said, "There's a chap down the road, you know." You know, it was bizarre—my parents' farm was about a half mile from William's. So that weekend he was having a "Good-bye to the Farm" party. He'd just got divorced and was having to sell his farm, so he had a party to say good-bye to it. He was staying in the area, and the farm was on the market—he didn't want to sell it, but he had to. He was hanging on to it by his fingertips and he had a friend living there with him, another divorced man, a wild man—these two divorced men living there having a great time! My sister hadn't actually met William, she just knew about him, but my mother had. She'd met him at the cattle market, and he'd outwitted her over buying a cow. My mum is very good-looking—and he'd actually pinched her bottom, which diverted her attention, and he'd made the winning bid by then!

I went, but at that time I was seriously thinking about going off to Canada for a while to work. What I was really thinking was, "Either I'll settle down, or I'll move on." So I went to sort of check out the guys, and the only person I fancied was William, but he was out of the question because he had this girlfriend . . . Unfortunately, his mate who was living there with him liked me and I did see him . . . But he really was completely awful! We went out a few times. I offered to go round and pick him up so that we could go out for a drink because I had a car, and I found William sitting there . . . So we checked each other out and I found myself not wanting to go out with his mate. I thought, "I'd much rather sit here and talk to William." I knew I'd been attracted to him but people were warning me off him, you know: "He's just separated and is shagging anything that was around . . . He's a terrible philanderer!" Well, we both did like each other.

One day I was walking down the lane with my sister and he came up in his Land Rover and I suddenly had this jolt—you know? You know how you do? And that was when I suddenly thought, "Oh! I really do like you!"

He had two young children whom he saw at weekends. They were at boarding school, but their mum had care and control. Still, he saw them when they had weekends at home and on holidays. I remember at first getting quite upset because he did have them at weekends and I wasn't really included then. I was being totally selfish—I remember a row, with me saying, "I want to do this," and him saying, "No, I've got my children," and then me saying, "But I want to do this!" And one time after we'd been going out for about six months, I think it was one night after sex and we were all lovey-dovey and he said, "You must remember, there's no commitment because there's no way I'm getting married again and there's no way I'm having children again." I was absolutely devastated because by then I knew that he was the guy, and I knew I could not bear not having children. I didn't know quite what to do. What do you do? . . . I thought, "play it cool." And I just hoped that he would come to realize what I already knew, as well. The more we were with each other, the more we realized it really did work. But it was a gradual thing.

So we started to see each other and I'd go out to his farm from my flat in York on weekends. My parents knew him and liked him. They were, though, a bit worried that he was divorced—weren't even sure if he was. It was funny—they drove past his farm once, my mum told me, and she said to Daddy, "Oh, Diana's probably there for the weekend," and my father was slightly shocked. But still, they liked him. William would come to theirs with me for Sunday lunch. But there was a bit of pressure after a while around whether or not he was fully divorced and would we get married? He wasn't actually divorced till a year after we began to go out. That didn't really bother me. What bothered me was his saying that he didn't want to get married or have kids.

We were first at this weekend stage and then it was practically every night. I had the flat and then I sold the flat in York because I'd decided I wanted to live near him. I mean, I was there practically every night and we did try living together but that didn't work, as he'd bought a tiny little cottage. And I don't think he was ready for me to be there full time. So I bought a place nearby. And then we made a mistake, after about two years.

I got pregnant—it wasn't planned and it wasn't because we were taking chances, but it was an accident . . . but I think subconsciously I wanted it. Subconsciously, I thought, "This is it." I was about twenty-seven at the time. It's still quite a thing between us. He regrets what happened terribly . . . I knew we weren't really ready to have children then. I went round to my mother after I did the pregnancy test and William just—well, I wasn't prepared for his reaction, which was totally negative.

I took the day off work and spent the day with him and he said, "Look, Diana, I can't have children. This is the wrong time for me. I'm not getting married and if you have this baby, it will be totally by yourself." And I just couldn't. Nor did I want the pressure with him thinking, "Oh, well—I'll give in." Because I think he would have stayed with me—I know that in retrospect—but at the time I wasn't absolutely sure of him. I didn't want to be together just because of that. To me the relationship with William was so important. More than anything. Now that I'm a mother I would feel differently. I can see now how it would have worked out then. But he wasn't totally committed then and I think that was what it was. I was but he wasn't.

So I had an [abortion]. I was actually feeling terribly sick the whole time before and I remember feeling the morning after it, "Hey! I don't feel sick!" William came in with a bunch of flowers and I remember I'd been thinking, "How am I going to feel when I see him? Is something going to change?" I was relieved because I was so pleased to see him. It was an awful time and I went back to live with my parents for a time, I was so upset about the whole thing. But you know, I don't think I thought even then, "I don't think we're going to make it." I don't remember ever thinking that. I do remember thinking, "I wish it had worked out. I really do." But I also could see it was the wrong thing to do. I couldn't bear to have had any doubt—that he'd be with me just because of the baby.

But that was a turning point for William. He said, "I was so worried about coming to see you—whether you'd still want to see me or not." And I said, "It hasn't changed my feelings for you one bit." It really didn't. After that, I think it probably took another few months, he was more committed somehow. Soon after that we bought our own place—not thinking of marriage at all. We both sold our cottages. I did then get pregnant again and I lost it. He looked after me after I came back from having a DNC. As soon as that happened, we both decided, right, this is it—and we tried, actually tried, for a baby quite soon after the miscarriage. By that time I'd reconciled to the idea of not being married. I said to him, "Okay, I understand about the marriage thing, but I really want children. I really do." I couldn't envisage a life without children. By this time I was twenty-nine—I had a real urge. And he said, "Okay. That's fine. Let's try." I think because we'd lost two, in whatever way he was more sure. We were much more settled. We'd bought a house together.

That pregnancy and birth was also traumatic: I had preeclampsia. I had to have a cesarean. I nearly died and the baby nearly died. The day before the doctor had rung me and said, "I've just had your tests back—I hadn't been diagnosed with preeclampsia yet and I was feeling fine. Have you felt the baby moving recently?" So my heart started pounding and I thought, "Oh my God. That's a terrible thing. God, it's dead." Then I was desperate and my blood pressure went sky-high. The midwife came out to see me, took my blood pressure, asked me how I felt, and I just kept saying, "Fine. Physically I feel absolutely fine." But that's apparently a thing about preeclampsia—you feel brilliant. The ambulance came to take me to hospital but I didn't want to go: it was six weeks early. And the ambulance driver said to me, "Well, if you're going to lose the baby, it's better to lose it now and start over again." Isn't that terrible?

They tried to induce it. I was on Valium. And I was having a baby, so during that birth, when I was conscious, I was so happy to be having a baby at all . . . When I woke up from the anesthesia, there was no baby. I didn't come around until everyone had gone, including William. I thought the baby had died. I was desperate to see him. Or should I say, "it"—I didn't know if I had a boy or girl. I made William describe the birth over and over again. At least one parent was awake and witnessing it! I kept saying, "Are you sure this is my baby?" I couldn't quite believe it had worked, and that I'd had a baby. We were both—the baby and me—in the special-care unit for about two weeks afterward. There is one thing that was . . . well, one feels . . . when I had our son, it was my firstborn and wonderful but for William it was his third. Though he'd never say that, because he loves our kids and obviously with them he's been much more involved . . .

One night I was allowed to go out, and William came to get me and the doctor and nurses called him "Mr. Hood"—that's my maiden name. So the question of names came up, and I said, "Well, our son will be called 'Hood'—we're not married." And William said, "Well, I want him to have my name." So I said, "Look, I've been thinking about this, and if you want to call him 'Patton' that would be okay. He can be called 'Patton.' That's fine." So William looked at me and laughed and said, "Well, that's okay—there won't be a problem, because we're getting married." And I said, "Hang on a minute! Look—are you sure? I don't want to put pressure on you." And he said, "No. I really want to marry you." So we'd gone out to dinner from the hospital leaving our baby and came back with William having proposed. It was wonderful. Being married hadn't been such a big thing—I'd adjusted—but my parents would bring it up every now and then—sort of, "Oh, what can I call William? He's not my son-in-law." And my grandparents—it was hard for them seeing me pregnant, waddling around, bizarrely not married. Even at the antenatal classes I was very conscious of not having a wedding ring. Because of his past experience William felt vulnerable, so we did draw up an agreement about how to split things if we should ever split up. I'd said, "Why do we need that?" but he said, "It's just to look after both of our interests, really." I was happy to do it.

My parents have always made it possible to keep things flowing smoothly with William. I'll confide in my mother—not so much in my sister or brother, as we're not very alike, and we've got different sorts of interests and social circles. I can't imagine not having my mother around. She's very wise. My parents have been very involved grandparents. My mother always knew, and said, how important it was for William and me to preserve our intimacy. They had something of that in their own marriage—though I don't remember them ever going to bed in the middle of the day, which is something we do! But she's very open about the fact that they've had a very good sex life. When we got married, we had a honeymoon—and that was when Jonathan was only nine months old. They took him for a week and we went to France and had the most wonderful, restorative honeymoon. We were so exhausted after the baby and just having some time on our own was amazing.

After Jonathan was born, I gave up work. I'd loved work, but I wanted to be with this baby, and decided not to go back. And I've loved staying at home too. Less than two years later we had Laura. I would push the pram around with these two babies, going for long walks, and when Laura was born, we'd moved into this house, with land all around, and being with them outside was wonderful. When she was about a year old, we bought this house, by the lake. We've spent a lot of time and money doing it up. We bought it cheaply because it was a real wreck, but it became our dream house, and it was something we did together with pleasure. It's like the houses we grew up in— big, old farmhouses. Both of us are pretty handy and like doing things up. He developed the vegetable garden, which he's very proud of, and I do the flowers . . . Last summer was the culmination of our efforts. My parents had their golden anniversary here. All my cousins and relations came, and it all looked perfect and lovely.

I did go back to work and did one day a week for the marketing agency I'd been with for a few years, but then I began doing interior design, first training in it, and now I've set up my own business. I do a lot of that from home. I earn the money for holidays—that's sort of my motive. And since I'm back where I grew up and so are a lot of people I grew up with, most of whom run their own businesses around here, we have a close and wide circle of friends. The funny thing was that when I first met William, he was friendly with all of them—I'd just returned, and he'd got friendly with my friends in my absence!

Our children have definitely helped in terms of my stepchildren. It got easier when the little ones were born—they feel close to them, and love them, and my children adore them. But, really, if I'm honest, the major bone of contention between us has always been the stepchildren . . .

His first wife isn't really an issue. She rings up sometimes but she's never really been horrible to me because I was never really involved—I mean, they split up long before I came on the scene. They still have rows over the phone; she can still get to him. But she's actually always been very nice to my kids. She only came between us in the beginning in the sense of his feeling he didn't want to be married again. But he does say that he never thinks that he actually loved her properly. I do not feel like a second wife at all. I think that's probably because they got married so young and they really shouldn't have got married. I think he knew quite quickly that it was a mistake but he was going to try and make a go of it. And I feel like this is his real marriage and I think he feels that way too. William is a lot more tolerant of me and puts up with an awful lot that he wouldn't from his first wife. She was pretty appalling—depressed, unable to make decisions, immature. I can be appalling but probably not in that league. He's really very forgiving of me. When we have a row, he won't harbor resentment in a way that I probably would. He's the one who will come to me and say to me, if I'm smoldering in my room, "Come down. It's not so bad."

William's children from his first marriage, I think, have a sense of entitlement and bitterness and they seem to want money and things from him all the time. And they ought to be old enough now—they're grown—to be more self-sufficient and not to have that attitude. If we take our children on a skiing holiday, for instance, William will get "You never did that with us, with our mother!" In the afternoon, when our kids were little and would have naps, William and I would do what we do here on the weekends—go to bed. We close the door, and we're in our bedroom. Our children are completely used to it—it doesn't bother them at all. We've always done it. His older kids were upset. They resented the fact that we did that. Perhaps it was because I wasn't their mother. I think they thought till not too long ago that they'd get back together again . . . It was also hard when they came to stay: they weren't respectful of some of our traditions and habits, doing things like cooking their own meals when there was going to be a family one—their own mother didn't used to cook for them when they'd come home from boarding school or university, apparently. And their mother fuels a lot of their resentment, complaining when she hears about any large presents that our children get. She also accuses William of not being in touch with his children enough. It's really unfair—he tries hard to treat each of his children equally and does make the effort to talk to his kids.

There are still a lot of unresolved issues there for all of them. The kids—one in particular, really—are resentful; when she comes to stay, there is always a row. I try to stay out of it but then feel very sidelined. I just feel, oh, I don't know, that they're really nothing to do with me, that they're not my problem, which is awful. I know I shouldn't say that . . . I usually end up taking a book up to my room and going to bed while she's here . . . They're grown up now and I wish they'd be making their own lives but I do realize that they still need their father. Nothing's ever going to get resolved.

I just have to try not to talk about it . . . I mean, it's like he said at the very beginning: "Look, the children come first." I can't ever help that. I mean now . . . the older I get, the more I get to know my own children, and the more they grow up, you have this wonderful feeling that your children are part of you and anything that comes between you and them you just can't bear it, really. And so William has got that but tenfold.

I don't tolerate the changes and adaptations we have to make easily. I get cross with him, like when Christmas gets disrupted by things to do with his children. I take it out on him—I don't talk to him. And sometimes it carries over into other things. I get frosty with him. I know when I'm being horrid to him and feel stupid but it becomes a culmination of feeling tired and disappointed . . . I think I could trace most of my irritations back to this one central issue because it feels so out of control—I can't control it. I can understand it, see it, but I can't control it. I guess I do want William to be totally mine. Maybe if they weren't problematic people, I wouldn't find them encumbrances and I'd be able to be better about this, though. And though William is a very tolerant person in most respects, on this subject—his first children—he's not at all. He gets defensive and he thinks I resent them. So we end up not being able to discuss it. That's the main thing that's always between us and can get other resentments going. It's really the only thing, though, even though we seem to be rowing about other things.

When I get cross and we get frosty, I can bring myself back to a sense of loving him again. He starts being very helpful, for instance. Like the other day, after we'd had an argument, he began to help me with a project I'm doing—it involved shifting furniture around and he helped me do it, and then he lit a fire so it was warm where I was working, and got the coal; he enables me to do things. I started working and that also calmed me and all that helped me. Sometimes I do get to feeling "I'm so fed up with him I don't want to be with him anymore." And then I feel, "But I can't be without him!" I start thinking about friends who are divorced. They're all so unhappy. The husbands, mind you, are all right: they've all got new women! Also I think about the children. When we do have a row, especially my daughter gets very upset. I mean they know their father has been divorced before . . . and a lot of her friends at school, their parents have split up. So you suddenly think,

"Oh God—we can't do this! How stupid are you being! We love each other!"
Then we end up cuddling up to each other. First William comes up to me.
After our last row, he said, "Do you really want to split up?" And I said,
"God, of course I don't!"

I know William would never go through another divorce—I can push him
to a great limit. That's terrible of me. I don't mean it when I threaten him. I
don't necessarily always tell him how much I love him, but I do it in many
other ways—I always have things he likes to eat ready for him. I make things
nice for him around the house. I am volatile, and he is a bit too, and we do
have great rows, sometimes not for ages . . .

Money—like for holidays—is a bit of an issue, because William has to
give his money to them, too, even though they got a big chunk in the
settlement back when he divorced. I do understand it—it's his money and
their money, just like my kids. It's fair really. But that's different from time,
which is at a premium for us as he works away, and there's not so much of it
for just us. But I mean after rows and difficulties he comes up and I do just
melt and I do remember that I love him. He's suddenly all kind and loving—
but that's often after sex.

He does find it hard to say "sorry." I find myself yelling at him about
something he's obviously done—like the other day when he let the dog out
and it ran off. So, I yelled out, "the dog!" and he said, "You're always
shouting and nagging at me." So I said, "Look, why don't you say, 'I'm
sorry'?" He then gets into my personality: "You always shout! You always
nag!" So it escalates and then I go to bed! That stops it. I'm the one who will
go away and that will end things—he could carry on batting things around
and around. Then he'll come in, after a while, and ask if I want a cup of tea. I
can tell by his voice that he's all right, and that means he's sorry. It's his
"sorry." Presumably he's calmed down during that "time out" period too.
After he makes the approach, we'll feel closer. Sometimes it will end in sex. It
takes me a bit of a while to feel close enough for sex.

Sex is very important in our relationship. Funnily enough, sex wasn't all
that brilliant to start with but, because we felt very comfy together, then it
did get brilliant. It's better now than it was, though it's not as frequent,
obviously. Now we're a bit more adventurous. We do use marital aids, and

that actually is very good. Because it's sort of more, it's . . . it gives you more depth, I suppose . . . and often, you know—it's a bit difficult to talk about it—he'll pleasure me lots to start with and then again afterwards he—well the aids can help, as he's not such a young stud anymore! So, I suppose in the old days we had sex and I didn't always have an orgasm, although it was lovely. But now, using marital aids, I can have amazing orgasms and it's brilliant. It means we're exploring now. We're both very at ease with each other. That's great.

Often we'll have a quick making love in the morning, you know; that puts us in the mood for the afternoon—you've sort of had a taster in the morning. That happens about once a week, once a fortnight, depending on whether he's away up in Scotland during the week. It's better when he's been at home. Because when he's been away for a while, I sort of hold him at a distance to start. He'll come home all lovey and cuddly but I can't do that. It takes me awhile—it's as if he's coming into my territory again and I have to make room for him. So by the next day we're okay again, and back into a routine. I think he realizes that I can't be all over him when he returns, even though he still wants it, so still tries. He's more demonstrative than I.

Sex does help us feel close again after we've been irritated with each other, and it often becomes part of the process of making up, once I feel close to him again. I think you sort of split apart when you get too irritated with each other and then you suddenly realize when you've had a bit of time and a nice cuddly afternoon, when you've had sex, you suddenly realize, "Yeah, you still love this guy and he makes you happy and he's everything you need."

. . . We go away together on our own, and always have . . . We make sure we have enough time for each other so we can feel intimate together and that helps keep our sex life alive. My parents have always helped for that.

We both read too, though not the same kind of books, but we'll often sit together reading our books. Sometimes there's a crossover: he just got William Trevor's *The Story of Lucy Gault* for me and that's something he'd read and I would too and we'll talk to each other about our books. We love entertaining and have great parties. We've got great friends together. I think we have a similar sense of humor.

Actually, I think one of the things I was thinking about the other day, which would be very difficult if you split up, was your joint past humor—the things that have been funny, your in-jokes and the things that you say together. I could say something to William and he would know exactly what I meant . . . You get to have an in-joke thing that is a shared history. There are things that make me laugh that don't make him laugh but then when I'm laughing at them, he'll laugh because I'm laughing.

He's very easy to get on with. He's a lighthearted person. Things don't normally get him down and that's what attracted me to him, actually. I think he was attracted to me physically first. He respects me and we're on a par, intelligence wise. I read papers and we talk about issues, though there are some things we don't share. I mean he wouldn't have a clue if I said, "That's Cate Blanchett." You know, he'd go, "Who?" which can irritate me; or, for example, he hates science fiction and I love it. But, then, he'll come along to the latest *Star Trek* movie. He'll come along and fall asleep in it. We've got a very compatible life.

There's nothing missing, really. I'm happy now with my more creative work; he's home working some days and that's brilliant: I love it when he's home. And then I like it when he goes away, because I get my space, though he doesn't like being away. He does like his job and likes the way it's structured, though—it's not nine to five. He says that as long as I'm happy, he's happy. When he retires, I think he'll always have to have something do, like run his own business, but that's not for another ten years or so, at least. He's always wanted to write. Perhaps he'll do that—we'll both want to be doing something creative. I don't think we'll stop—I want us to come together and develop even more.

7

The Hard Work: Living with Differences, Managing Conflict, Trauma, and Distress

RICHARD and TINA MOORE
NANCY AARONOVITCH and ANNIE HART

"OPPOSITES ATTRACT." "Like with like." Which is true when it comes to enduring love? Can people who are very different manage to bridge their gaps, empathizing with each other enough to understand their differences and enjoy happy lives together? Or do you have to be with someone very similar to yourself in order to feel good together over a long period of time? Some of the couples in this book seem to have similar temperaments, though others are almost at opposite ends of the temperament pole. Some couples share politics, others report voting differently. Some choose different books, laugh at different television programs, and come from different ends of the social spectrum. Others share similar social histories, tastes, and styles. What each couple in this study does have in common is the ability to find ways to bridge their differences and to reframe the fact of those differences as a potential source of strength. Moreover, sharing similar core values seems to be key to overcoming and living with any apparent differences.

Being a Muslim and from Pakistan and my wife upper-class English and Quaker, the divide seemed unbridgeable. But our love for each other made everything else secondary. Deciding to live here, I wanted my, or rather our, children to be part of this culture. They would have been part of the Pakistani culture had we gone back. There has been no conflict as in many mixed marriages and so the children had a clear and smooth and sure and a secure way to grow up.—**Qasim Patel, 64**

Differences in style and temperament, as well as ones of class and upbringing, can nevertheless produce a happy fit.

> We both bicker. All the time! But, neither takes offence at all for any length of time. We argue but don't normally hold grudges and I let him control the TV remote control . . . I like to cook, while he's good at washing up; I know he'll do the ironing, but we both know it's me that cleans up the sick!! It's a jigsaw.—**Lynne Rutherford, 43**

Indeed, complementing each other through differences means two lives, blended, operate more fully and efficiently—sometimes because of the differences. Difference can lead individuals to feel grateful and interested, as well as admired and appreciated. The flip side of this is that differences can yield frustration and misunderstanding.

Difference in who does what in a relationship is, of course, the source of many arguments. When it comes to keeping conflicts over how much each person puts into a relationship to a minimum, it is important to take the long view (past, present, future). Simmering sparked by dishes left unwashed may be soothed by remembering that your partner took the car to be serviced. Credit accrues when there is historic perspective, so that, for instance, an argument over the messy bathroom is a single incident, not a festering, long-term wound. You have managed to get over such things in the past; you know you will again.

> If we've had arguments or conflict it is usually about silly niggles—having spent my life cleaning up after farm dirt, mud, etc., I get angry when dirty shoes are worn in the house—I don't like being taken for granted (no one does). I blow my top and on occasion have walked miles to get my anger out of my system. Once sane again and calm, I

know I couldn't find a more kind, reliable, honest loving chap and the grass is not greener on the other side! We say sorry, and make up.—
Claire Hoxton, 56

Differences and conflict can sometimes, but not always, be bridged through talking. Most stories mention talking, talking, and more talking. In fact, many couples talk about how much they talk. Some are clearly very good with words. Women are typically more verbally fluent, but some couples thrive on words because both partners are at ease with them. Perhaps surprisingly, communication can be good if there is at least one, but not necessarily two, comfortable with words. Frequency, per se, of productive conversation does not seem to matter. Instead, research on good relationships[25] and good communication[26] shows that what does is being clear, direct, and open about most important things, and feeling "heard" by your partner. People need to feel soothed, or reassured and "attended to." Good communication apparently consists of partners feeling that they have talked about important things and that they have been listened to and understood, outcomes that themselves bring about appreciation and affection, as each partner feels restored to the emotional equilibrium and good will essential to feeling cared for and caring in return. Crucially, agreement itself is not necessary.

Not every couple "talks and talks." Some find talking problematic, with different styles making it difficult, as Iona and Jamie in chapter 6 testified. Indeed, some have noted that they take pains not to discuss things at length, feeling that would be like scratching a wound, as Pam Johnson in chapter 8 suggests. However, what is clear from the couples in this study is that, as prior research suggests, they think about what the other has meant or might be feeling. What this could mean is not necessarily talking it all through, but instead, as one interviewee said, "putting some things away," perhaps bringing them out later, but often just putting them away. One couple comments on an additional component of managing conflict well: part of the process is taking responsibility for managing your own hurt feelings before they escalate and cross the boundary of irreparable harm. Some cooling-off mechanism within the couple, managed and accepted individually, is necessary. For some this means leaving the room, others the proverbial counting to ten, yet others gesturing for time-out or peace. In all cases what results is a break from each other and a chance to cool down. Once the physiological fight-or-flight response dies away, people have access to other feelings and gain the ability to think more clearly, opening up the possibility to consider another point of view.[27]

> In the beginning we were too poor to part and had nowhere to go separately anyway. If we had a fight, one of us just took a long walk, and we did a lot of walking in those early days.—**Rita Turner, 42**

Received wisdom suggests both that blazing arguments are bad and it is good to talk. This is not always true. Research indicates that when the proportion of conflict to harmony is too high, when difference or conflict breed contempt, when partners do not feel their differences are honored or respected, and when physical harm enters (domestic violence) in the wake of conflict, then arguments are not only bad, but also talk is not enough and can even antagonize.

The same body of research also shows that, while usually couples can be characterized as mostly handling conflict in a particular style, often they use an assortment. Some shout, simmer, and finally reconcile, not necessarily reaching either agreement or compromise. Others do the same but, through discussion, come to either a compromise or an agreement on one person's position. Others do not raise issues overtly, although they are aware of dissent or disapproval. Instead of openly discussing conflict, they mull over the other partner's position independently. Sometimes attitudes and behaviors clearly change as a result, other times this process will bring simply a respect and understanding for the other's position. Still other couples discuss the conflict area from the beginning, talking for hours, perhaps picking it up over days, with the aim of a negotiated compromise. In all cases, though, the partners have felt heard, or acknowledged. Reaching an agreement or being proved right is not necessarily the important thing, though often agreement is reached. As one interviewee said, in the end, "Peace at home is more important than any issue that divides us."

We are both fiery people and neither of us finds it easy to either admit we are wrong or to be the first to say sorry, but one of us always does. Even so, maintaining a relationship is *serious* hard work. There has to be a lot of give and understanding and an inordinate amount of love to make it work. You have to be prepared to admit you are wrong—even if you know you ain't. We have been through awful times but every hurdle we come to is passable, if we approach it together. We are not at all religious, but we have total faith in each other. I truly believe that if you are lucky enough to find someone who loves you and understands you as much as you love and understand them, then anything is possible.—**Susan Mulligan, 43**

Other research shows another, more fundamental point about trauma, difference, and conflict.[28] If you expect your relationship to feel good all of the time, you are not likely to learn to adopt the attitudes or the kinds of acts necessary to manage your distress or to feel hopeful and do whatever it takes to ride out the storm and get the relationship back on a better keel. The stories here suggest anything from portions of days to weeks, months, and even longer periods fraught with difficulties. It is the proportion of good to bad, pleasant to unpleasant, that counts, as well as the expectation that difficulties will both occur and recede.

If this sounds as if some couples might brush things under the carpet, it is in fact the opposite. The couples who succeed are those who approach their differences as inevitable and ongoing, but also use each new conflict as another chance to chip away at the bone of dissent or disharmony that keeps arising between them. They see their difference as a lifetime challenge: each time recurring issues arise it gives the couple the opportunity to achieve a little more understanding. As Sue Fox said, "I knew what I was getting with Bob when I married him. He is what he is"—and so, the things she finds maddening, difficult, dispiriting about him, the ever-present issues between them, arise again and again, with new ways for her to understand and handle them.

But disharmony is uncomfortable, and misunderstanding and conflict can hurt. So other research has found that what is also indispensable for happiness together is to employ what's called "repair mechanisms."[29] These include the simple but often magical words "I'm sorry."

> We come from two very different backgrounds. We have managed to make a success of our marriage despite dire warnings from parents and some of their friends beforehand . . . When we have rows I storm out, bursting into tears. I either walk around the local streets or hide in the house (pathetic isn't it?). After about a half an hour or so I come back with equanimity restored, and almost immediately we are apologizing. He will make a cup of tea; I will ask him what he wants for supper. A day or so later we may go more fully into what caused the row or sort matters out.—**Patricia Patel, 63**

Most of the stories mention either a verbal "I'm sorry" or gestures (a cup of tea, a hug, or a smile, for instance) to indicate a truce. Some couples note there is one member who usually initiates reconciliation. Initiating repairs, itself, does not have to even out fairly—instead, fairness lies in a mostly equal number of repairs being made, eventually, to both partner's feelings. Repair mechanisms (expressing both regret for hurt caused and awareness of the hurt experienced) are often conceivable because largely the apology is for the hurt feelings: for the wounding during argument, rather than the points made within it. Once one side expresses this, the battle lines recede. You are allies again, and it becomes more possible for the other to apologize and even for the actual contentious points to be considered, at least eventually.

Having the perspective that the relationship is bigger than the issue, and not having to be "right" or to win seems to be crucial to the happy love story, as is the perspective that allows differences to feel distant and manageable as time passes.

> We met at the seaside. I was eighteen and he was twenty . . . we were so in love! We married against our parents' wishes . . . Tim had a really bad temper on him those days. But you see, I'm no pushover either, and so there was trouble . . . We had this terrible, really terrible fight and the police had to come. That was it, though. That was a turning point.

Never got like that again . . . He does lots of things for me that show me that he loves me. It's nothing to him to fold the washing if he sees it, when he knows I'm in the middle of it. He'll wash the floor if he sees I've done it and it's got dirty again. If he sees the ironing's out, and he's not doing anything, he'll pick up the iron—he doesn't do it very well, but that doesn't worry me. He doesn't need to tell me, like, in words, you know, how much he loves me—he does that too . . . really, yes. He just comes along and hugs me too, whenever.—**Lorna Davis, 48**

Living with difference is one piece of the inevitably hard part of remaining coupled and pleased to be so. What can feel even more dispiriting and difficult to surmount is trauma or severe distress. Some of the stories recounted for this study imply that love has "saved" them, others that love itself has needed saving under the weight of trauma. Clearly trauma or an accumulation of multiple stresses that feel unrelenting can break a relationship. It is well documented that when a child dies—the single harshest event research claims a person can endure—a marriage is often so tested that it can crumble under the strain. When terrible things happen, it is normal to wish our partners will be "rocks." But sometimes both partners need "rocks" of different sorts, even at the same time. One grieving parent may need silence to nurse grief: his "rock" is someone who leaves him alone. Another grieving parent might yearn to talk, to reimagine, continually, scenes of loss, so that their immediacy and power are lost: her "rock" would talk constantly with her. Each "rock" is not only defined differently then, but also can be at cross-purposes with each other.

Sometimes partners are amazing emotional heroes, giving what is needed even when it is hard for them, putting aside their own needs, even adapting so that they are differently met. For some couples, therapy has been used, or another outside source: a doctor, cleric, or friend. Richard Moore, whose story follows, mentions that he turned to therapy—initially because he felt so unhappy at law school, and then subsequently with his wife, Tina—to gain both insight and techniques for managing and understanding the contributions each individual family's legacies had made to the tensions that recur between them.

But not everyone needs, has access to, or is disposed to calling in another, and sometimes external sources can be less than helpful, anyway.

Ed had been working away from home from Monday to Friday. We had three children under five and we had little help. Our second child was diagnosed with Asperger's syndrome, a mild form of autism, and had "challenging" behavior. It was very hard, and (at that time) we did not communicate properly. At this time we had some counseling—not something I'd be in a hurry to recommend. It did have the effect of bringing us together because the woman was so horrible to me that Ed became very supportive, and because he had to make time to attend, and it was nice to spend some time together. We (now) communicate effectively, and sometimes we choose not to communicate at all—an element of privacy is important. Ed always treats me with consideration; he is always polite and caring.—**Alison Homewood, 38**

Not all partners can be emotional heroes; yet these enduring and happy couples do sometimes relate tales of crass or pusillanimous behavior in troubled times, which are generously forgiven through an empathic under-standing and acceptance ("she wasn't well" or "he was frightened" or "I knew he wanted to be able to do something else but just couldn't"), demonstrating another sort of emotional heroism feeding love.

Well, Eileen told all about what it was like [her periods]. But, you know, it was okay—I loved her, I knew her. I just said to myself, "That's not Eileen talking, it's the hormones, it's the time of the month talking. It's not my Eileen." It wasn't her. And that was right: I knew I'd get the real Eileen back, and I always did! And, now, look: she's cured. She's back. And she's kind, and patient. She loves me. I love her. We do things together, we have fun, and she helped me through my depression, she did, when I lost my job. "Never mind, Jerry," she said, "it just gives me more time with you!"—**Jerry Todd, 42**

The first part of a love story is the easy part. No one deserves a medal for falling in love. It is in the ensuing chapters, when differences emerge, and distress and severe upheavals disturb the dream of the relationship, that the real heroism of enduring love stories unfolds.

Richard and Tina Moore

Richard and Tina Moore live in the middle of Philadelphia, in a period house filled with artworks done by Tina and various friends and relatives, jokey finds from thrift shops, exotic mementoes from travels, and wild juxtapositions of color. Richard, fifty-four, quiet, thoughtful, athletic-looking, is a lawyer. Tina, fifty-three, petite, effervescent, and artfully stylish, is an artist who also teaches classes for children at a local museum. Their son is at university, while an older daughter, graduated, is living with them temporarily. Richard and Tina met when both were university students during a summer break traveling in Europe. Their stories show them making enormous leaps over different backgrounds and temperaments to forge happiness, even using these differences to their advantage when they face tragedy.

Richard Moore:

I was the younger son, by five years, of a Philadelphia Quaker family, on both sides. I grew up in Philadelphia, in a well-to-do enclave. Most of the people I was surrounded with were also Quakers, whom my parents and their families had known for years. We belonged to clubs—tennis, swimming . . . We had a summer house at a lake . . . Most of the friends I had in school—I went to a Quaker private school—were also from this set. My mother's family had quite a bit of money. My father's family owned a lucrative business. He started at Princeton, but in the Depression the family business began to fail, and his father was primarily a businessman, who felt that his son ought to leave Princeton and come home and help with the business, so my father had to leave Princeton in his second year. He was very smart, and he had a chip on his shoulder about that. He took over the family business. He did well with it for a while but it eventually failed; his explanation for it was that it was a family business and he couldn't get his family to stop interfering with his management techniques. I don't know if that was true or not, but the fact of the matter is that it failed with him involved. That was emasculating. My mother's family money was what carried us through. He also had had rheumatic fever as a child, and that meant he couldn't get into the service in World War II. One of my touching discoveries about him after his death was when my brother and I went into his office to clean it out, we found in a desk drawer a stack of documents . . . that detailed his unsuccessful efforts to get into the military, as if he had been waiting in the intervening thirty years to answer anyone who said, "You coward"—he'd then pull out the papers in reply. That was very much my father.

I felt close to him because he was the more emotional of the two. He was the guy who would get teary—he'd tell a story that was poignant—and he was just a warmer, juicier presence than my mother—or than his two repressed sons at that point in their lives. He was certainly interested in us, probably to a suffocating degree. We felt that our lives were vindicating his failures. We had to be the best in our class, proof that even though the men in his social circle were more successful than he was, his children were more successful than theirs. It was never said out loud, but it was apparent and felt by us.

My mother is surprisingly down-to-earth for someone who came out of such privilege. She has no interest in ostentation, values all the right things. There's a lack of pretence about her that makes her stand out. She graduated from Vassar and worked for five years as a microbiologist at a medical lab before having children. In another age she would have gone to med school. But she became a housewife without much to do till the business crashed, so she sat on boards of charities, working very hard. She's almost ninety and she still works two days a week at a hospital. She is very practical. She's not a hugger. If you were sitting near her, she wouldn't reach out and caress you; she's not emotive like my father. My father—particularly when he had more time on his hands—could talk excessively, while my mother would use the phrase "too much of a muchness," which irritated my brother and me, meaning you were spending too much time on one subject. Being impolite, or excessive—those things were key to her. Her social clock turns off in about sixty seconds—keep it polite, don't let a lot of feeling contaminate a social situation. Unlike him. When they would drink—there was social drinking— he'd bring things up, like sex, to be provocative, and my mother would sort of go "darling," with her jaw muscles vibrating, "that is not a topic you need to discuss at the table." And we would just keep quiet, rather than side with either one.

But they had a pretty good marriage, though it didn't seem sexy to me at all. He really respected her intellect, they had the same values, a lot of friends, and they could make each other laugh. It was a relationship that worked but one I didn't want for myself.

He died in his sleep one night, one of the only times she wasn't there with him. She is a trooper and just sort of carried on, though. And then the wife of one of their best friends died a year later, and for the next sixteen years, till he died too, she and John were together, not married, but very happy. It cheered me up and enlightened me. It was good to see that you can live different lives. Some of the things that she hadn't gotten out of the relationship with my father she got with John, and she adapted at a mature age. She showed me how to deal with a crisis with an attitude of let's see what we can do to make it better, a better approach to life.

I have never wanted to disappoint her—she's a pain about social conventions: you had to write the thank-you notes before you unwrapped the gift. You had to do things her way. As my brother and I became closer in college, as the five year difference mattered less, and then continued to be best friends for the rest of his life, my mother was the endless topic of conversation. I remember ending many long evenings—and by that time both of us were married—with saying, "Oh, my God, we just blew a whole evening talking about Mom! When are we going to grow up and get out from under this thing!"

I also had an English nanny who lived with us till she died—I was the last child she looked after, and I loved her and she loved me. She delighted in me. My father also showed delight in me—in my achievements—but I kept him at a distance because his delight was unbearable.

I went to Princeton, fulfilling his dream. My brother had gone to Harvard
. . . I was going to go to Harvard. It was a highly complex decision for me. I
didn't want to be a clone of my brother, but then Princeton meant fulfilling
my father's dream. It annoyed me that everyone thought I'd choose Harvard.
When I'd been there I'd thought it had an intellectual, removed quality, and
Princeton was a place where people threw their arms around you. That was
very appealing. Immediately after arriving at Princeton I felt I'd made a
mistake: it was all-male then. I felt very lonely—very sexually lonely. I didn't
really have a girlfriend till I met Tina, just friends from school and home. I
had no confidence in that area at all then.

Then in the summer vacation after sophomore year I met Tina. I was
traveling in Europe by myself, trying to catch the ferry from Wales to Dublin,
hitching, and at the last minute got a ride. The boat was literally pulling away
from the dock and I jumped on, over open water. She and her friend were on
that boat and saw me jumping. It turned out we were all headed for the same
hostel in Dublin. We sort of teamed up, spending the week together hitching
around Ireland. I was totally smitten with her. I didn't know then she'd be the
love of my life, but I did know that she was the one out of the two. I then went
over to England. I knew I'd see her when I got back to America. I wanted to
pursue it without the awkwardness of her friend being there.

It felt very easy being with her. Very warm. And with her friend being
there it had to be social rather than sexual, so we got to know each other. I
had my guitar and, because of the summer camp I'd gone to as a kid, I was
totally consumed with the folk world and culture then, and she knew all the
folk songs I sang. She wasn't from my world, my parents' world, at all—she
was from a big Italian family from Brooklyn, not wealthy. Here was this art
student who was sexy and interesting and spontaneous, emotional, fun to be
with. Great! I never knew a woman could be like that; there was nothing in
my own history to make me think such creatures existed!

She was at NYU and so when we got back I invited her to a football game
at Princeton, which she didn't like at all. But we had a great time together.
Love blossomed for me very quickly. The distance made it hard. And she was
going out with other guys, which I found very threatening. We had a
tumultuous time that year because of it. We spent the summer together in

New York City and that was great, seeing each other all the time. But in the fall we went back to how things had been, and the other men in her life in New York made it very difficult. I remember going to New York for a peace demonstration that we were going to go to together, and her brother—who's a major figure in her life—was there, and I was late getting down and he was impatient and they didn't wait for me. They went off. I was stood up in the peace movement . . . So I said, "That's it. You've chosen against me." And we didn't see each other for a long time after that—for the rest of the year, which was my last year at Princeton.

I saw other women too, but it came from her; she just said, "I am too young. I should be experimenting, not commit to one person. I'm here and you're there and there's so much going on here." I could appreciate that but it was excruciating. That two-year period was marked by the greatest happiness and the greatest pain that I had experienced so far. We'd break up and one or the other . . . would make contact again.

If I had taken up a fellowship after graduation, that would have taken me to San Francisco . . . We were broken up at the time of both our graduations in 1968. But my draft board turned down the fellowship as a draft exclusion and so I ended up doing teaching in New York instead, and she was then working there too. A different chapter of our lives had opened—the issue of other people wasn't around any more—and we got married at the end of that year, in 1969. But the issue that rose during the beginning has colored our whole life: license to do what you want versus responsibility.

Her family is great—they were all embracing and I loved being with them. They were different ethnically: southern Italians. Her father was just a wonderful guy, as easy a person to be with as I have ever met, generous, friendly. There were lots of cousins, lots of family events, and these were fun, unlike ours . . . And our families managed to mesh. My father loved meeting people of different ethnicities and liked them a lot.

Because of the draft I taught for a while and then I went to law school: I gave myself a narrow spectrum of career possibilities and it was the most appealing choice. But it did seem to be that the people who had the most interesting public sector jobs—I knew that that was what I wanted to do—were lawyers. So it seemed that law school was the admission ticket.

My father died when I was in my second year. I hated law school. I hated the way it was conducted—the autocratic, traditional method and style—and somehow I crashed that first year. My brain turned off in the second semester, though I was doing nothing visibly different. Tina was teaching and painting, living a completely different sort of life. We spent many hours of the day apart and she had no connection with what I was doing, and what I was doing was something I didn't like. I got to my final exams and it was a terrifying experience. I had an anxiety attack: some complicated question about a plane crash over two different states and I thought, "I don't know how to begin to answer. I don't know what the issues are." This propelled me into therapy. I had never talked about any family issues—particularly the burden of things with my father. He died in the middle of it. It was sad, but in some ways easier for me then; that is, life was easier without my father and that was a revelation. After that first year it got easier in law school and I didn't have trouble again. I finished and got a job in Philadelphia doing work in the mayor's office, stuff on corruption, which was wonderful—not straight legal practice.

When kids arrived—ten years after we got married—it just added to our intimacy; they never got in the way of it, nor made it fade. I was very determined to be influential as a parent and I loved having kids from day one. I never had a minute of their lives when I said it would have been easier without them; I loved the activity in the house, the kids around, and it actually made my life with Tina even more interesting and it gave me the chance to do things my way and get my point of view across. With Tina there had always been the point that I was an adult and so was she, so I couldn't impose my views so much in our relationship, as I'm more reticent about stating my needs or feeling a sense of entitlement in our relationship. But with the kids, I could get my two cents in. Tina wasn't going to dominate, and actually that helped our relationship.

Meanwhile my brother had become a lawyer too, in Philadelphia, and he was working for a man who was one of my father's old friends. He was being the perfect son. He worked for the man who had always seemed like . . . the apotheosis of success. My father had worshipped this guy. I stayed in my public sector work, and meanwhile my brother, who was now a partner in that firm, approached me about joining him. I had two little kids by then. But instead, another, more exciting job with the city, right in the thick of things, came up, special counsel to a commission. And just then my brother's cancer—he had had colon cancer that seemed in remission—spread to his liver. Within two months he was dead.

He had two teenage children, and was only forty-five. We lived right near each other, did lots of things together. He hadn't gone for a checkup in four years and his wife nagged him to get an annual checkup. He checked out fine, and then a test came back saying he had colon cancer. They operated, removing some of his colon, and there had been some spread to the lymph system, so he had to have chemo. I remember celebrating the last month of his chemotherapy. He had had a goal: ten treatments of it, and after that he'd be home free. Then a scan showed that he had this major tumor, undetected, no physical sensation . . . they had to excise a large part of his liver and we were on liver watch for a week to see if the liver would regenerate. It didn't. In a week he was dead. It was the worst thing that has ever happened in my life. We were so close, he was my closest friend as well as my brother, so it was awful on every level. It was horrible to see the devastation that it brought to his family.

But for me—the gift of my brother's death has been that I have been much less bothered by little shit than I was previously. I try to focus on the larger issues. And that was a life-changing thing for me. I appreciate what I have tremendously. It sort of feels like every day my kids and wife and family and I are healthy is a gift. I continue to help out his family. I took over some of the things he did for my mother, like her finances, and I deal with the uncles and aunts and so forth. And Tina has been amazing. Her role in helping in this case was and has been huge. She would go and sleep in his wife's house with her, sometimes in her room, the nights after my brother died, so she wouldn't have to be alone. That's not something that would have occurred to me to do, or that I could do, as a man. She would be in the bed with her, comforting her physically, as she is so capable of doing. Because of her sense of family, she just shows up for things. If someone is in the hospital it is effortless for her—or it seems effortless—to sit with them and make them feel better, and brighten their day in a way that if I would do it, it would be labored and it wouldn't come as naturally. And I am tremendously grateful to have that.

I went to my brother's office after his death, to clean his desk, and my father's friend, my brother's law partner, said to me, "Why don't you come work here? At my age I don't want someone new, I don't want to bring a stranger into the practice. I'll teach you the business, and it's yours when I go." I agonized over that decision for months, really, much longer than he wanted me to . . . there was a sort of inevitability to it. It was like, this is what I have been trained for, this was the whole point of my upbringing, and so what choice did I have? And so I took it on, and for the first time in my life I had a job that held no interest to anyone that I talked to . . . When I said, "I have a small general practice that emphasizes trusts," people are nodding off before you finish your sentence. And that was true at home too. I had always had some stories to tell, and suddenly neither Tina nor our children have had much interest in what goes on in this job . . .

Now it's fine. I had inherited a partner—a third partner in the firm—who was a witch and it got impossible, and in 1992 we severed the partnership and I moved the practice. Just as my marriage was a liberation from a sexless dreary past, and my brother's death was in some ways liberating, for it made me focus on more important things, the new practice and move has been like every day is a day in the country here. I've achieved some selfhood in this; there is the stamp of who I am. And I've organized things so that I do the things I'm good at and farm out the ones I'm not. I like my job now and my life. And I have a new partner, who Tina loves, and she is now more accepting of what I do and it's more integrated into our life together.

Tina had a stake in my being the sixties guy she'd married. I, like her, hadn't gone into traditional things, despite my Ivy League background. The message to me was that there wasn't anything sexy in what I was going to do if I took on my brother's job. So it was risky on those grounds, taking this job, as it meant losing her regard, and she burst into tears when I told her my decision. But we talked and talked and she did appreciate the other things that were compelling about it. A huge part also was that our two children were starting school, and they needed private schools as we were living in the city—it was also a financial decision. Tina makes very little money from her art and writing. She's actually a very successful poet, but you don't make money out of publishing poems. And at that point she wasn't really working much—she'd worked in a library but then having the kids meant she was really mostly at home, though she would be making things and writing there too.

Some of the therapy I had back then was relationship therapy, where we talked about the issues that have always been around for us. These have been there from the beginning, as have the things that have been great. Because of who we are, it is very easy to fall into the reverse roles of my parent: I am the provider and regulator and Tina is the free spirit. And in many ways it is the free spirit that attracts me and turns me on, but it is also infuriating to me, and not good for me or healthy for our relationship if I get locked into the role of provider and regulator. So that has been the dominant theme of our marriage—how we negotiate that.

Tina is prone to excess, in general, and I can get too often in the role of regulator, which I do not want. When we're out, Tina would drink more than she might want, and perhaps get flirtatious without meaning to . . . Or she would talk too much. I despise the role of being a cop. Yet it enraged me if she did drink too much or got out of control. I've always had trouble with "entitlements"—what I am entitled to expect from a situation?—and I err on the side of not demanding enough, or not imposing my wishes enough, and then feeling enraged. But over the years I've gotten better at speaking my mind. In fact, we rarely have blowups in our relationship, even though Tina is very hot. I'm very hard to fight with—I don't blow up fast and I use humor to deflect things. And I don't always bring things up even if it would be on my mind. Instead Tina might have felt remorse for her behavior and say, "Oh, how did I act? How did I act?" and I would say, "This is not a job I want; I am not going to be the morning-after judge." She worries about my opinion of her, and she reads me, but sometimes she'd go, "Oh, screw you," if she's had a couple of drinks, "I'll do what I want!" And then she'd apologize afterward.

Another example is that Tina is easily disappointed: she wants things to be perfect and then is upset if they don't work out. I have always organized myself so there's another plan in my back pocket as a way to cope with disappointment, not getting too excited over one thing. There are always two or three other choices. I was always having to come up with something else for her—I don't love that role, the being the "make it better" guy all the time. I'd get impatient with her, and she would also see when I'm disappointed. We both have moved toward the center. I am better about expressing enthusiasm for things and she is more resilient about things not working out. Also I read her less reactively than I used to: keeping Tina from being disappointed used to be my life's work and now it isn't at all. She keeps herself better, and when she gets disappointed, it's her problem, not mine.

Now our kids are gone, though our daughter has moved back in just temporarily. When they left, I was frightened of what that meant for my life. Did that mark the end of a fun, youthful period? So I set about to do other things to fill the space that they occupied. I joined a chorus and I do yoga and tennis. All of these things plus my work means there is somewhat less time with Tina, which used to be time around the kids. But we see friends a lot together and family, and she does a lot of her own things too.

And Tina makes things special. She works to make them. She entertains and generates fun. And certainly the vacations that we take—we are well suited to them together. We both love wildlife-related things, we love different "ethnic" settings, we love cities—she loves museums more than I but we accommodate that. She makes events special. It's a quality that I saw right away and appreciate more with time. The flip side is that she crashes after, but that talent of hers has enriched my life and I have learned from it. She is a fun person to be with.

As for sexual fires: well, we're in our fifties. Tina has some arthritis. She has always been accommodating about sex, but it happened earlier for her, that the sexual fires sort of were less. But we've never been without it, though there is less heat. I am feeling it, to my great chagrin, too. But it is a fact of life that that arena that has always worked well for us, we have to work harder at now. That just means we have to think about it, and that is depressing because it makes you feel old . . . So, it is a new time for both of us, and Tina's physical issues, arthritis, are really frustrating for her, visiting a succession of doctors. The aging thing has scared both of us. Of course I've thought about other women—I'd never want to have the mind-set that I couldn't: one of the pleasures of life is being sexually interested . . . I think Tina's more doctrinaire about not having affairs—too much guilt, couldn't do it. I've heard too many stories about people who have had a magical moment and acted on it because it was there and available or whatever . . . but neither of us has had affairs.

We talk. I'm a good listener. We talk about emotional things, lots of things; Tina's a better talker than she is a listener, but she certainly knows me well. And she is available. If I say, "Listen, I need to talk," she is there.

She does have a talent for making life special. Two summers ago our older daughter was in Argentina for the summer and Tina and our son and I went down there for a family vacation during her last two weeks. It was a big, expensive vacation and it was all planned in advance. In the last part of it we went up to amazing waterfalls in the north. We deliberated if we had the money for this or not and we did it. It was the end phase of the vacation and I was already thinking of the office but Tina wasn't ready to let it go and she was looking for something to prolong it. We were at the end of a trail of Jesuit missions, and Tina wanted to fly back to the beginning of the trail. It meant an extra five hundred dollars. It wouldn't come naturally to me to do anything like that, but it did to her, and we did it, and it was a great part of the trip and the kids loved it. Like the credit card ads say, "You can't put a price tag on it." So it was great.

I am very much in love with her. She's not the same girl I fell in love with . . . there's a change there in both of us. We've moved to the center. The entertainment portion of our life she has taken care of, and that is great for me, so she is filling the responsibility there, and I appreciate that a lot. I'm not the only "responsible" person. And she'd say she appreciates me taking care of the business side of things. But I think I've moved to the center too. I also do my own things to facilitate the good times, or something like that. That occurs with the kids, or with the cooking: Tina has no interest in cooking and I love to cook . . . it's sort of a sensual, welcoming thing that I bring in, not just "business." I'm not just business nor she just spirit and entertainment now.

Tina Moore:

I grew up in Brooklyn, the second of four children, in an Italian family. We had a two-family house. My aunt and uncle and cousins were next door; we were in and out of both houses. Boundaries weren't exactly a high priority. We all spent summers at a lake in New Jersey—my family, my relatives, my cousins, aunts, uncles, you name 'em. I've got sisters and brothers and cousins who are like sisters and brothers—all very close. Sometimes too close: my first cousins married each other—that was a little . . . a little weird after they got divorced, but . . . My sister, my older brother, and I were and are very close. We live near my sister and we see her a lot . . . I had a close relationship with both my parents. My mother's full-on, very warm. We see a lot of her. We have vacations with the two mothers, Richard's and mine— they get on really well, and we take them away with us about once a year. My father—he died a number of years ago now—was totally wonderful and I know I idolized him. My parents had a good relationship, lots of talk, lots of spark. My father was a wonderful, bright, affectionate guy. A rock. He was a plumber and had his own business; my mother didn't work—she was at home. There was music, art, talk, emotions, all the time. One thing—you were never lonely. That's for sure. The problem was feeling crowded in, not having a private, quiet—a place, you know, alone with yourself, without voices all around.

I went to college to study art, but I also was open to other things— writing, crafts, into nature and conservancy, and wildlife. I went to NYU in Manhattan and did art and art history. In the summer after my sophomore year a friend and I went hitching around Europe together. We were on the ferry from Wales to Dublin and we saw this cute guy . . . and then when the boat was pulling out, just about to leave, we saw him jumping, jumping onto the boat! He could have missed it . . . Anyway, we started talking on the boat and hanging out together, and both of us really liked him. There was no question that I wanted him—and I knew he liked me but she liked him too. When we got to Ireland, we just kept on together. We ended up spending about a week together traveling around Ireland . . . He was a combination of this rustic, folky type—he knew these folk songs that we knew—and he was also very bright and extremely articulate, and, oh—he was adorable. He wanted to see the stuff we wanted to see; we'd go have lunch, have a beer; he had the same interests . . . There was this beautiful old house I remember where we had lunch . . . It was just like meeting someone, and seeing something—well, it was like, "This is something I want." It was just this feeling that grew over that week.

I think it was clear that Richard felt that too, but it was awkward because my friend was there, so we couldn't talk about it. Then we had to go back on the ferry to go to England. We were off to Scotland and Richard was going off then to London . . . so we got on the ferry—and Richard slept on the floor, and there was a sense of missed opportunity. It was three o'clock in the morning and I just said, "Do you want a back rub?" And he said, "Sure." I felt real guilty—it was like, "Jump now! Go for it!" I was a real nut—I was only nineteen years old—so he got on his stomach and I straddled him and I gave him a back rub, and he said, "Do you want to go on deck?" So we did . . . and nothing happened. We were just leaning over the railing, and then we heard this voice say, "Hey, what are you guys doing out here?" It was my friend.

I just said to myself then, "I want this." I need to make it clear to him, and when we said good-bye and we left him, we gave him our addresses. And we went off to our separate journeys.

When I was back at college I got a call from my mother and she said, "This guy called Richard Moore called. I'll give him your number at school." And I remember saying then to my roommate that I met this guy this summer and I really think I love him—there is just something about him. And I was also furious! Because I didn't really know him—I was going out with other guys! I was too young! . . . Maybe a month or so went by between the phone call and when I saw him. He asked me to the Harvard-Princeton game and I thought, "I love this guy" . . . let me see what this is like. And I looked at him wearing this plaid jacket, and I thought, "He is just so cute, and there is something so eager about him and young, and optimistic, and a kind of openness," and it was kind of like, "Oh, the world is open to him!" He was so glad to see me!

I was so young but I was touched by how young he was. We had the same kind of . . . of . . . *sense*; there was a sense of curiosity about him. When he was happy you could really tell. I loved his face—and I still love his face: so cute, just so cute!

But I was a little intimidated by all this Ivy League stuff and I still am. It was hard because he was Quaker, and he wasn't like the people I knew . . . at all. I'm talking about the class thing. I liked it, but I was also intimidated by it. And I was also a little snobby about it. My house was just much more tumultuous. On the other hand, his father was interesting . . . They were really bright, which I liked. I was intimidated by his mother. But his father was great—I liked him right away. His mother—she takes time to know. But I love her. I think his parents loved each other, like mine did, although with his parents there was a tension, mostly because of his father's failed business.

I knew my parents would love Richard and I didn't want them to. It was really about, if you ask your mother, "How does my hair look?" and she says, "Great!" it's like, "Oh, no!" I wanted something edgier. He was wholesome, and I thought I wanted to be with the edgier guys. But it is something that makes me laugh, and makes him laugh—you know, "You're too good and I'm bad." It comes out in very funny ways, like, if I come towards him with scissors toward his hair, there will be this panic in his eyes because I am capable of doing something then—it is part of my over-the-topness. I think I needed someone who *wasn't* dangerous, who *wasn't* over the top.

I understood in my soul why he loves me when I met his father, and his second nanny, this big, huge black lady who used to clean house who was very interested in him, who loved to talk. He was very close to her, and when I met her, I could see he didn't want someone—like I didn't want some-one—he grew up with. Like I could have married an Italian. I wanted someone who was a little odd, and educated, and he didn't want—he wanted someone who was more emotional and vibrant. He loved my family, and I loved his contained, articulate self.

But I got increasingly angry with him in that period. I hadn't slept with anybody yet. We went out but we started to break up because I needed experience. He didn't have any more experience than me. By this time I was in my junior year—we both were. I don't remember the exact chronology of things but we ended up sleeping together and it was bit awkward because we hadn't had much experience, but it was fine, gentle, and then we went out and went out. And then it was like it was annulled: it was, "I am going to marry you, but just hold on!" I was just angry with him, which wasn't fair. It showed by us having a hard time together. We broke up for a while.

I don't really remember how we got back together. He wasn't in New York, and I can't say I missed him—I wanted to have experience. But he was there, he was always *there*, and I knew that. I don't remember longing for him so much as knowing that this is the person I want. There was some confidence in me. Some kind of inevitability about it. I was just trying to hold off. My history with guys was that they would like me more than I would like them, and I always thought, "I am not going to like these guys." He was the only person I thought, "I am not going to get sick of this person." I didn't really say to myself clearly that I loved him—that came later. What I did think was, when I met him, I thought, "I think I can love this guy for the rest of my life," and that is scary at nineteen. We ended up getting married when I was only twenty-two and he was twenty-two. We spent most of our senior year together and then we decided that was it, we had to be together. And he came to New York to join me in 1968, when we both graduated. We ended up living together one year after college. And then we just thought, "This is nuts. Let's just get married!" I said, "Um, so, let's get married, don't you think?" and he said, "I have to think about that for a couple of weeks." He wanted to get married, he just wanted to do it in his own time. I was furious! So then he said, "Let's do it," so I said, "all right."

I didn't know what to do with my life. The public library had this program for people who didn't know what they wanted to do, and so I was a librarian; you didn't have to go to library school but you could be a librarian, and I actually loved it. Richard eventually applied to law school. He was teaching and he ended up being a teacher in Brooklyn. He did that for four years before law school.

In general, in that time it was mostly good. But we had times—Richard has had career things that have made him miserable, and I have had career things that have made me miserable, and then we had small kids—but the general thing was good. We waited for ten years before we had kids. That was pretty conscious and that was good; we were both pretty immature. We needed a lot of growing up. I was pretty neurotic. I don't think I had a handle on who I was and where I came from—not a lot of stock taking.

Recently I was watching the movie *Gentleman's Agreement*, and thought of Richard—Gregory Peck—but also had some flashes of the two of us in the early days of our marriage. We did have some annoying fights, which usually began because of my feeling that Richard wasn't behaving the way I wanted him to—i.e., like my wonderful father. This, of course, took some time to realize, but we actually figured it out ourselves. An example: We were on an extended trip to Europe, which lasted for the summer. We had been through Ireland, again, England, and then to Norway. It was wonderful. Towards the end we were running out of money and had to really watch our expenses. We passed a carnival and I wanted to go . . . it sounds incredibly childish but I got mad at Richard because he thought we shouldn't waste the last bit of cash on something so foolish—and he also hates carnivals. The dynamic had been, though unspoken, that he would "take care of me," and I guess the assumption was "just like Dad," who I idolized and felt unconditionally loved me. After feeling ashamed of myself for being such a spoiled baby, but also annoyed at Richard for being so "responsible," I handled this in my most grown-up way: I got furious. I remember sulking a bit and arguing, and then actually talking. Richard got to be the disapproving father and I got to be the unsatisfied child . . . Nice!

We also had some camping trips where Richard didn't set the tent up the way good old Dad did and other ridiculous things, but as the years passed I grew up a lot—and had many sessions on the couch, as did Richard. I think the old dynamic of Richard taking care of me is still alive and well, and I still struggle with my feeling babyish, but I do realize that I take care of him in many ways too.

I also think that we had a yearning to merge with each other. That being such different personalities, Richard the "solid rock" and Tina the "flamboyant, free spirit," together, we could be one perfect whole. When that vision clashed with reality, we got stuck. Little did we know how simplistic and very young we were. And that life is much more interesting with its lack of black and whites.

We went to Philadelphia after he finished law school because Richard got a great job with the city, in investigations. He was a lawyer for them, and he was so happy with that. His father had died fairly recently, and he had hated law school—that was an unhappy time, and I was teaching and doing my art and having a good time in my career then. Actually, his father's dying wasn't such an unsettling thing for us; it sort of released Richard from the complicated psychological burdens of his father. And his mother was in pretty good shape. She got together with his father's best friend. I think the parallel things in our lives have been the career stuff. That was like that up until ten or twelve years ago. I have always had a conflict around my career— you know, what do I do, how do I earn? He had a similar thing, of not really wanting to be a lawyer, but that job working back in the city was very exciting and he did some good stuff there. Then he became a commissioner for the city. He only did that for a short time because his brother died.

That was tremendous, a monster in our lives; a horrible, horrible thing. They were very close. And he had kids. When he died we took care of them, his sister-in-law and the kids. When he first got sick—the first time we thought it was over, and it wasn't; it was a long, drawn-out thing. We had small children. Everybody was trying to get over this, and it was dreadful. We talked, we had them over all the time, we were there. It hasn't really left us. It changed all our lives.

One dramatic way it did was that his brother and he had always talked about becoming law partners, and, of course, they never did. But his brother's partner, who was an old friend, asked Richard to be a partner and to go into his brother's practice. That was a big step: it meant him taking on responsibilities for a lot of family friends and his brother's family, because the practice had managed their businesses, and it meant Richard stepping back into his family in a big way, and out of the job that he'd really loved. He had gotten along really well with his brother, very close. I get along well with his family, though I didn't have a lot in common with a lot of them, and I love some of Richard's cousins a lot. We would go to Christmas Eve with my family, which was big and tumultuous, and then we'd come back in the morning, get dressed up, and go to his family —very warm and things, but very different.

When he got offered this proposition initially I didn't want him to do it. I thought it was going to be stodgy and boring, so I didn't want him to do it. I know his sister-in-law really wanted him to do it, because that would carry on his brother's thing.

Now it's okay because I am getting this bigger picture . . . I find it hard to remember how it was then, what I felt and how it got better. I'm not good at context and continuity. Richard can remember things and say when they happened and why and I don't. I just know that I think it's fine now. Since he started his new firm, with his wonderful new partner, who I love, and the new partners and people who work there now . . . It's fine now.

His father drank, and he drank in the afternoons and would get depressed, and I get depressed; I can go up and down. I'm flatter now. I haven't been depressed in a long time. I was depressed, for example, when the kids were little. I could go for weeks feeling low. He notices and it upsets him. He gets quiet and concerned. He is not afraid to say, "Let's talk about this." I tend to blow things out of proportion. He tends to say, "Okay, this is bad. Let's put it on the table and look at it." When he has these career-crises things, I do try to do the same for him. I tend to think that Richard is often right about stuff. He is like a sounding board for me. The only thing that makes me angry is that he is so rational all of the time . . . he is so balanced.

Richard has always described himself as a lonely person—deep down he is lonely, as much as he is connected, as much as he loves—which I have never really understood. I understand it, but then again, I don't, because I always think of myself as the opposite, because I have people in my head and I can't get them out of my head, so I never felt that I was lonely; I still don't often feel that. But Richard feels that there is a loneliness that is deep down. As close as he was to his brother, there was something in his family, because maybe of the too-intense attention of his father . . . That was the opposite of my family . . . because the boundaries were almost too low. He is very healthy, but a core of, of Richard, is this. His brother was his main link to his family. And I am his link to being not lonely.

He says that his happiest moments have been coming home at night through the door, knowing that we are behind the door—I have worked mostly at home—and so when he comes in the door, he has a family. And to me, that is normal because my father did that. When Richard would come through the door, he would come home and say, "Hi!" He comes back about the same time every night, around seven thirty. We wait for him. When the kids were little, he used to come in and test the waters: was it a good day or a bad day? He wants to see if everything is okay, so he comes in and is, like, "Hello?"—a tentative hello. And he will come into the kitchen and see how I am. He was the one who was most upset about the kids leaving. I wasn't. I feel that I love them, and they are okay, and I have them in my head anyway. Richard was nervous about them but it's okay. Our older daughter has needed to come back and live with us for this year to afford living with a not-very-high-paying job for a while. We got used to just us, and now, but well, she and I are so much alike that his relationship is similar . . . He says, "Why does she have to say everything that comes into her head?" I think that Richard has this containment and I have this nonboundary thing. It was just what he needed, and I think that if he married someone like him, he would have been lonely.

He does "lose it," though, sometimes, and when he does, it is really scary—like my father. He was the one in my family who didn't get angry. When he died—the legacy of his death: he was a wonderful man, so we missed him—there was a real hole. Richard's brother was someone whose legacy was similar—about his father, or family stuff, they spoke the same language.

We don't have conflicts, or tumultuous things going on. I mean, Richard's mother would have gotten after his father because he talked too much. And sometimes we have that because I drink too much and get into discussions that sometimes get out of bounds. We went to one of his biggest client's once . . . and the husband and I were having drinks and we started to talk about politics. We talked about Bush, and I drank, and he was trying to stop the discussion, and I had had a glass of wine, so I started pushing rather than dropping it, and Richard walked in and later he said, "How could you have?" . . . And in the end I think he was right; I was a fool . . . Part of me doesn't want to be like Richard and Richard doesn't want to be like me. Part of me adores my overdoneness and it gets me into trouble.

Often what I'll do in this kind of situation is say, "What did I do?" and he will say, "I think you should have stopped." And I will say, "Oh, God! I feel really awful!" and he is angry at me. He won't say, "Don't worry about it." That is how I know: he will say nothing. And then I'll be really upset because if Richard gets angry, then you know he has been pushed to that level. And I feel really badly, like I haven't behaved well. Part of me thinks, "Oh, God, give me a break, I am not a child." But then I do think he is right about this, and I will feel guilty because I didn't hold up my own. It just goes away after a few days. I will feel really terrible and I will want his reassurance that everything is going to be okay. And a couple of days later he met that client and she was very generous about it, and he did feel bad—because I did take the guilt. He felt for me. He knows I have problems in that area.

I think we have less of these problems now, but they crop up, but I think getting older has helped. I try to be conscious when I walk into a situation of these kinds of conflict areas—of our personalities, of me talking and saying something I shouldn't say, being out of control. I am more difficult because of the nature of my personality and Richard is so rational. He is more concerned about appearances, much more than I am. There is something about him that makes you want to please him . . . You want him to like you . . . There is this kind of—he has a sense of dignity and decency and he is not stodgy, he is just who he is, and I know a lot of people want to please him, and some are afraid of him, but he is not scary at all. But you do want his approval. It was part of what I liked in him. I like being around someone I respect so much . . . He is *humane*. His humanity is in his—I think of him as a tree. There is a solid elegance to him. And the kids are all concerned that they will disappoint him because his standards are so high. He is really quite unjudgmental, though.

. . . I have never doubted, even when I am angry, I have never felt like I have to get out of this. This is the one I want to be with. I have never felt anything like, "I hate this person," or anything; I feel annoyed, but I come back. I have always come back.

Sex has been good most of the time. I don't think of us as having a fabulous sex life, but a good one. He has always thought of me as sexy. It makes us really depressed if we don't have sex. More than the actual doing it is the idea of it! And we know we don't so much now, because things get in the way: someone is sick, or the kids are here, and we think, "Oh my God—

how long . . . ?" We say it. He says it, too. As a man, he has always wanted and needed more sex. It makes us feel connected, so when we don't have it it makes us feel scared. We are getting anxious about our lack of interest at the moment. We've lived together so long that we know this . . . We don't have to work at sex itself, though. We can go for weeks without it, but we try not to. We'll say, "Friday night we have to stay home. Or Saturday morning."

But if I think he's not happy, I couldn't have sex. I am more conscious as I get older—before he would initiate sex more than me. Richard doesn't say much. And now I say it, and he feels better that I have actually thought about it. He loves to be taken care of.

He said to me that my coming into his life made him feel sexual. I would say the whole package is sexy. I would say that initially I was attracted to his face and then it was more who he was. So, yeah, he is sexual to me. We aren't very physical all the time with each other. We don't hug and kiss a lot, don't usually hold hands. Richard is more romantic than I am. Being together so long it is just weird to be romantic.

We aren't separated very much—he goes off on camping trips without me maybe once a year. We do more separate things now since the kids have grown and we are older, but not a lot. Sometimes once a year I go off with my sister but, no, we don't take separate vacations. We have a very traditional marriage in that respect and others. He has always supported me financially, which I am not very happy about and I think it would be a nice thing for him to have the burden taken off. I don't think he'd like it for very long because it's the whole thing of being a man, but I would love to do it. Maybe as we get older I will.

I would love to make enough money from my art. I haven't made a lot. Richard is incredible about this. I do know that there is a discontent about me not making much money but whenever it comes to the point where I say, "Okay, I'm not doing this art anymore, I'm going to get a real job," he says not to worry. We do have retirement funds, but money can be an issue for us. I do know that he gets a tremendous amount from me, because he tells me, and I take care of him. I make things fun for him—and people have said, "Oh, you are so much fun, you're so good at 'people' "—it's not a talent. It's who I am. Some of that I've developed in relation to being with Richard. I have always thought I was lucky to be born into this time, this place, this family. In most ways Richard thinks the same. I think he feels lucky that he is who he is.

I think Richard gets a lot from that in me, as I do him. I work hard at taking care of him in my way, as he takes care of me in his. I think he is doing okay now. This is a good time for him. For me, I would like to be working more, but as much as I would like to be working more, the older we get, the more grateful we feel for what we have. We are alive and happy, and we love each other, and our children are happy. The themes that come out in our life together are Richard being "strong and silent" and my boundarylessness—and we have similar interests: wildlife, traveling, reading. He watches baseball and reads the sports section—I don't. And above all, we share family, an intense interest and involvement in our family, and our common friends.

In terms of our marriage, I think we were lucky to have been on the same ferry, and we noticed that we actually saw something in each other; we have chemistry. Richard needed someone like me, and I needed someone like him. I think the specialness of our relationship shows in the way I see myself in the world with this person. I don't see myself without that person. Everything I say, I feel in my heart, this is the right person. I have never doubted that.

Nancy Aaronovitch and Annie Hart

Nancy Aaronovitch and Annie Hart have lived together for thirteen years. About four years ago they moved into their present condominium in a complex in the suburbs of Phoenix, Arizona, a community for "over-fifties"—with a recreation-community center and pool at its heart and pleasant landscaping all around. Annie had only recently turned fifty when they moved; the women are seen fondly as "youngsters" by many of their neighbors. But it is a conservative community and Annie and Nancy hide the nature of their relationship, hoping the fiction that they are sisters will last. Annie, married and divorced twice, has a grown-up daughter who has recently moved back to Phoenix. Annie had been in another long-term, live-in relationship with a woman that ended before she met Nancy. This is the first time Nancy has lived with anyone. They are large, expansive, warm women who are affectionate with each other. Nancy talked freely about a life colored by sadness, violence, and loss, and the shier Annie gingerly divulged a similarly turbulent story. Both are currently plagued by chronic pain. As we talked all together at first, they watched each other protectively, scanning for signs of trepidation about what was to follow, or approval that to go ahead would be okay, or for support for the interview ahead, for each knew that that interview meant revisiting anguish. Yet they live cheerfully, delighting in each other, feeling lucky, and largely crediting their mutual love for their capacity to do so. When the interviews ended, they bounced on their well-stuffed sofa, arms around each other, and each crowed, "She's the love of my life!"

Annie Hart:

I grew up in Arizona, near Phoenix, with an older sister—she now owns her own business. She lives in North Carolina, not real close, but we try to see each other when we can. My dad died after I was married; I got married out of high school. I grew up with both parents. They stayed married; my mom remarried after. My dad was a quiet man. We grew up really respecting him, but we were a little intimidated. My stepdad was, like, the master-of-the-house type.

I'm fifty-seven now—I graduated in 1963 and got married in 1964. My husband was someone I knew at school—he was a nice guy. I did think I loved him. But, really, I guess it was my sexuality that led to the breakdown of my marriage. We had our daughter when I was twenty-two, about three years after we were married. It was really before I had her that I began to know. I knew I wasn't content. I was trying to be, but it wasn't working for me. I mean, I cared about him, and about our marriage, but it just wasn't there, for me.

We tried a few things. We were actually nudists for a while. There was a camp up around where we lived. You know, it wasn't a sexual thing, like people think it is. It was just sort of a—a *living* thing. So we went up there and tried that for a while. We left, but we'd met a couple up there. They were wife swappers. They knew we were kind of having trouble in our relationship and they'd talk to us about it. So they talked about their wife-swapping, and I thought, you know, that sounds interesting . . . I was in my twenties then. I thought, "I'd like to try that." And I started having dreams—it did appeal to me. I'd had dreams, sort of, while I was growing up, but not really like that.

This was in the late '60s—before any gay movement. I began to feel tormented by it. I felt guilty. I thought there must be something wrong with me to like this. I was tortured by questions: "Why do I like this? Why am I different?" I knew I had this little problem but it never occurred to me that I was gay. By this time I was a mother. And I did feel that I loved my husband too. He knew about my feelings for women. It wasn't a secret between us or anything. But it clarified to me that I didn't have sexual feelings for him. So eventually I left him.

He was upset because he loved me. He was a good man, but I just did not want to be with him—or, as it turned out, any man. I left not thinking, "I want to be with a woman." I left thinking I just wanted to know who I was. But by then I had a small child. Single mothers weren't so common then. So I found myself wanting to remarry. I married a man I actually did think I was attracted to, at least at first. I don't know—I really don't know. He was nice to my daughter. About a year after my first marriage ended I was remarried— it was really a rebound thing. And then it turned out he was sexually abusing my daughter, who was five at the time. Within two years I'd found that out and we were out of there.

It was awful. Devastating. I still can't talk about it. I still cry—and that was almost twenty-five, thirty years ago. I discovered it because I found her locked in a closet—she'd freaked out and was all upset and we went to the doctor and it all came out. We called the social services and the police, and he was prosecuted. He pleaded guilty and got two years probation . . . He was definitely a scary guy. I moved, changed jobs, got out of there. We moved to a different state, stayed with my mother and stepfather for a while.

So that was all going on. My sexual feelings hadn't changed. I was in very bad shape. I mean, I was a single mom, tormented with these feelings, thinking all the time, "How could I have married that guy? It was my fault." All my fault what happened to my daughter—I was the one who chose that bum. Even though I'd felt I was marrying him for her. That was like the ultimate lesson. So my daughter went to live with her father; I thought it'd be good for her. That was a terrible, terrible point of my life. It's hard to talk about this even now. Her father and my daughter are very close. We'd stayed good friends. I did see her a lot.

I still went out with guys—I was dating several guys in the next year. One of the guys I was dating wanted to go to a gay bar, so we did. I met this woman there and she told me she found out late that she was gay and I was interested, and I remember feeling frightened. But that opened up a lot of doors to me, because then I knew who I was. I realized that this is who I am. This is what is normal for me as a woman. And I really straightened out my life then.

My daughter came back to live with me, and we lived near her father. She's had both of us. By then I knew I was a lesbian. She was about eight or nine when I told her. This was in the late '70s. I gave her a little lecture about being a homosexual or a heterosexual, and she said, "It's okay, Mommy." She was really sweet. And then she said, "But I like boys. Is that okay, Mommy?" She was just so cool about it, and actually she still is. There was this song called "Here Come the Lesbians, the Lesbians"—it's a coming-out thing— that we sang!

The first woman I was really in love with was in 1979. She had broken up her relationship and we weren't together for very long, but I felt real love for the first time. Then, the second one, with Jane, lasted longer, and when it was ending, she couldn't handle being in a relationship anymore and then also didn't really want to be my friend anymore, and that was hard. I was just crushed. Soon after, I got involved with a woman, Hope, who'd been a friend. I was with her for about nine years. Some of that time my daughter lived with us, some with her father, and then she left home and joined the navy. Hope had been interested in me and she broke up with her partner when I broke up with Jane. We'd all been mutual friends, and at first we started going out as friends. She was older than me and had her own kids. In fact, I was the same age as her oldest daughter. In some ways she was like a parent, but she also began to control—there was a power struggle there. She didn't make more money than me, but she took control of my money. When my daughter was about fifteen, she went to live with her father. Hope wanted more of me, and my daughter wanted me—there was a struggle there between them, and I was caught in the middle and it was really uncomfortable. My self-esteem was really low, really low. I might have figured out who I was in terms of my sexuality but I was still selecting partners who I was letting control me. That was a lot like my mother.

Then I found out that Hope was swinging with other women, including some of our best friends. I caught her. I finally said, "This is not the way it's going to be. This is not what I bargained for." It took me about a year to end it and move out. But we had property together—a house—and I'd let her control all the money. So I stayed until the following September, living in the downstairs of the same house with her. She got all the money from the house. I had my job as a claims adjuster, thank goodness. I make a decent salary. So I found another place, and was living there, and just looking for friends now. I joined a gay women's choir. My daughter had left home. I was by then in therapy, for my very low self-esteem and my guilt over the sex abuse, and I was also very angry. I was very untrusting. You know, when I moved in with Nancy finally, it was like, "This is mine!" about everything I brought in.

So about a year after I'd moved out, I met Nancy at the gay women's choir. She couldn't sing at all. It was at a party afterward that I had at my house that we met. That was another terrible thing. My niece had just been killed in a car crash. I was having this party after a concert at my house, and I had to go ahead with it. I had some photographs that I'd taken—some of my niece who'd just been killed—up, as well as other ones. And Nancy's a photographer—she was an artist before she had all her health and other troubles, you know—too, and so she really liked my photos and I could see that she had an eye and really appreciated the things I do by her reaction. I was still grieving. But I did feel a connection.

I wasn't going to move in with anyone, though! It was a few months till we got together again—it was at a gay women's choir picnic. She was just the kindest person, the sweetest person I'd ever met. And she really appreciated me. She is very tender. When I think of all the terrible things she's had to go through, I feel so sad. It's so sad when she talks about her father and what he did to her.

Nancy had recently arrived in Phoenix and very quickly we got to know each other. She didn't hide from me the fact that she'd had a history of hospitalizations and illnesses. But I saw how brave and good she was. She told me about her past—her mother's illness, the abuse from her father, and how he'd terrorized the whole family. I knew that she'd had physical problems too and was on disability. But she'd been stable for a long time. She'd moved out here for good reasons, and was getting more stable and healthy here. I do admire her for all she's done and been through and stayed so kind and good throughout it.

We didn't move in together for about three months. I knew she'd never lived with anyone before. But then she said, "Look, Annie, I am not trying to put pressure on you, but this is the truth: I am saying it to you now. I can't say it will hold true forever. But right now, I want you to move in with me." I had wanted to wait. But she said, "I don't know about later. I only know about right now."

She was like a little kid. She was so fun to do stuff for. She'd never even had a real birthday party—I gave her one on her forty-ninth birthday! She was just so sweet. I don't think that anyone had ever appreciated me like she did. She was so kind. I would do anything for anybody but doing stuff for her—and I know she's an adult, but, well, she's like a little child. She has a kindness and sweetness that is so wonderful. That is what I fell in love with. I had never had that before; she adores me. It is wonderful to be adored. And she hurts with me when I think of things like the sexual abuse of my daughter. She feels for me, she really does.

When she said, "I don't know about later. I only know about right now," I did move in. But, it was without full trust for a real long time. And that was shaken by some awful things that happened a few years later. Nancy's problem is that she has bipolar disorder. It wasn't diagnosed correctly for a long time. She was given the wrong drugs and put in the hospital, getting wrong treatment a lot. By the time she moved out here she was finally fine, on the right stuff. But she's on disability and public medical insurance. So her doctors sometimes change—you know, that's when things can go wrong. That was the problem. Her new psychiatrist gave her the wrong drugs. He wouldn't listen to her family back in Chicago. They were trying to tell him.

She got real bad again. And one of the things she does then is spend wildly, which meant she spent our money wildly. More terrible, though, is she gets real paranoid and aggressive—says real nasty, real frightening things, and to me too. I was real scared. I didn't know what to do, how to make it better, if it would ever be better. I had to protect myself. I felt terrible, real frightened for her too. This wasn't just a few days—this went on for a long, long, time. I wouldn't know what to expect one day to another. One day she was hauled in by the police, who found her doing things—they thought she'd stolen something but she'd gotten into some argument in a store and left and it was all confused, and they caught up with her and held her. And then they called me. It was a terrible, terrible mess. So she ended up being put in a hospital, with an order. We would talk on the phone but sometimes that would be worse. She would be crazy on the phone. I knew that she wanted to know I'd be there—but I couldn't promise her that then. I needed time to understand and to get my head together and think. My mother loves her but even she said I should come home for a while, and so that's what I did. It was real confusing, real sad and awful. When Nancy came out, we had couples therapy; it was for a long time, till I could understand and till she could understand what my issues were about it, before I moved back home.

We've been fine since. Except for things like the money, which we now have a plan for. That was about six years ago. I think Nancy learned more than ever how important it is for her to keep on her medication and to be clear with her doctors. She won't let anyone fool with things now. She certainly knows the effect on me. Now I am in charge of the money. We're thinking about her not having a car—it costs her a lot and we probably don't need it. We don't have a whole lot of money but we try to plan for what we need and what we will need. But this is an agreement we've come to together. We're trying to make sure that she won't be tempted—she overspends even when she's well too.

When I introduced her to my mother, my mother just loved her. This was the first time she'd ever approved of any relationship with a woman. She advised me when I was thinking about whether I should move in or not, she said, "Just do it." I was so shocked! My sister loves her too—right away she thought she was great and was interested in getting to know her. And she's great with my daughter—she lives near us now with her boyfriend. Nancy is interested in what I think are the important things—like nature, animals, the good things. She's very caring. She's helped me think when I wake up in the morning, "I have the answer to the world: just love each other. Just open up our hearts." We saw the same things in each other—and that we could trust each other.

We live together easily now. We have a kind of routine for our jobs at home. I like to see things and rearrange them, stuff like that—moving things around. I like to see our things so I rather enjoy dusting. Nancy hates dusting. But other than that we just do all things, both of us. I like a real clean house. Nancy's become a lot neater. I might sort of prod her along into things, but we both do them. We both do cooking. We plan vacations together—she's better with the Internet and doing the research, but then we discuss it together and make the decisions together. She's used to fixing things—I mean she's been a super in buildings and can do that type of things. We do keep our bills separate. We've got individual checking accounts and a joint savings one. I think the individual checking account is important for individuality and stuff. The joint one is for extras like vacations. Things don't necessarily have to be equal in finances. We passed that a long time ago. We used to be arguing about how everything had to be equal. Because I make more money and, at least for now, she doesn't earn—it doesn't matter, it's just not a big deal at all. We own our condo together, and the mortgage happens to come out of my paycheck. But it still feels about equal. I pay the utility and phone bills because I make more money right now. But that's now. She pays the vet's bills. We have had a beloved cat that sadly died last year. We tried everything to save her, and in the end she died. We took out a loan for the vet's bills, of five thousand dollars. Nancy takes responsibility for that. We both pay the condominium maintenance fees. And we discuss any major purchases.

Because of her condition she's given me her charge card and more control over money. That's her choice. I am not a spender and I am more practical. But that's changed—for the first five years of our relationship it was pretty much like, I paid my own bills, she paid hers. Then when we bought the condo together, she decided she wanted control of the money and that was not a good idea to me. Because you turned your paycheck over to her and then she was in trouble with debts. I don't want to do that anymore! I don't want to control her money or bills either, I mean, but she likes the idea. If I have anything left over at the end of the month and she needs something, I give it. If I have it, it's no big deal.

Sexually, things have changed, and a lot of that is due to physical things. When we first got together, Nancy had a bad back—she has had a chronic bad back and that's meant she's had to leave jobs because of it and got disability because of it too. That meant that we always have had to be careful because things could be painful. I didn't have that then, but I had a car accident in 1994 and tore a ligament in my shoulder and hurt my back. I also have a lot of other health problems and can't do much physically. But we enjoy sex a lot. Now we have two bad backs and that sort of spoils the sex part. Because of pain and disability we can't do a lot. It's maybe now a few times a year.

We used to have a hot tub, our personal one, in the beginning and that made sex easier. Now we don't, so it's harder. But we are still very physical— we cuddle all the time. We are very warm with each other. We love being in bed next to each other. The quality is still good when we have it. I'd like to have it more often though. I do miss the sex. It bothers me that we don't have it so much. I wish I were in better physical health; I don't sleep well and have a lot of physical deterioration. I can't walk far, and my knees are a problem too. I feel older than the fifty-seven which is my body. But it doesn't mean love is any less or that the intensity is any less.

A thing that gets in the way is that we live in a very straight community. It's of mostly retired people. They think we're sisters. They wouldn't approve. When we moved in, we were carrying boxes in and people asked, "Are you two sisters, or what?" So I said, "Yeah, yeah." Nancy's family is in Chicago, mine's in Arizona, but we're sisters . . .

We feel very close. Most days when we wake up I'll go and take a bath and get dressed for work, and Nancy will always powder me after a bath; I can't reach behind and bend down that easily. We always hug and kiss before I leave for work and when I come home. When I come home, I go lie down to have a little "alone time." Then we'll talk about the day, watch TV, go to bed together. On Saturdays we'll clean the house. We have a group of friends we see, some of them going back twenty years for me, and get together, and do stuff on the weekends. And we'll go on trips or out for drives in the country to take pictures—the birds, the bunnies, the animals. Our cat, Sonya—she's our new one—is something we share deeply too. It was terrible when Tasha—she was our cat before—died.

We are respectful of each other, but we have differences, and if we do, we talk about things. We don't really fight. We tell each other all the time how much we love each other. We say how lucky we are—it's a mutual-admiration society. I have found the love of my life and I say that to her and she does to me. I am grateful. I never thought I would have another relationship. Nancy is the best relationship I've ever had.

Nancy Aaronovitch:

I'm sixty. I grew up, first, in a kind of blue-collar suburb of Chicago. When I was out of high school, we moved to a nicer house in a nicer town next door. My mom was just wonderful—kind, sweet, fun, warm, smart. But she had a very hard life. She married my father out of high school. She should have gone to college, but she was always a dreamer. Very impractical. My father was—then—very good-looking and charming. Swept her off her feet. She was the daughter of Jewish immigrants, hardworking, good, kind people. They hated my father. With good reason. My mother was willful. She decided she was going to marry him, so she did. She was once really beautiful and I always saw her as beautiful but she got worn down by her hard life. I had an older brother. He died—he was pretty young—a few years ago. We weren't in touch for a few years—he had a lot of problems and so did I. I'm close to my cousins and my aunt, who died about ten years ago, and that's my family. I stay in touch with them but don't see them much. It's hard to travel and expensive. I love them very much and I feel loved by them too.

It was a hard childhood. My mother's family were close by. My parents separated for a while when I was very young—about three, I think—and we moved in with my grandparents for a few years, maybe three or four. That was a good time. Then they got back together and we moved to the apartment where I grew up. I think my father was having an affair and he said he'd ended it. He never did, I'm pretty sure of that. After my mother died, he moved in with someone with the same name of that girlfriend. He gave her all my mother's jewelry. I knew it was the same woman.

My father was a terrible man. My mother had a lot of pride and wouldn't tell her family hardly anything about what went on. They'd just tell her to leave him, but she didn't think she could. I think he'd just threaten her and beat her up, and she was convinced she could never be free of him. He beat my older brother up regularly. My brother used to get into trouble at school, played hooky all the time, hung out with really bad kids, and finally dropped out at sixteen. He joined the army, and fought in Korea, and then when he came back he took night classes, finished high school, eventually got a college diploma and worked in insurance. He had a kid young. He did stay married for quite a few years. But he drank. He lost his job, though I know he got another one and had another marriage and was okay in the end, but I only know that through a grapevine. Unfortunately he sort of dropped out of our lives. He couldn't take everything that began to happen, including with me. I understand. I don't really have any hard feelings about it . . . I'm just very, very sad. I will always feel sad about it, and I do miss him and wish we'd been able to straighten things out before he died.

You see, he tried to save and protect me while he was still home, tried to help me with my father, but then all he'd get was beat up. I was very close to my mother and she confided in me. Like she got ill with cancer when I was fourteen and I was sworn to secrecy. She didn't want her mother and sister to know—they would just worry. So I kept this secret with her and I would go to her doctors with her. She died when I was twenty-four and it was a horrible, painful death, and my father made it worse. He was still beating her up when she was sick.

My father used to beat her up like he did my brother. It was just terrible. He was a drunk and a gambler, and a control freak, and he just controlled all of us. When I was about eleven he began to abuse me sexually. I didn't think anyone would believe me. I do know what it must have felt like for Annie with her daughter. It's terrible. I don't really remember much of it—I only remember clearly one time, when I was eleven, but doctors of mine have suggested that it might have been earlier too. Because I would wake up in the morning at four A.M., screaming, with my father standing over my bed, scaring the living daylights out of me. That I do remember. My mom must have heard me . . . I don't know what she was thinking or what she did . . .

But you have this little kid who's scared to speak out against her dad . . . He tried sexual intercourse—not just molestation—but my mom walked in at that point. That was when I was eleven. She called the cops. They came and I was too scared. I said it wasn't him. I said it was in her head. The cops said, "You have to give the story straight." My mother tried to divorce my father at that point. My brother tried to get me to talk in the courts. By that time my brother had started going over to his friend's house all the time so he was never home; he thought at least he could protect himself that way. But he was scared for me. I was scared to speak out against my dad, I was just a little kid, and yet if I didn't, there is nothing they could do. I was horrified by him, so in the end I wouldn't. But I was horrified, and so that's why later on, when my mom got really sick, I did stand up to him.

That was when my mother was sick and I called the visiting nurse—I had told her she might get a call in the night, and just know that you will have to come—my dad has this habit of if I call for help, he will grab the phone from me. And so when he was beating her up when she was home recovering from her operation and very weak, and she was dying, I called the nurse, and said, "I am going to kill her!" She knew that she had to come right over. I told her that so that she would know to come right over, this is an emergency, no time to talk, just come, and I didn't want to say anything about him while I was on the phone. She knew this was the call she was going to get. He did pull the phone out. She tried calling back and all she got was a busy signal. So she knew. I thought he was going to kill her, really. Yeah. And she'd just had surgery and all.

So that was when my mother went into a nursing home—the visiting nurse found her a really nice one, and that's where she died. But she had saved up and bought us this house in the suburbs. My father always had a job, a skilled-worker job, but she worked as an accounts assistant downtown and had saved up so we had a nice house. And he was in it, with me. So my brother and his family moved back in with us for a few months, saying it was something about not being able to afford the mortgage on their house. It wasn't that. There were so many lies going around.

I was an art student then. When I was nineteen I was on diet pills because I'd always had a problem with my weight, so I got put on these pills, and they were barbiturates and I had a breakdown. I was hallucinating. My mother was terrified. This was during her illness. I was put in the hospital. No one asked about the diet pills. I was diagnosed as schizophrenic. I kept taking the pills. I kept having more breakdowns. I'd go out and spend things—once I bought a motorcycle and I got it into my head that I wanted to have some ducks, so I rode out to a farm and I was riding around with boxes of ducks on this motorcycle and the police pulled me over . . . Lots of stuff like that going on at the same time as my mother being ill. I had a boyfriend, Bart, during my early twenties, and he was very kind and caring with me. He once picked me up from jail because the police had picked me up . . .

I kept trying to finish my art school and it kept getting interrupted—a lot with me being in the hospital. I also had to get jobs to support myself so I'd do things like be a debt collector, and take courses at night. I did have some jobs in commercial art. But after my mother died I started drinking heavily. I was drunk a lot of the time. I could no longer work as a commercial artist because I had the shakes. I got a job in this debt collection agency for a while. That was where I had my first experience of sex with a man.

It wasn't exactly rape, though it depends on how you look at that. The boss asked me to work late. He would train me. He was double my age. I couldn't really fight him off because I was too drunk. He'd brought out all the bottles and he knew I had a drinking problem. I didn't know that they had this back office with a couch and everything, and a bar. Bart and I were broken up and just friends then. I hadn't had sex with him and after this incident I felt really guilty for not having sex with him, since, you know, I did it with that man. I'd had relationships with men—I'd been popular in high school but I never really saw anyone "like that." You know, no matter who he was, he couldn't kiss me.

I think I've always been gay. When I was in grade school my mother was called in continuously around second, third, or fourth grade and the teacher said to her that I was gay and if they didn't let me be gay I would be a "latent lesbian." I don't know what they were talking about but my mom came home and she was talking in Yiddish, which is what she did when she didn't want us to understand what she was saying, and I heard the word "lesbian." Apparently there wasn't a Yiddish way of saying that. And then I heard "latent lesbian." I don't know if my mom said that in front of me on purpose or not. I was chasing the other girls. At break time we would play boys against the girls and I would play with the boys, so naturally I was a little boy against the girls, and when I caught the girl, I wanted to kiss her just like the boys because that was the reward of catching a girl.

In my twenties, during all those years of being in and out of the hospital, I was in therapy off and on. I was in this therapy group, a "confrontation group." It was a new thing. I was living in Chicago on my own. My mother was about to die. We would be in this group and the therapist would sit back on the sidelines. They didn't get away with this kind of group for very long because there were too many suicides . . . Anyway, I was sitting in therapy and saying that I had been dating all these men and couldn't find any one for me, and that he could be the richest man, the best man, but it wouldn't do anything for me, and then this one person said, "Oh, you're gay. You know that." And I picked up my chair and moved back, out of the way. I didn't really know what that meant. So I said to her, "What does that mean?" And she said, "Oh, well—you like women." Then she said, "I'll take you to this bar and you tell me if you don't feel anything." She was straight but lived in Old Town, which was where a lot of gay people lived at that time—she knew what she was talking about and all. So she gave me the address of this bar and we met on the corner. "Bonnie and Clyde's" it was called. We sat down at the bar and I was a nervous wreck. They must have known I was just coming out because I was in this dress and you didn't really wear that in a gay bar. So I was at this bar, in my dress. I ordered a Scotch and then these two women came back to the bar, with my friend next to me, and they sat behind her and began making out. Suddenly I felt tingles like I'd never felt in my whole life. And I thought, "My God! This is the reason!"

My first real relationship was with a woman I'd see only at weekends. I didn't have her phone number, but she had mine. She was definitely in control. She would be driven to me by her male gay friend and he'd come with us on our dates. He was like our chaperone. We'd go dancing. I was still drinking, and if I was still awake, we'd have sex. I wasn't capable of any real relationships then because I was drinking. It went on for a few years. Then I became sober. I started going to AA. I met Carolyn there and we went to an AA party. She said she wanted to learn to dance so I took her out onto the dance floor and we started dancing. It became a monogamous relationship. But she wanted to move in and I didn't want that. I wasn't looking for that kind of closeness. I still wasn't completely regulated on my medication. Things were still not completely stable. I was working doing IT stuff. I'd taken a course and become certified in fixing IT hardware. I've always been good at making things and fixing things. So I worked for a big company and would be sent out on jobs, and then my back began to be a problem for me. So I had to take sick leave, and then I lost that job, and I had to sue, and that would start off my emotional problems . . . I won, eventually, but only after many years, and was put on disability, and my back never got better . . . Anyway, Carolyn ended up staying over a lot, so I guess you could say we were living together, but I always made her go home for a while.

I was afraid of relationships—my mom had had such a bad one. You date people, it's nice, and as soon as they move in, bad things can start. So we were together for a few years. It was while I was with her that I hurt my back and I had all that stuff about my back—and then I realized she was cheating on me. I knew she was lying to me when I asked her about it, and I kept trying to get her to tell me the truth. She'd look me straight in the face and lie. It was like my father—another untrustworthy figure. So I ended it . . . that had been a confirmation of everything I was afraid of in a relationship.

But I then met a high school teacher, Jewish, which was nice. But she had problems about commitment too. She was called Barbara. She was fine about my not wanting a committed relationship: "Oh, you don't want a relationship like that, that's fine with me too," she said, and that was comfortable. We dated for three years. But then I began to want a monogamous relationship. She didn't. She'd say I was her favorite, but she couldn't settle into a monogamous one. So I kept trying to break it off. She'd show up at my door. Around that time I decided to move out of Chicago. I'd started having other symptoms, and was diagnosed with diabetes. I'd been getting work doing stuff like being a super in buildings, which wasn't great for my back, but it would mean I'd get housing. Then my back would be a problem again, and the stress would build up, and I'd be in bad shape again—though by then I'd been diagnosed correctly with bipolar disorder and after a few years finally was on the right medication and I stopped going into the hospital.

I needed a less stressful life. But before I left, I said to Barbara that I'd found out about a great couples therapist who could see us for a few sessions and give us her opinion of whether our relationship had a chance or not. We didn't even go the three times the therapist had set up for us. It was too late, and she wasn't capable of the kind of relationship I then wanted. I'd decided to move to Arizona, and we promised each other we'd remain friends, and we did. She's actually come and stayed with Annie and me.

I was forty-seven by then, and I knew that I had to do something about my health or it would be too late. I wanted a place that was as stress-free as possible, with no humidity. I had these two friends at home in Chicago, two gay guys, who I was talking to, and they said, "Hey! Arizona is the place for you. The cost of living there is less, there's a gay community, there's sun, there's theater" . . . They got out a poster and showed it to me. It made the place seem possible. So I said, "I guess I'll have to make a trip out there" . . . I felt better as soon as I stepped off the plane. By the end of the week my back was feeling better and I felt great. I saw a Realtor who took me around, looked around the food shops, looked in the paper and saw there was some cultural life, and went to a gay AA meeting. I got the story on the gay community here from talking to people there. I had a pretty good time, so I came back and decided that I'd move here.

I moved out here and got a job as a super in a building. It helped me with housing. When I moved out here I didn't want a relationship. That is not why I moved. I moved to a little place with my little kitty and that was that. I just wanted all the aches and pains in my body and soul to get better. Then I heard about the gay women's choir because I made friends with people who were members of it, so I went along. It was a social thing, and I like listening to the music. No, I can't sing. But that was all right. That was where I met Annie the first time.

She had this party. She had just lost her niece, and she went through with this party, trying to be a wonderful hostess, and her daughter was there too, and I saw her photographs. She had such a wonderful eye. You could see the pain that she was in, and you could see how she tried to cover it, and throw this party. My heart just went out to her. I saw something beautiful, and that is what I wanted. I thought, "This woman is really sweet," and "sweet," to me, is everything. That is what I saw in Annie. Just look at her, at her smile, and her eyes are so honest. You can just see it. It isn't like you have to test it, really. It just comes out, and you know, as we have gotten to know each other, I know more I have made the right choice. I waited till I was almost fifty years old.

Annie would never abuse me. She would do anything for me. When I talk about my father, for instance, it really hurts her—she just feels so sad. But it hurts her even more because of what her daughter went through. We had a different kind of pain, but we both got through it. It's all about caring about each other. I just love having someone to love who is so sweet, kind, and caring, and lets me be me. I get along really well with her family too.

We had two bad times. I had one short period about two years after we moved in together when my doctor was changed and the medication was changed a little and I began to get paranoid, and when I get like that, even Annie seems to be against me. It was very hard for her—I also was spending crazily, which was hard for her too. We almost broke up then, but we went into couple's therapy, and we made it through. But that was a pretty short period.

The worst was about five or six years ago. The same things happened. I got a new doctor and he wouldn't listen to anyone, and he said I wasn't paranoid, and I didn't have bipolar, I had a personality disorder. And he said I was on the wrong medication and he changed it. He wouldn't listen to anyone. I tried to get my family to talk to him, because they understood—my cousins know about this stuff: they work in hospitals, one's a doctor. He wouldn't even return their calls. It took them threatening to sue him till he started listening. In the meantime it went on for a few months this time and I was very bad. The police got involved. I must have said some terrible things to Annie, and I know I did do things that scared her. I can understand now why she wasn't immediately prepared to come back, and I am just so lucky that she did, and that our couples therapist helped us get through that. I don't think it will ever happen again. I really don't. It had been a very long time since it had happened before and I think we all know how to make it not happen again.

So, except for that terrible time and the fact that money is always a problem for me, and now I think it's right that Annie is in charge of our money, and I'm getting a lot better about money, anyway, we live together very well. It's easy. Usually Annie gets up first; she gets ready for work. Annie goes and takes a bath and I powder her before she gets dressed. Whoever gets up first makes coffee and brings it to the other one. We have our coffee and we talk about the day before or our dreams. If there's something else going on, like with Annie's mom, who lives nearby, she'll give us a call. Then we eat breakfast and our kitty is with us, and the kitty and I say good-bye to Annie. We always give each other a hug and kiss—if the kitty doesn't manage to run out in the hall first.

I'm home and I'll have a project I'll work on—I still make things, build furniture or bookshelves, or make picture frames, or gifts for people like stained-glass things, or I'll be doing my photographs and developing them, or fixing things in our house—some project—while Annie's at work. Then I'll shop and cook or whatever and then phone Annie during the day and we'll talk for a while and then Annie comes home and we kiss. I don't know how many straight couples do that every day . . . you know, hug and kiss when they say good-bye and hello after being apart for the day, every day. You know it really does make a difference.

Anyway, at that point Annie goes and lies down. We decided it's good for her to have a little bit of "alone time"—a little bit of space. So she goes and lies down for maybe five to ten minutes. She doesn't have a long time. Then we have dinner, and talk about the day, then go watch TV usually, and then bed together, some more TV and have some ice cream. And then sleep. During the weekend we usually have company or meet people for dinner, after we've cleaned the house. We used to go on nature walks but we find it hard to walk now. Both of our backs have gotten worse, and Annie's legs are bad. Now we take drives and do some photo shoots. If we don't have time to go on one of our drives, we go to the parks—there are usually geese and birds there. And we have our kitty, our new one, who looks exactly like our old one that died last year. They kept telling us they could save her . . .

Our health is not great. It gets in the way of things for us. We moved into a sort of senior citizens' complex—it's for over-fifties. It's great, but it is a very straight community and they think we're sisters. It's a bit hard that way. But I'm home a lot so I can do things. I clean up—I'm so-so at it, but I'm much better than I used to be. I was always the slob. I'm not the slob now. Annie likes a real clean house, so I always clean up, especially when we're expecting company. Annie kind of cushions me with warmth—she'll say, I'll dust today, when it comes to Saturday, and then I realize I should dust. She sort of probes me along.

Our routine varies. We each do whatever needs doing. I do the shopping. I have the time. I look up the bargains. We each have our own car but we're probably going to give up mine because it's too expensive. Annie goes off to work and I can drive her, and then have the car during the day. When we plan our vacations, I do the research and Annie does the booking, after we've discussed it together. And discuss it again. And again. I'm the more mechanically minded, so I fix things around the house. We've got two individual checking accounts and a joint savings one—that's something straight couples could learn: it's good to have individual ones in addition to the joint one. It's the best, the best way to do things. I'm not earning anything at this point so there's nothing extra from me that goes into the joint one. But if there's anything left now, I buy more food with it, but when I am making some money, that's where the extra goes. Right now Annie pays more and puts more into the savings. Right now, anyway. At this point we discuss just about anything we buy. It used to be we discussed just the major purchases, but because I could just keep purchasing, I discuss just about anything other than food things I like to buy. Even gifts and things. I've given her my charge card. She's just more practical and she is not a big spender. We have our cars in both names so that we get joint car insurance—it's much cheaper. For the longest time we weren't going to do it, but it makes one-hundred-dollars difference every month, so we did.

At the beginning we had our own private hot tub in the backyard where we lived. That was very good for my back, so it helped with sex, physically. I could really enjoy sex more then, to be honest. When we were still at that house, Annie had her car accident and then she wrecked her back. So now we had two bad backs and that sort of spoiled her sexual part and also her shoulder was wrecked, or rather she had some deterioration. That all got in the way of our sex enjoyment and for a long time we really couldn't. Annie and I cuddle a lot and now we like to cuddle more even, and touch more. But as far as sex goes, now that we are living in this place, over community gardens—we don't have our hot tub. And that was a big part of where we'd be able to have sex.

We still have sex once in a while. You know, but thank God, we stopped this thing about planning it—you know, Sunday at such and such a time, because it just didn't work. It's better, we found, to be spontaneous, to go for it. But we don't have it too often because it isn't okay, it's too painful, and so you don't feel "just go for it." So we have the warmth mostly without the sexual activity. We hear that with some of our friends they have separate beds. We would never think about having separate beds.

When we do have sex, though, which is only a few times a year now, we enjoy it just as much. The quality has improved. I think it's that, well, it's like when you don't have sex for such a long time and you know it could be painful for both of you, you kind of want to take your time, but yet you don't want to stretch it out too long because that would hurt. So, what I mean is that I think that there is more sensitivity to each other than when you go at it all the time. It's more sensitive, and so that makes the quality better.

Annie, if she tells the truth, would want it more often. She's not in good shape either. But it could be more often. We had and have a good time sexually. Once I took pictures of her in sexy positions and it was very funny because her cousin came to visit and was looking through our photographs and I suddenly realized those pictures were in there. Annie keeps the albums all nice—they weren't in there, they were in boxes, and this cousin looked through all the albums and then was looking through the boxes . . . I don't know if he saw anything and he's real sweet so he probably wouldn't say anything if he did!

I think our neighbors think something like my mom married her dad—if they think at all, because they must know our families live in different parts of the country. I hate to tell you all the lies I've had to say. I'm the one who's home and I wish I didn't have to talk to them. Sometimes they push it too far and I have to come out with something. The story changes always!

Family is very important to us both. Annie's daughter has moved nearby with her boyfriend and her mother's around here, so we see them. My family's far away. You know there's a myth about gay people that they don't value family ties. That's a farce. Sometimes families don't accept them, and that's horrible. Annie's family—we're closer to them because they're around—don't care at all. They accept. I remember when I came out to my father, it was in a Chinese restaurant in Chicago. Every so often I would meet him for dinner after I moved out, after my mother died. And I came out to him at the restaurant. The waiter had just put down the order and I said, "Dad, I am gay." And he slammed his fist down on the table. "No! No," he shouted and he stood up and was ready to grab me. The waiter put his head in between us and said, "Is there anything I can get you?" And my father slammed his hand on the table and the water went all over the place. "You know, don't ever say that again!" he said, and I said, "Okay, I won't." So that was the way he reacted to my being gay. That was about a year and a half before he died. I came out about six months after my mom died and he died two years after her. But the rest of my family—my cousins are the ones left—is fine. I love and value them and they love and value me.

I think what makes our relationship work so well is that when we do have differences of opinion, we can always talk them over and we always respect each other's opinions. We have this very mutual respect for one another. We also say things directly to each other; we tell each other how much we love each other and how terrific we think the other one is. You know, how good we feel, how lucky we are. We always say how lucky we are to have each other. I say it to her, she says it to me. Always. She says it's a mutual-admiration society. I say to her, "You are the love of my life." I remember the first time she signed a card to me with "love," she said, "that's not quite right." She said, it should say "the love of my life." That was just before she was going to the choir for a rehearsal and I said, "Tell them! Tell them!" And she said, about me, to them, "This is the love of my life."

She still says it, and I say it to her too. "It's a good thing I met you," I say to her, "or it would have been just me and Goldilocks"—that was my kitty then—"forever!"

8

The Delicate Balance:
Sharing Lives Without Losing Selves

PAM and CARL JOHNSON
ALICE and CHRISTOPHER JOHN

E ACH OF THESE happy stories carries themes of sharing. Ongoing sharing of important values, pleasures, and activities, and finding common time in which these activities can occur helps keep great relationships renewed and refreshed. The couples in this study share family, values, goals, humor, interests, tastes, people loved and loathed, stories, recreation, hobbies, homes, customs, habits, projects, history, and intended future.

Some couples share almost everything: children, leisure, work, politics, and friends. While all of their joined interests and activities are deeply enjoyed and treasured, it does raise the question, what about the individual? Bookshop shelves bulge with volumes urging individual growth, reminding us to "look out for number one" and "cultivate your own garden." While well-being can be mined through living within a secure, happy relationship, individual hardiness is also important. A central task for couples is getting the balance right between psychological health through individual pursuits and joint ones. Maintaining the right balance does vary both within couples and over the life cycle, and is an ongoing task for every couple.

I gave up the idea of having my own social life and just dedicated myself to Ron and my family, and Ron did the same. We've never regretted this, and now that we're not even old yet, we've got time for ourselves together, which is great.—**Rita Turner, 42**

While this quote shows little room for individual pursuits, other couples describe relationships that are not so exclusive, claiming that separate friends, separate interests, and time alone are part of what breeds relationship happiness.

I do not always share my wife's interests and vice versa, but we let each other do "our thing" unhampered. Not always easy but better than not!—**Oliver Tyler, 82**

Couples even manage to share across surprising sorts of divides, apparently prioritizing autonomy over sharing, but still share domains central to their identity as a couple. Most couples do live together; normally intimacy is easier to come by and foster through the daily business of living. But there are outliers in these stories of enduring love.

Our relationship is unusual—but special because we have managed to survive dealing with being single parents who have always put their children first. While the children are at home, we live separately. Steve has always understood that I need to look after my child above all else and I have tried to do the same. We have trusted each other enough to live separately and not always want to know what the other person is doing. Sometimes we don't speak for a few days, and because I feel confident in our situation, that is fine. I just know that he is there in the world—geographically very close, because he only lives five minutes away—and that I can reach him if I need to. There's a lot of freedom, but a lot of closeness.—**Joanne Long, 40**

These vignettes in this book convey the differences across couples in how much sharing and how much independence is tolerable. They also show that amounts of sharing and independence usually vary according to changes in life circumstances: having children or not, children leaving home, the degree of overlapping interests, and relative health, for example.

couples, however, override this with the comfort of knowing the hours
are numbered (however large), and use this sense of security and
ort to carve out their own things in a piece of their own time.

my subsequent career I traveled widely. Sometimes we could go
oad together—once for as long as a year. Other times we'd have to
separated—once for as long as eight months. These separations
e tough. But I think that during our "testing" times such as these we
e dealt with them more as opportunities to be grasped and used to
advantage . . . We have tried to share everything that can be shared.
've shown mutual appreciation and expression of appreciation.—
tair **Crawford, 82**

matter the amount of autonomous time and energy and how many
mous interests the individuals here claim, their stories demonstrate a
set of core values, or important beliefs that guide their lives. Being on
ne track, and—to mix a metaphor—singing off the same hymn sheet
go, is part of the narrative thrust. Couples point to shared politics,
of life goals, cultural pursuits, humor, pleasures, tastes, friends, and
interests, but most overarchingly, shared bottom-line values such as
, humaneness, and charity, and in some cases, religiosity.

have shared a belief and we pray together and are both practicing
stians. We have shared so many things—wonderful and delight-
-in our years of marriage.—**Marion Alfred, 75**

ing a home and working out a mutually comfortable style and set of
s well as raising children jointly according to key values and goals,
most couples' central projects, but other ones also can share center
grossing each partner equally and giving both people another set of
nt shared references and objectives.

ly after we moved in together I started up a food supply business,
Debbie's part-time help. She helped encourage me in this, made it

Not having children gives us more free time
pursue our interests. After work, Rich will gc
and I will read or write. We lead rather sepa
are very quiet at home, the house often in si
own interests—then come together over mea
discuss and talk things through. We also sp
example, we are in a samba band that meet:
practice—thereby giving us a social situatioɪ
Leah Banks, 34

For most couples, the proportion of time sp
shifts from a lot in the early period, to less if
increased time spent at work, to more again
independence and eventual departure in particʋ
and energy. For some, this largely enhances
reading, playing computer games, or developing
Happy couples spend the new resources on t
increasing the time given to or the intensity of t
of marital satisfaction show a dip after childrɪ
remain together, a rise after they leave. Many att
and focus on each other, deepening friendship,
and pleasures. A yearning felt in the first flu
resurface (if more gently): the longing to be iɪ
while mourning the lover's absence, a fundame
normally suppressed—not wholly, but routine
rearing years is now allowed a renewal.

One Friday night I had to attend my best fɪ
get drunk, etc., I remained sober and droʋ
however, stopped for speeding and fined .
with Katy—obviously I can live with the
rather travel for two hours at eleven P.M.
with my wife than stay in a hotel.—**Rich**

possible. But it turned out that the person I went into business with was a con man—I struggled to find a career/employment and tried to start a new catering business with Debbie. Our customers loved what we produced. But the hassle of getting up at four, together with the effect it had on our children, meant that we decided not to continue the business.

During those four years we also had a great deal of work done on the house, but eventually we almost lost it because our finances were so tottery. During these difficult times Debbie, an extremely accomplished cook, kept us alive on "stone soup." She was determined not to go out of the home to work while our two younger kids were preschool, and I was in complete agreement, so eventually I obtained a place on a government-funded retraining scheme and this led to a job as a computer programmer with a major international engineering company, a company I've been with ever since.—**Terry Carlson, 48**

To share deeply and widely, whatever the proportion of joint versus autonomous time and interests a couple works out, is a risk, the tremendous risk at the heart of love: with almost absolute certainty one of you will die before the other; one will take what you have given and shared to the grave. It is a noble risk, taken by these couples.

While such sharing as these couples describe contributes to a strong relationship, it also strengthens the individuals within it. Happy couples' relationship stories stand in stark contrast to those of couples who are alienated or separating. They emphasize the affirming nature of the relationship and its growth at the same time as they affirm individual growth. The speakers attribute a good deal of their sense of security and safety to being in the relationship, as well linking their personal development to the liberating sense of being loved and understood.

We don't get under each other's feet, and pursue our own activities (I am involved in several community projects as well as helping her). We love each other very much, but in a very dynamic way; we are a mutual-admiration society rejoicing in each other's separate successes as well as

mutual ones. There are far too few hours in the day, we are so busy . . .
Even after more than twenty years I am still in love with her.—**Andrew
Lovington, 73**

If nothing else, Martin and Dennis's story in chapter 4 show the power of
love to transform the individual. Because falling in love with another man
clarified and liberated each of them individually, their story illuminates the
fact that love can bring profound individual growth, drawing out of people
and requiring of them the possibility to stretch and know themselves more
profoundly. Each man made fundamental, sometimes challenging-to-the-
core, adaptations because of his desire to be with the other. These changes
yielded individual wisdom and welcome challenges. Their story also challenges a widely held assumption about "personal growth"—i.e., that
individual happiness lies in pursuing individual goals. Instead, it suggests
the sum of an individual's personal happiness may consist in large part in the
pleasures of sustaining a secure and enriching, enduring partnership. Indeed,
research on happiness[30] and marital sturdiness concur.[31] Apart from the fact
that it was through their relationship that each could accept his sexuality,
increasing both men's individual happiness, because of their commitment,
Martin's planned career in academia was exchanged for another that has
given him real satisfaction.

Sharing is often thought of as a baseline component of intimate love.
Some sharing is necessary. But what that looks and feels like is not
straightforward, as the variation across these couples' stories indicates.

Pam and Carl Johnson

Pam and Carl Johnson have been together for thirteen years and married for
twelve. Pam is fifty-four, Carl seventy-three. They are both energetic,
friendly, good-looking, and stylish, both African-American; both have spent
their adult lives, from their early days in the civil rights movement,
promoting African-American social justice. Carl was happily married for
twenty-nine years to his first wife, Thelma, who died of cancer. They raised

three children, all grown before their mother's death. Pam married first at seventeen, divorcing four years later, marrying again at twenty-eight and divorcing eight years later. Neither marriage produced children. Carl, a professor of medicine and political activist, is a nationally known leader in civil rights, while Pam, a former television producer, heads a research think tank on humanitarian rights issues. I met Carl in his university office suite in New York City for his interview, and I met Pam in her Midtown office, where the interview was punctuated by messages about the event occurring that evening: the Carl Johnson Lecture, an annual lecture sponsored by a local university featuring and honoring an individual whose contribution to social justice has been significant, an honor bestowed on her husband in the year of its creation. Pam chairs the board administering both the award and the celebratory dinner.

Pam and Carl Johnson's lives were joined originally around politics and social change. Because they met in middle and late-middle age, respectively, the question of how much to pool and how much to keep separate in already well-functioning lives became central to them.

Pam Johnson:

My life has been a lot more nonlinear than Carl's. That has been helpful to our relationship, because, in a lot of ways, being a professor at three different prestigious colleges, you really live in a rarefied air. He's had challenges—but he has not had to really hustle. Even though I know that I was gifted and fortunate in many ways, I have, more than he, lived in the "real world."

The most unusual thing about me, which a lot of people who know me . . . don't know, is that I've been married three times. I first married my high school sweetheart when I had just graduated high school. We got married too young. I grew up in Akron, Ohio. We were an interracial couple and he was one of the most brilliant people I have ever met. I went to a school where I was one of two black students in my graduating class and I was one of the top students—had we not been in the spotlight, we would probably not have married so young. He went to Duke University in North Carolina and I to Spelman College in Georgia because it was sort of close to where he was—

that was a primary reason for my choice. And that was the first time I was with a lot of other black people—I had never had a black teacher before. It was while I was there, in the mid-sixties, I got involved with civil rights.

Most people don't remember this, but a lot of Southern states had miscegenation laws, even then—blacks and whites couldn't be married. We were married at this point, and when I would go up to visit him, I was challenging those laws. Because I was a good student my college let me stay and do everything even though I was married—usually you weren't allowed to be married then as an undergrad. I'd had less sex than anyone else I knew, really, then—I hadn't had sex before I got married. I was very straight. In 1967, two years after I got married, a Supreme Court decision struck down the miscegenation laws. But till then we were essentially cohabiting, rather than being married in the eyes of many states down south. We were both committed to civil rights. Had it not been for Rick, my husband, my life would have taken a different turn because I grew up in a family that didn't have much education, even though education was the primary goal. My original plans were to go to college, then travel around the world for two years . . . then my life took all these turns and twists. I became very active then in civil rights, in the NAACP.

My parents weren't activists. They had to work all the time, just to feed us. My dad was involved in the church, and they believed in feeding the hungry, in taking care of the community, and my mother just by sheer goodness, really, took care of—well, she gave birth to three kids, and took care of nine more. And when people were hungry, they always came by our house, even though we didn't have much money. My father had other children, so my mother made a decision to take care of his kids. They stayed together until after I left home, when I was seventeen, and a year or so later they separated, after all those years together. My mother left because she felt sad for who she was. Part of the reason I am so driven is partly because of the opportunities she never had.

And also because of my schooling. We didn't go to the city schools. We went to the county schools, which were the excellent ones—I had an education that was better than most people's private one. Because there were so few blacks, we were not treated any differently from everyone else. I never thought that I couldn't compete, because that is what I did. In my high school there were only four black students, all women. All three of the others have died—one of breast cancer, one of kidney failure, and the other when she was still very young. I'm the only one left, a sort of standard-bearer. I feel I cannot let the side down. And I feel that with my family too; I'm the oldest of the three full siblings.

At any rate, Rick and I were young and foolish, and we divorced four years after we got married. We had really split up long before we officially did. I did move up to be with him before I graduated, which meant that I didn't graduate then. I had to take classes elsewhere, and finally ended up graduating later, after we'd divorced . . . I took an extension degree through Antioch College, a really alternative, flexible program that let me do it mostly where I was based, which was by then in Washington.

I began to work in television then. I was working for NBC in Washington as a producer, and married, this time an Afro-American, older than I, when I was twenty-eight. He had two children, a son and a daughter, and I became very close, in particular, to the daughter. He was alcoholic and very possessive and competitive and became very abusive to me. I tried to have children with him, but miscarried and that was one of the reasons the marriage broke down. After eight years I left him. By then I was doing a lot separately. I'd become head of a production company, and was also doing quite a bit of lobbying, eventually moving into political and public relations consultancy there, and I was very well connected politically. In fact, even though Carl is very well-known nationally, when he'd tell people in Washington that he was going to marry me, they'd say, "Oh, you're the one who's marrying Pam"—that is, I was the one who was well-known there! We got beyond that competition, by the way.

I met Carl over the phone. He will tell you his version of the story. He was writing something for a book and a big conference I was organizing and I had to talk to him a lot over the phone over a number of months. I fell in love with him through that. So I sort of proposed to him on the phone after a while. The only disagreement I have with the way he tells the story is what he doesn't say. He doesn't remember, really, that I took back the proposal. He wavered, because he had people telling him it's too soon after Thelma died and you don't know her very well . . . At one point he said to me, "Maybe they are right." I knew about the talk going on in the background . . . I said, "If you can't be committed to me, then it is not going to work." So I took it back. Then we went on vacation and we were driving along the road and then *he* asked me to marry him. And we stopped, and I said, "I have three conditions." The first was "Do not pull rank on me because of either your stature or your age." The second was "The children do not live with us"—he had three grown children and two of them hadn't really gotten themselves sorted out and were still sometimes living back with him. And the third was to set goals and expectations for them, our children. I felt that he had brought his children up without having to worry about food and shelter, and they had not really been challenged enough. They didn't have any initiative. He was frustrated by this about them too. He has found it hard to make changes that would be necessary for this to change, and I have pushed harder than he, regarding our children. It has created friction, and it has also been helpful. Sometimes we can't talk about it—we have to put a "pin" on it.

Though there was a lot known about Carl, I didn't really know anything personal about him. At the point I needed him to write something for the book and presentation I was putting together, I hadn't read his book, but he'd been recommended to me . . . by a lot of people. So I read his book then. I called him at home and introduced myself. He said, "I really don't have time to do this. My wife has just died." And I said, "Oh my God. I didn't know. I'm so sorry." People found it hard to believe that I didn't know, but I really didn't. And then he was so concerned about me, being so shocked and embarrassed, that he said, "Oh, of course you didn't know. Are you all right? Are you upset?"—and he called back. And I thought, "Wow! What kind of person is this?" And so I was not too upset then to say something like, "Well, if I find something in anything you've written that would be relevant, can we just update it?" And he said, "Oh, you won't be able to find anything, but sure, go ahead" . . . So I did find something and I rewrote it and he said that he really didn't have time to look at it, but, of course, he did, and he called and told me I got it all wrong. He said, "You don't understand the context. I don't have time to work on it right now, but if I do, I will send it to you." So, of course, he did, and it went back and forth, over a few months, and that's how it started. And from that first telephone conversation I couldn't stop thinking about him.

I didn't have a picture of him in my mind . . . I hadn't really needed a mental image of him to feel I was falling in love with him. I just had a spiritual one.

I had lunch during this time with a man who's been something like a father to me and he said, "How are things going?" And I said, "Well, fine, but I think I've done something very unprofessional." So he said, "What do you mean?" And I said, "I think I have fallen in love with someone I am working with." And when I said "Carl Johnson," he said, "Hey, I hear he's got women all lined up to be with him." So I said, "What do I do?" And he said, "Well, if you really feel that way, I have known you a very long time, and you are not a flighty person. Go with what your heart says."

I am fairly self-controled. In our conversations I certainly didn't tell Carl about my two marriages right away. He'd gone into more depth—he's much more open than I am. He talked loads about his first wife, Thelma. After we were married I got close to Thelma's sister. She said to Carl, "You should stop talking so much about Thelma to Pam. It isn't good for her." So he asked me about it. But I didn't mind. It was good—it was most of his life, and they had a good relationship. No, it was fine with me, and I wouldn't have had it any other way.

So one day, when we were having one of our long phone conversations, I said, "Now that I've read your book and talked to you, I know that you are the person that I want to be with." I don't remember the exact words, but he does. I said, "I think we would be happy together." Then he came down to Washington, not exactly to meet me, but because we had a major press launch and he had to come down for that. At first he'd said he would be too busy to come for it but by then he had become intrigued enough to come to this press launch. I had made a terrible mistake becoming smitten with Carl, as it meant that I was forgetting things professionally that I would never have done otherwise. Like I'd made a mistake in judgement: I'd let a person who shouldn't have been be in charge of setting up the mics and she hadn't done it, when we had all the major TV channels covering it! This was discovered with only two minutes to go. He saw me recover the situation. I took charge, while meanwhile the line producer was getting completely hysterical. And he said that if he hadn't been interested in me before that, that would have done it, because "You take charge." That was the moment that he fell in love. He said he couldn't believe how I processed information.

Then it was a short time until we decided to get married. Before we actually met he went out to the West Coast to visit a friend, a woman writer who's very close to him. He was interested also at that point in another woman, also a friend, someone he'd been attracted to during his marriage. So he was out in California for a few days talking about whether or not he should go for it with this other woman, when his writer friend said to him, not having yet met me, "You know that woman in Washington that you've been talking about? She seems like the one for you. She's the one you need. She will take care of you." And he listened to her.

Before he came out to Washington, during the Christmas holiday, we were talking to each other on the phone. One of his dear friends—he has lots of good women friends, and I don't worry about them because we don't *do* affairs—was talking to him and he mentioned me. And she said, "Oh, I know her. She is a *serious* woman." So there were all these things sort of lined up in his mind before he met me and making him feel that I wasn't crazy. Because he *could* have thought that, given what I'd done—proposing to him that way! He could have thought that I'd lost my mind.

It was a committed relationship then from near the time we met. Not seamless, but the biggest thing was the commitment. We had bumps and then we got committed to each other. It was seamless in one respect: it felt right and it felt positive. But it wasn't seamless in another, because you had two adults with formed lives, styles, routines.

At first I didn't have contact with the children—I didn't have a contact with them, just with their father. And, in fact, the youngest one didn't come to our wedding. He felt it was too soon, less than two years after their mother had died. While I thought it was selfish of him not to come to our wedding, I didn't mention it for eight years. In fact we are very close now. It came up in a sly way, when one day he was saying, "I've never been any trouble for you, have I?" and so we had a short discussion. But in some ways that discussion has made us closer.

I refer to Carl's children as "our" children. The youngest refers to me as his mother, the middle as her stepmother, and the oldest is really too close in age to me—fourteen years—to do either. I have adopted my mother's attitude. It's what you do that forms a family. I also have learned from my mother that in a group, you can pull something special out of each one of them, from each child . . .

I have to say that as close as possible we have an equal relationship. But really, the way I see it, he is the senior partner. That is how I have tried to accommodate it because there are certain times when I feel he needs more. I know he will care for me, but I think that because of his age, well, sometimes he needs more caring than I do. Maybe that is sacrifice. I know I have gotten into this with a couple of my women friends who feel that I always defer to him. I don't. He also defers to me. But there are certain things . . . well, he has earned my respect, and sometimes I do think, "What's the best use of his time?" He does a lot of the cooking—he doesn't think he is too good for those things. Look, taking out the garbage isn't the best use of his time—it's not the best of mine, either, but . . . But the other thing is that even though this is a man-woman relationship, I am with someone who has earned his place in history, and still has a lot to contribute, and I can help him do that.

And in a way that is part of my own contribution, helping him to contribute.

We both have a commitment to social justice but his is the more public face. Sometimes I will push in other areas, though. For instance, a few years ago, during demonstrations against police brutality, he didn't want to be part of that and take attention away from those who had started it. I met a woman involved and she didn't just want it to be about poor black women, so she asked me to join them, and I said, "I'm there." And I was arrested. He then joined in and a few weeks later he and a whole lot of other doctors, lawyers, professors, got arrested. Most people will remember him getting arrested, not me, but that's okay. Recently I went down to Washington on a peace rally; he didn't have time to go.

This award—the Carl Johnson Lecture—we're both very active and involved in that, of course, throughout the year and in helping it get set up. So we share that commitment and activism, but we are also very romantic.

Carl is more than me. He does the grand gesture, rather than buy flowers and things. We had most of our dinners by candlelight when we were first married and that is when we talked and talked and settled things. I find that because I am doing too many things most of the time, I bring papers and schedules to dinner. That is like bringing snakes into the Garden of Eden. He is definitely more romantic . . . He puts everything away, everything down, when we eat. He is still easily seduced by the sound of the ringing telephone and so he will answer the phone, but only to say he'll call back. And that's when we give each other full attention.

We also have lots of friends in common. Some of the friends he has had over the years were friends he had with Thelma. Some of them decided not to continue the friendship, but for the most part, there's been an acceptance of me . . . And my friends, they all love him—that's been easy, really simple. That moved him. I think he is a sweeter person than I am; not a nicer person, but a sweeter one. He does say to me, "I am a better husband to you than I was to Thelma."

I think at this point I talk about her almost as much as he does. I have a lot of respect for her. I do recognize the marriage with me is easier for Carl, though, for a number of reasons. First, the children, who weren't always easy, and who still have issues around independence and initiative. Second, because of all his training and being primarily an academic, they moved about eight times. Thelma's parents had died when she was young and I don't think she had the same ability to fight for her own space as I do. When I feel my space being invaded, I fight back. And life for me is easier as a result. Theirs was a very traditional marriage. She cared for him and the kids intensely and he was a wonderful father and husband. But he was traditional. And in a sense, in our relationship he is a little less traditional both because he has allowed himself to be and also because I fight for that. That is something that I learned in past relationships—if you don't have a sense of self then you are not going to make it, not going to survive.

Also, we enjoy a very nice lifestyle. We both still work too hard. The problem is that there is too much to be done . . . Sometimes we have to remind ourselves that, for a couple, we do actually spend a lot of time together, but Carl often thinks we don't.

We have a house in the country where we go on weekends. If he's doing a publicity tour if he's written a book or something, I go with him if I can. I have to plan a lot in advance—and actually that takes time away from him . . . He doesn't always see that the planning . . . is part of our being together. He sees the present and I see next week. He'd want me to be with him more. He says that, but if I stay home, he is on the phone, then on *his* computer, and I will leave and then go to *my* computer. It's kind of cute.

Carl and I have some strange conversations sometimes. Some of his colleagues who are his contemporaries are old. He's seventy-three this week. I'll be fifty-five in a few months. When we got married twelve years ago, one of his friends asked him, "Aren't you afraid of some young guy taking Pam?" which I thought was absurd. So we had a conversation about this, and he said, "Well, you know, if you did have an affair, I would forgive you." And I said, "No! You can forget about that! I am never going to have an affair— you can't put that one on me. I can see you now, polishing your halo, forgiving me for, for this great transgression! I am *not* going to let you have that pleasure!" So we joke about that. Because he intellectualizes things, he still sometimes brings it up, and I will say, "Carl, just stop. This is a totally absurd conversation." But it is funny. And when we were married seven years, people said, "So what about the seven-year itch?" And I said, "No, we've itched already."

Two years after we got married I got breast cancer—devastating to Carl because of Thelma too. Carl says that it's always amazing to him how in couples, if the man gets ill, the woman would always take care of him and how when a woman gets ill, the man—well, the woman would be alone, and it seems like that happens a lot. But that isn't what has happened with Carl with either Thelma or me. Then four years later Carl got an almost-fatal case of pneumonia. In fact, when we got to the hospital, the doctor pulled me aside and said he might not make it . . . I can't tell this story without crying . . . He stayed there for three weeks and I essentially moved into the hospital because I'd read all these stories about doctors not washing their hands . . . and it's true: except when they were around me.

And with my breast cancer, when I was taken into the operating ward and given the anesthesia, for some reason I started flatlining, and so I had this awful instant that has never occurred again . . . They thought I might have had heart problems . . . and they brought me back. If I had had any doubts whatsoever, that period was when I knew I could trust the relationship and Carl completely, and his love for me. My mother and favorite aunt also died within three months of my diagnosis. He was right there, in all of that. When going to radiation, he came with me, every time, and I said to him, "Carl, no one else's husband is coming. Please don't come too: I felt like a little kid." And for weeks at a time he would come. And when he stopped coming, when I said to him, "Don't come, I have to do this on my own," all the people said, "Where is your husband? Is he all right?" And so I had to ask him to come back, I had so upset the poor people working there! I had a lumpectomy—a quarter of the breast removed. It also gets all discolored with radiation. But he has just accepted it. He's so good about it—he didn't think of anything else except that I was okay. And when he was so ill, I stayed at home as much as I could afterward, making sure that we both ate properly, paying more attention to the basics. So we have had those trials and I feel that we have been tested and proven true. And so anything else—we can figure out how to get through.

He took care of me, and I took care of him. And we also take care of the sense of self . . . and the sense of integrity. It really means a lot to us to try to be good people, and when we aren't as good as we would like to be, or should be, the other person steps in. For example, Carl is very quiet and patient, but when he loses it, he can hurt someone and doesn't realize it and it hurts more coming from him than most people, because you don't see it coming. So when I see that he is at that point, I will try to step in.

You know, in terms of sex, I thought that marrying someone so much older I'd have to curb my appetite. That is not at all true. It goes back and forth a bit in terms of frequency. We've both had major illnesses. We had breaks for a while because of our illnesses. In the last few years he's been a bit more concerned about the frequency and the frequency of my desire but I'm not. I said things are fine. I talked to a friend who also had cancer and she said that she didn't want sex and her partner did, and I told her that he obviously didn't see all the throwing up, the feeling terrible, more throwing up . . . But they got through it and so did we.

That's one of the secrets—that you can be resilient sexually.

He is frugal, but that is partly what enables us to have a good lifestyle. We don't have money problems at all, but Carl tends to worry about money more than I do. He was a Depression baby. The more money we have, the more he worries. So we have little disagreements about that. He'll do a whole printout of every penny and make suggestions to me about how to be more frugal. And I will say, "I have never done that"—implying I'm not going to start now. So we have had to get beyond that. Because of his age, he wants money in reserve, while I'll want to roll the dice, even though, actually, I am conservative. He never gambles. Sometimes I go to Las Vegas on business and I will spend fifty bucks, and he'll think it's a real waste of money: he'll say, "Why would someone want to do that?" It isn't because of his children—he's set up trusts for them. And I make good money—that's part of the reason I changed jobs to my present one. I say to him, "I grew up poor; you don't know poor." And he'll say, "But you always had enough to eat." I remind him, "We didn't always." So I have my secrets about what I spend and when, but he doesn't push it . . . What he wants to know is . . . the bottom line . . . of what's there. I do resist it even though what he wants is simple.

Another thing: we try to talk about everything that comes up. I have a quicker temper than he has, and I have learned to say to him, "I can't talk about that right now. I'll talk about it later." And then we'll have a cup of tea or glass of wine, later, and we'll just talk. What I do is that, if it's significant, I'll think about it when I go away, but if it's insignificant, I put it out of my mind—I mean, why push it at that point if you don't want to talk about it? It never goes away really, and it always comes back. Even if we say we're not going to talk about it, we do.

Once Carl said to me, "If we were just living together would you still be you?" and I said, "No. Because the most angry that I get, the most frustrated that I get, I remember that we made a commitment, we made a deal—to be mature, loving people, and to work it out. And that, to me, is what marriage is all about." And I said, "It is not more complicated than that."

Carl Johnson:

I think that much of who I am in life, and in regard to women, stems from my mother. I had a great relationship with both parents. I never wanted to embarrass them, never wanted to disappoint them, because I recognized that it was a struggle for them to stay together. They had differences that used to result in fights early on, and once I remember my father packing up and moving out . . . There were a few physical fights—I remember them rolling around on the bed—not serious injuries. This was in 1932.

My mother had graduated from high school and was supposed to go to college, sort of an "upper-class-poor" black family. Her father was a cook on the railways and I think he was a cook for the president of the company, and her mother was almost white—very light-skinned. Her father was very, very dark. They both died when I was quite young. One of her brothers had been killed in World War I. Another had a great struggle. He wanted to go to medical school but couldn't get in. He finally went to school to become a pharmacist instead, but couldn't get a job. He worked as a waiter. This was the racism of then. He had worked for a family of doctors, who encouraged him. Another uncle didn't have an education but was very smart and tutored people, encouraged people. When I was into stamp collecting, he got me a book. When I got interested in recording, when the first real recordings came out, and when I got into photography, he set up the dark room, he got me stuff. There were two boys—we were two years apart, and then fifteen years later my parents had another child. I was the oldest. We were encouraged. There were ambitions.

. . . I thought I was great because everybody told me that I was and it came out in all this support from uncles and aunts and cousins . . . All of us went on to college. My brother became a pretty top musician, having gone to Oberlin Conservatory. He had his own quintet, and has made records, and is still performing. We have little contact now—I really do love him, but . . . My sister became a teacher. My mother died only a year ago, at age ninety-two. I think I might have been the one who was closest to my mother. My brother was probably a little closer to my father, learned to drive trucks like him, but, then, I did all my father's bills.

We lived in St Louis. I went to St. Louis University, a Catholic school, and did medical school and the beginning of my clinical training in St. Louis. My parents wanted me to go to college. My father had only had a sixth-grade education. When I graduated from high school, though, I was immediately put in the service because it was the Korean War. I was stationed for a year in the South, the Deep South, first, and my father was very concerned about me. He bought me a little car and I made the payments on it, and then of course I offered to drive one of my white classmates down there with me and there was some difficulty with that on the way down. I was stationed in Louisiana—there were still the Jim Crow laws. Still segregation. Still riding on the back of the bus.

I'd met Thelma in high school. We'd competed for grades—except I really can't say we competed. She helped me on French . . . When we graduated from high school, Thelma wanted to be an actress, and wanted to go to Carnegie Tech, but her father didn't think that was proper, so instead she went to Washington University, in St Louis too. But I was in the service . . . After I came back, she'd gone, to do a master's in Cleveland, and I was in St. Louis in college, on the GI Bill. I had another girlfriend, Jeannette, who I'd been writing to while I was in the service. I wasn't really ready to move forward. I assumed that being married would be a burden on my desire to be someone. So when I came back from the service, I told her it wasn't right. She forgave me and she married someone else—but it was clear that she was still in love with me. I didn't love her, though.

Thelma and I were both churchgoers then, though in high school not the same one. But it was church that brought us back together. I went to Pittsburgh and was on the faculty teaching medicine, earning fifty-four hundred dollars a year, had my own apartment, and I was the man about town, I would invite them all out for dinner and serve ginger ale and grape juice—so sophisticated! But during that time Thelma called and said she'd moved to Pittsburgh . . . she said, "There is this new church—why don't you come with me?" They were meeting at the black YMCA. It was segregated—this was in 1957—that's why they were meeting at the Y. So I went.

There was another woman I'd met, and we went to concerts together . . . and Thelma was more my "buddy." But when she asked me to church, that was the beginning. She was a social worker, and there were men chasing her. It was clear then that Thelma had had much more experience than I had. I said to her then, "Thelma, about your men . . ." After we'd been married, I said, again, "Thelma, tell me about some of these men you have been with," and she said, "Whenever you are ready, I will tell you." And I never got ready!

We were trying to fix up this room in the church, and we were painting together. We'd go out to the minister's house; he was a social activist and knew Martin Luther King, and had left a very prestigious church because he said they were never going to do anything. But to leave that and then start this new church, it was really something, and we would go to church; he was married, with three children, and it just seemed to me . . . well, he and Thelma had these tremendous arguments and Thelma was ready to take him on any time, and I would sit across the church with his wife and we would just shake our heads. But it dawned on me then that this man was as great a man as I hoped to be, and his marriage was not a burden, but a support. I saw that it was possible. Moreover, Thelma's sister saw me as the Perfect One, and she had her child call me "uncle," and would send for me to have dinner with them. So it all began to seem possible . . .

. . . It dawned on me that I loved her during that period . . . That summer she took a job at a camp. I had worked there too and loved it; I thought being a camp counselor was the best thing to do! I still love camps, but it didn't work as well on my children. I would visit her at the camp, and I proposed to her there. I think it came slowly, but I realized that she had a lot of—I was so impressed that she had the ability to characterize someone that she just met after about ten minutes. I was very impressed. And she was a worldly woman. When I introduced her to my parents, I said, "Dad, Thelma can drink you under the table." I was impressed with her all the way through our long marriage. Marriage has its problems but she was somebody who was going to be there. And she was . . . She followed me from place to place, not always happily, but she did it.

. . . She had no interest in sports: she never learned to ride a bicycle, she could not swim, and when I learned to sail, she was always fearful about going out. I did more of that with my kids, at least to some extent. In those pursuits I felt lonely. I like jogging; we would argue if we were going to a restaurant and I found a place to park and it was a block away! We always fought about directions. It was amazing to me that you could have a wonderful sexual experience and then get dressed to go to someone's house for dinner, have poor directions, and then by the time you got there you weren't speaking!

By the end of the evening, though, we'd be speaking. That would be just because we both enjoyed time with people, and I love a woman who can do that and who you don't have to stay with—she was confident with others, including other men. I would look over and there would be three of them around her and there she would be holding forth. She was very socially adept.

We had three children, the first after we'd been married two years, in 1962. At that point I was already involved in national civil rights actions, and on the board of a major national organization. I learned a lot working with the boss of it, about the technicalities of school desegregation. He was a white man who committed his life to the cause but I never got the sense that he really respected black people. We got along. I became a spokesperson.

I went into academic medicine in part to encourage black students. I'd worked in a big national hospital in Washington, and then I was approached by the university in California, and I said, "Yes," I was interested in teaching, and they told me I could start by being an adjunct professor of medicine. It worked out because I learned that I did like being a teacher. Then in 1968 Martin Luther King was killed and I got all these offers. The pressures . . . they all wanted to hire, and I decided that Yale was the best school. I was still in California, and Thelma was moving around with me and the kids for all these jobs. She wasn't employed during this, but she was doing volunteer work. Before the babies she worked in Pittsburgh and Washington as a social worker. It wasn't a picnic, and I'm not sure I fully appreciated that. I think I prioritized my work—I thought I was doing God's work. By that time I was going to the South a lot, and being in some kind of not-so-safe situations. I wouldn't imagine taking my children with me.

And I have regrets about that—about not having been around so much. Waiting too long to introduce the kids to stuff, not being sure to give them a sense of proportion and value. Our greatest challenge, Thelma's and mine, was to get them over a sense of entitlement, which is still around to one degree or another . . . Once we drove along the California coast and rented a cottage, and the kids went running through it and said, "Mommy! Daddy! Here is your bathroom. Where's the kid's bathroom?" They'd never been in a place where they didn't have their own bathroom! . . . Though we did see my family, because on July 4th we had family reunions, so they knew there were others who didn't live like they did.

Thelma died in 1989. She first became ill with breast cancer in 1970, had surgery, radiotherapy, but no chemotherapy. She went for checkups regularly and there were about seven or eight years when she was free of it. And then it came back . . . She was ill, very ill, for about a three- or four-year period. She didn't want to talk about death, and me neither, and it was only in the last year when she had given up on the chemotherapy . . . the night of my mother's birthday . . . they called. She was put in the oncology ward and then she kind of brightened up; some people came to visit. She had a very bad night, and I had gone out at two a.m., and I sang to her, and it seemed like she calmed down, and the kids came and then I said, I will take them home and give them breakfast. And she died while I was away. I felt horrible. It happens a lot.

So it is hard to overcome. The woman who had done so much. But also, she had always said that if I die first, I hope you marry again. "It will be a compliment to me" . . . I do understand now what she meant when she said "it will be a compliment to me." If the marriage to Thelma was good, the fact that I was willing to remarry indicated that I wanted more of an enjoyable relationship. Also, that she recognized that I was a better person with a complementary person . . . I'm someone who relates, who likes talking. We talked a lot. We didn't just coexist. We got into each other's lives . . .

. . . There had been a lot of grieving for Thelma before, as she'd been very sick for so very long. I had this great minister. I said to him, "She doesn't want to talk about dying." I didn't have many people to talk to. It was a time of great pain. We'd been together for thirty years, and known each other from childhood. I would have loved for her to get well, but when I knew she wouldn't and saw how much she had gone down, that when she died, and I got back to the hospital, and the nurse said, "Oh, she has died," and was crying—it was not what I had hoped for, but it seemed to me that she was free from all that pain. And I had the sense of having to carry on . . . I had taken leave from Yale because of a protest I was leading about tenure for black professors, and Thelma was sick during this, and some friends were pissed off that I was doing this while she was sick and thought Thelma needed me with her. I told him that Thelma would have been less happy if I'd given up this protest, and would have been guilty because of it. I later saw it was the same kind of support I had had over the years. She was pleased and also very proud. The protest went on, after her death. There was loneliness then. I am such a workaholic that I filled a lot of the empty space, after the rituals of death were over.

Pam asked me to marry her, but then withdrew her proposal. I kid her that she had a backup—this white guy who was an academic, who later married someone else. She denies it, but I say, "Oh, that was your backup." Pam called me first about the book she wanted me to contribute to in October, and Thelma had died in August. We talked on the phone over a month. It was always a pleasant conversation. I never thought, or said, "Oh, when are we going to get together?" I certainly wasn't looking for someone. Pam was talking to a good friend about it, saying, "I really like him, but his wife just died," and this friend said, "Listen, there are women camping out." That is what prompted her. So she called me and said, "Look, we haven't met, but I love you!" It was extraordinary, I know. I can't remember what I told her. But another friend who knew Thelma came up to visit from Washington for New Year's and I told her about Pam. When I told her her name she said, "Oh, everyone in Washington knows her!" She listed all the things Pam had done. And you know, I saw, this is not a flighty woman. Based on that, I went to Washington for the press conference for the book and I just watched her function. She dressed very severely. I noticed how she was.

We met in 1990—in January—and married in 1991. We were pretty much together most of that year. I asked her to marry me in the summer. About a year after we were married, Pam was diagnosed with breast cancer too. She has not gotten ill since.

My first response to her was "Well, be glad you're married to me because I have been through this!" People would say "Oh! Oh no!" And I would say, "No. *I* didn't have it! *Now* I just should be a better caregiver." It was just, just a matter of keeping up with her. I would go with her to radiation and chemotherapy. She asked me to stop going because her oncologist and I would get in these conversations.

I have had health problems during our marriage too. In the last couple of months I've had health issues and it turns out that I have a cancerous tumor in my small intestine. It's a rare kind of cancer that affects mainly black males. At first it was very hard. They could do the MRIs and the CAT scans but couldn't get a biopsy. The main thing is that it messed up my digestive system. This cancer may not be life-threatening but it is life-debilitating. My physician said he thought I was ready for the next step, which is an injection, and so I got one in my arm first, to see if I could tolerate it, and it looks as if I can, and this week I go back for the regular ones. It may just be placebo, but I think I feel a bit better.

Earlier on, about seven years ago, though, I had something much more threatening. And Pam literally saved my life then. I had viral pneumonia. And almost died. My doctor—Pam talked to him and explained to him what was happening, very carefully, to get me correctly diagnosed. It was really bad. On a scale of one to fifteen, it was fifteen. And Pam was there, watching, waiting through the whole thing. She slept outside, she monitored, she went over things with the doctors, she went out and bought towels and soap . . .

She also has always been so active in the field I'm in, committed to the same ideals, the same projects, and always has been, on her own, and now with me, and she is as committed—and she is so single-minded—working then, and now, particularly, given the state of the politics of this country now . . .

We're together on all these things. She is now very occupied, busy in her work, not sure how happy she is in it at the moment, but she goes out of her way to go to the protest marches and that's added on. We have done that together, especially in the past. I do wish that she didn't work so much now and that we now had more time together, though. Though the other part of that is that I need to get work done here, at the university, and beyond. I'm seventy-three and I am as busy as I was, maybe more than I've ever been. I published a book in the early 1970s about black human rights and health and that made a big impact and I never knew then that here, thirty years later . . . and now I'm working on a new one, also in the same area . . .

I'm not sure that if Pam worked less, I would, but I'd have her around more! We share a lot. Late dinners—with candles and wine—whenever I am home, and that is a time to talk, and we do it. Mondays and Wednesdays I take students to dinner. Sometimes she shows up too. We eat late—last night I got home at nine forty-five and she got there ten minutes earlier. Every once in a while she'll come and listen to me lecture. A lot of her job is about public relations and communications, which aren't things I know so much about, but when I can, I get involved with her work. She also has a lot of editing skills and experience, so on my books she has helped in the editing.

We don't have that much of a social life. We'd like to do more than we do, but the couples we like are also busy, and deadlines loom. But sometimes she will say, there's this thing, and I really want you to go. There are a lot of things she'll go to by herself or with a friend. On the weekends, we work—at our house in the country often. For a long time we didn't go to the same church. I had met this minister up in Harlem and I would go there. But he died this year and now we go together. Pam's a more regular churchgoer than I am . . .

I resisted buying our weekend house. When Pam started talking about a house in the country, I was very resistant. Finally she said, "Thelma wanted you to have a country house and you said no, and I ask you and you say no. You have all this money in retirement and you are never going to retire—I think you should go along with this!" So now we go up there whenever we can . . . When we're there, we go to dinner, we talk. Pam takes the car and goes shopping. I say, "Do you want me to be with you?" when she does, and she says, "Absolutely not!" Pam likes to stay in shape so she does sports more than Thelma did. In the city we'll go to the park and she'll walk while I jog. I haven't been sailing for a while—I sold my boat.

My kids all love Pam. The oldest took to her right away. The middle one's a bit narcissistic: she reacted a bit negatively at first. The youngest, who was Thelma's favorite, he is a bit self-absorbed. Only the oldest is in a partnership at the moment. None are married. Two are gay. Now they all love her. She is a wonderful mother to them. Thelma would be disappointed in them—they all have problems with initiative, none are very enterprising, and all haven't had long, settled relationships. But Pam doesn't have that with them. She adores the youngest in particular. He didn't come to the wedding. Couldn't get himself to the wedding . . . But now he adores her. Her relationship with them is parental, even though they are grown up and she is only fourteen years older than my oldest. She has this mothering instinct. She helped her niece through college, helped her get an apartment, a car, to get a masters . . .

Our money is pretty separate. I get annoyed sometimes when I think of her earlier life with her earlier husbands, and her economic situation . . . She bought a house from her former husband in Washington and she put what she got from that into our apartment. Which she reminds me of at inappropriate times! I took money out of my retirement fund to buy a car, but not the house in the country, and she said, "Why don't you take more out of the retirement fund?" Now the house has greatly increased in value, and the retirement fund—well, the stock market, so . . . She doesn't hardwire, but you know, you definitely know how she feels . . .

I give a lot of money to my family, to my kids, to my sister . . . I bail the kids out. But last year I said, "Look, I'm not going to do this—I'll let you go to jail!" This is something we talk about a lot: tough love. My children are in their thirties and forties and I'm still bailing them out. So that's where the money goes—a lot of it. But Pam does a similar thing for her family. Look, we are not starving. How can I resent Pam bailing her brother out when I am doing the same? We make enough money to have a very comfortable life. But money does sometimes become an issue. I can get angry with her about how much she gives away to her siblings—eight of them! But then I just kind of let it go. She can get upset too about the amount I give away and to whom, and then we get into, well, "What about when you gave so much to your brother," and so on. So we then back off. Sometimes there is a silent day or something like that. Marriage is always fragile. You see people divorce after thirty-two years. Divorce is messy, and then you look for someone else, and then there are a different set of problems. So, as long as it's manageable.

There aren't too many issues, though, that divide us. She uses too many tissues, but that's not a big thing, is it? . . . There is so much turmoil outside, you don't want that inside . . .

Peace at home is more important than whatever issue. The time I was so upset that she was bailing out her brother—I was very upset and then she got very upset, and then there was quiet, not yelling, just quiet. We just go on, rather than sitting down and going through the various things. Or, sometimes we just laugh and it goes away . . . I am so appreciative of how much she brings that is positive and identifiable, that I may say a cross word, and she may, but that is part of living together. When we do say cross words, we just move on. We may say "sorry." We don't have blowups. But if there are cross words, Pam just kind of gets quiet. Maybe a month later she'll say something. The people who say that marriage is part business are right. You have to treat it as a relationship that needs attention, compromise, and forbearance.

She knows how much I appreciate her because I tell her. I think she would know anyhow. But she literally saved my life. I certainly told her how much I appreciated her after that. I told her I loved her. I tell her that. We talk about that time, still, now. I also buy her presents. I bought her a wonderful watch recently that I knew she wanted. I tell her I love her all the time. And I got that from her. She says it at the end of phone conversations. She thinks that there may be more times to say it, but you never know, and so I say too. I didn't do that before—the emotions were there, but you didn't voice them. Pam isn't very demonstrative but she doesn't want you to leave the house without a kiss. So there are a lot of physical affirmations.

I said to Pam, "You are a very attractive woman. If there was some situation in which, say, you were traveling, and you met somebody, and you spent the night together, and then somehow I found out about it, unless this is something that you wanted to carry on, I would forgive you." And she said, "Oh, no you don't! You are such a self-righteous SOB!" She wouldn't give me the glory! She said, "I'm not about to give you that chance!"

Look, that can always happen . . . the few times that I had had extramarital affairs—which were when I was married to Thelma—well, there was some upset. At some point I told her about it. That was a mistake. It wasn't so great that I should have risked the marriage for . . . Thelma, she kind of got over it, except on occasion she would say, "It's all right for you," and I would say, "Thelma, either you forgive me, or . . ." and she would say, "Oh, I forgive you, but I haven't forgotten!"

Out of that I can say that I am not going to do that with Pam. It never seemed to be that worthwhile. I think that with the other women, I enjoyed the charm, not the actual thing. I embed sex within a relationship. And with Pam that is how it is and is going to be. Now, does this mean that I can't go off and be someplace, and meet someone, no—but it is very unlikely and would probably be an embarrassment.

I had very little sex before my first marriage and I was almost thirty when I got married. I had sexual urges, but I didn't see myself like that. I couldn't dance . . . I didn't know much about what I was doing . . . and then, after I had sex with Thelma, I thought, this is great! And I think one of the things, she said, "Oh, I don't mind, as long as I am the number-one person." Well, I listened to that, and I was wrong. I took it literally. Thelma and I had sex all the time, until she got really sick. And then she said, "You know, I am not really up to it, but if you want to have sex with someone else . . ." And I said, "No. I am not doing that again. Even with your permission!"

After thirty years together it changed, but mainly in frequency. And, now, after thirteen, with Pam it is less frequent. We are older. It isn't slam, bang, thank you, ma'am. I am more attentive, more concerned about her, and I still enjoy it, and I think Pam, having gone through menopause, and the effects of the radiation, means that she is not as ready to have sex. I would like it to be more often. It is definitely not boring sex—that's something people think might happen in long-term relationships. One of the great things about our house in the country is that it is out there by itself and we have this lovely bedroom with a skylight, and just going to bed with Pam is sexual. And if we get up early in the morning and make coffee and then go back to bed, that, you know, is great. It is different now, but not less enjoyable or less worthwhile. There is more comfort with each other over time, and the actual sex act is longer. It takes a much longer time to build up. One of my friends, who is seventy now, said, "I think I have had enough sex; I think oral sex is better." You change over the years. You adapt. You realize that sex goes beyond sexual intercourse. You enjoy just being with someone else. Even with Pam's breast cancer, I want her to sleep without her top on . . . So you're with a woman over time whose body has changed but it doesn't make a difference in terms of desire. I find Pam beautiful without her clothes on. In fact, better—she's short and clothes don't really enhance short women. One breast is smaller. Even if she'd had a full mastectomy, it wouldn't have mattered . . . Her breast cancer hasn't gotten in the way of my desire. With either wife . . . I see other women and can appreciate their beauty but you can appreciate that without even wanting to mention it.

I get so much from Pam—particularly a sense of what is going to be good for the relationship. Thelma had that too. I didn't always. Pam has it. I think they both had and have a wisdom. I don't know if it's that women are better at having that, but I know that she is on track and seldom wrong. I think she'd say that my contribution is acknowledging that fact! There is this whole thing about men having more physical strength so they have to be in charge but that is all wrong. They have that, but none of the other things that a woman has. A relationship is a partnership, not subordinate roles, and there is a benefit to being married to someone who has that kind of wisdom. I learn something through it.

You know, I think that Pam and Thelma would have gotten along. So many of Thelma's closest friends are now Pam's.

I think a sensitive husband is always aware of inadequacies. One of the things that lets women have other women friends is a certain kind of sensitivity that they share. Relationships are not a matter of always trying to overcome things, but being sensitive and kind, about each other's inadequacies.

Alice and Christopher John

Alice and Christopher John are in their early and mid-sixties, respectively; they've been married for thirty-four years. Alice, now a child psychotherapist, met Christopher, a lawyer, soon after his first wife had left him, which was shortly after the birth of twins. Christopher had custody. At that time Alice, never married and having had a series of office jobs, had recently returned from traveling after ending a long-term relationship. At the point of meeting Christopher, she was in flux; she did not have a career or a university education, while, in contrast, Christopher was already a father, with a successful practice.

They raised five children together. Christopher has now retired, though he is active in voluntary work, while Alice continues to work at the profession in which she trained in early middle age. They live in rural northern England. Their story highlights another conundrum around sharing: how much can you expect to share when one of you already has children while the other wants to share and shape a family as well?

Alice John:

Our story started in 1969. Christopher was still married, though separated, when we met. Though, if it had been today, we would have started living together almost immediately, we waited two years, until he was really divorced. At that point I went to live in his house with him and his two children. Unusually, he got complete control and custody over his children, which had to do with the reasons he'd divorced his wife—she hadn't wanted the responsibility of children then and decided to take off to travel around the world. The children were tiny. In fact, I'd entered their lives from the beginning, when they—the twins—were less than a year old. When we actually got married, we picked the children up from nursery after going to the registry office, and we had a family party for our wedding, with a cake we bought from the local bakery. No time or space for a honeymoon, given the circumstances, but we went to a dance that evening and announced to our friends who were there that we'd just got married and had had a party with the kids to celebrate!

I myself came from a family with four children, in which my parents were very unhappily married, sticking painfully together for more than twenty years. My alcoholic father died when I was fifteen, which was both sad and a relief from the verbal and emotional abuse that we children witnessed my mother endure. I have more compassion for my father, who seemed to have changed toward my mother once children arrived, now as I'm older and I've had children too, and see how testing marriage, children, all of it, can be. But I didn't then. I just wanted to escape from the oppressive, emotionally brutal climate I felt emanated from him, and blamed him primarily for all the unhappiness I saw and felt.

Nonetheless, I did see how other couples operated, including parents of a friend, to counteract my parents' desperate relationship. They were a complete contrast to my own parents. But it was not just "good" to witness their happiness together: I actually found them embarrassing—watching their intimacy was too much—though, despite myself, I noticed that they were supportive, helpful, demonstrative, and affectionate, shared out domestic things, and clearly had fun with each other. Plus they were good parents. Obviously it was possible to be married happily.

I left home as soon as I could, eventually took a secretarial course, traveled around, had a number of jobs, and two relationships of pretty long duration, about two years each. Then I really fell in love with someone, and we were together for about four years—although looking back, I think lust dominated it, rather than it being able to fulfill me in other important ways. He was incredibly energetic, eccentric, sexy, and wild. His wildness was both enticing and also frightening, and finally I left him when I realized he—and the relationship—would never settle down. It was not long after this relationship broke up that I met Christopher.

I wasn't looking for another partner then, as I was still recovering from this breakup, and I can't say I was happy with my life. I was working as a dinner hostess, in a local hotel-restaurant, in which we met, in a small town in the north, "resting" in between "real" jobs, trying to figure out what to do with my life. I'd been traveling and planned to travel again, and this was a phase in which I needed to earn money, so I took this job and was marking time. I was pretty sophisticated and experienced at this point, in contrast to Christopher. A friend at the time said to me, "Leave him alone—you'll devour him!" I'd never met anyone like him before: kind, shy, sensitive, smart, caring—and with all that, also very good-looking. In fact, all those attributes made me want to run away. I think I might have agreed with my friend: he was too sweet and kind for me. He told me he was married and separated. I was skeptical about that, of course. He had two children, the twins, and was in the process of employing a nanny for them. I couldn't believe this—a man in charge of two small children, while gainfully employed? He also told me that he did not want a relationship. That's what they *all* said! So we became friends. We went on picnics with his children, which felt somewhat weird at first. It was different . . . and kept me interested. So much so that two years later we were married.

Christopher comes from a comfortably off family—he went to private school, university, and was a solicitor, used to a well-paying job. In contrast, as I couldn't wait to leave home, I only had schooling up to O-levels and then a secretarial qualification. By the time we met, I was already thirty, and had led a life in which I'd been able to live and be free to go as I wanted. Meanwhile he'd settled down with a solid job, marriage—admittedly broken down—and two kids. Then by falling in love with him, starting out as friends until finally about five months into the relationship, I realized it was more and I was falling in love, I became a mother to two babies and was with a very well-settled man. And two years later, by choice, I was pregnant with the first of our two joint, biological children. Three years after that we fostered a three-year-old child, and five years later legally adopted him. So I've ended up spending most of my life as a mother to a large family, in a large house, with many now-grown children, all of whom are "ours," all of whom we love equally and who make no distinctions between them as to who is biologically fully related or biologically related at all. They are all sisters and brothers, and all our children. My life, and I, were certainly changed by meeting this man back then and falling in love with him!

Indeed, motherhood, marriage, and family became themes. When I was pregnant for the second time—so that would have been the fourth child— we invited Christopher's parents to dinner, to tell them. At the dinner my mother-in-law said, "You're not thinking of more children, are you? You've got enough with three!" We told her, "Of course we are," and instead of being joyful for us, she was upset and angry. I was upset but also amused. We certainly then did not ask her permission when we decided to foster—as you can imagine—and then later to adopt that child! In consequence she never really accepted our youngest child as her grandchild—though I don't think she ever understood the concept of adoption. To be fair, later on she did come to appreciate and acknowledge him. The way I think she squared us having this brood of children was interesting: she has said that my husband, her son, had "more than his quota of children—and that's why his brother"—her other son—"has been childless!"

Children have been an obvious theme of our life together. Two of his with someone else, two of ours, one adopted, and we've got versatile styles of parenting, adapted to the needs of each child. But when there was a crisis with one of the children, we'd discuss the problem, and then more often than not, because they would know about it anyway, we'd hold a "family conference." I believe that all the children appreciated this—actually I'm not sure about the one whose crisis it was. I do know that they generally felt very supported, and even now, when they're in their twenties and thirties, they will often go to each other, because having had different sorts of parental relationships—i.e., not all having just us as parents; some having others as well—can give a different perspective on the problem. I developed a reasonable relationship with the twins' mother. What was difficult in the early days was her interference, or the perceived interference. There's no guidebook on how to deal with a situation like ours—including the adopted child, and the interference of his birth parents, as they tried to get him returned during the fostering period.

Our children have told us now that they see us as "interchangeable," although in reality our roles have tended to be fairly traditional: he's the practical one, he lends money, gives them advice on cars, houses, loans, etc., and I am the one who helps with emotional stuff. We take care not to side with any of the children, but to remain supportive of each other—even if we want to be critical. Even if you are being critical, you can be critical in a supportive way. And we have had to learn to support each other, to "stand back" with the children when we see our grown children make mistakes, and be hurt. We try to stand back and wait for them to come, as they usually do, in their own time, and we want to be fair.

And another thing that happened was that I married someone who was extremely supportive of my own development. Over twenty years I did mostly distance study while the children were still at home, and further courses later. I gained various degrees and qualifications, culminating in my employment as an educational consultant.

The theme of his support—of mutual support—and the importance of raising our family together was shown also during a time of terrific stress, which was when we'd decided to adopt our youngest child. We'd fostered

him, and after five years moved house, and when we did, that provoked the
decision to adopt him. The process took four years, including two attempts
at court orders to return him, precipitated by the birth parents, even though
they were not adequate to parent. Finally we went to the court to adopt,
which took three days and the adoption finally went through. Up to that
point he could have been returned to his birth parents, and he would have
lost a family and his loving four siblings, only to return to a very different
environment, and we would have lost him, as well. We fought hard, and it
was a terrible time for all of us. Even before that, as a new mother—that is,
after my first pregnancy—I thought that our baby daughter was dehydrated.
In fact she had gastroenteritis, and had to be admitted as a tiny thing to
hospital. I was by this time pregnant with our fourth, second joint, child and
very worried, which might have affected this pregnancy. It all worked out fine
but it was an early test for us—we developed a way of dealing with all this—
support and discussion. The acceptance of crisis, and development of ways to
deal with it, is something you can see was typified in response to our
children's "crises"—our joint discussion, our prioritizing mutual support
(the couple) and fairness during it—making even criticism supportive if
possible, and then sharing it during our family-meeting time.

Sex was extremely important for us at first, if infrequent, given that we
started out with all those children! Sex was important at the beginning,
especially so for procreation for the children we wanted. But the nature of sex
changes over a long relationship. When the children were small, sex—any
kind of sex—was difficult. We had four children under ten and were busy,
and exhausted, and invaded early in the mornings. When the children were a
bit older, we were more concerned with what might be going on in their
bedrooms than in ours! When they left home, Christopher had a real crisis—
when he retired—which made sex difficult between us for a while. And we'd
become middle-aged, and sex, while terrific and satisfying at many points
during our life together, had rather given way to deep friendship, companionship, and intimate closeness, and support. Now we are in our mid-sixties and
I am due for a hip replacement, so agility is not our strongest ally! We are
mutually supportive and interested in each other. Given our physical
limitations, penetrative sex has gone lower on the agenda, but closeness

and intimacy—physical and otherwise—have become more important, gone up in comparison.

As for fidelity, because Christopher's first wife left him for another man, I would never cheat on him. Nor would I tolerate him having an affair. But this is a decision, a choice for us to do it this way. We share a belief, worked out from the beginning by talking about it, that if the relationship isn't working, do something about it. Don't let it fester. Other people choose to live differently and that's fine for them. This is something we discussed thoroughly before we married, and it remains what we have chosen. Though I think that both partners ought to be able to have friendships with people of the other sex which are nonthreatening for the other—and if there is a tension, discuss it, deal with it.

We've definitely got a great relationship but we've of course had our testing times as a couple. The most testing of our relationship, I think, was when Christopher retired—early—at sixty. I had not realized until then how work-defined he had been. He went from wearing a suit and leaving at seven A.M., being in charge of forty people, to nothing. He'd never developed any other interest apart from us, his family. Overnight he became sad, depressed, withdrawn, morose, and comforted himself by drinking more wine than usual. This irritated me immensely—probably more than most people, as my father had been an alcoholic. He also lost interest in sex and intimacy. I was surprised, as I'd imagined that he was looking forward to retirement. We'd even been on a "preparation for retirement" course together. He went to his GP, who said "it will pass." Instead of us talking about our problems, which we'd done always before whenever anything had cropped up—for instance, around the children—he wasn't interested and communication was at an all-time low.

At this time our youngest child had left home prior to college, traveling around. I had a full-time job, well-paid, and I was the one leaving the house every day and able to pay the bills on my own. There was a real, practical option open to us of splitting up. We had a large house we didn't need anymore. We could sell it and buy two smaller properties. So I told him very clearly that his—and us together—continuing in this state wasn't an option for me. He could carry on being morose and closed down and drinking but I wanted something different. He was surprised and upset by this but it shocked him into action. We went into therapy together, and began to communicate again. He then went after other jobs. It's not easy to get one when you're sixty. So after a bit he became involved in charities, which he continues to be, and is very fulfilled doing this work, in which he feels appreciated and which he values. I took the step back from him at that time that we do with our children: I let him know what my limits and choices would be, and then had to let him find his way out of his dilemma.

It helped change our relationship, with me not being so responsible for his welfare as I'd been. We both became aware that I had the energy, will, and finances to leave the marriage. Staying has now become clearly a "choice." I'd lost trust in him during that period, and I've had to regain it—I never thought he'd lose interest in anything, including in me, nor turn to drink, something that he and I know would frighten me. So we've learned something about each other, and our marriage is one of a clear choice now.

We have found it very useful, during rocky times or moments, to remember what brought us together in the first place. I still believe that my husband is one of the most kind, sensitive, caring men I have ever met. We have three sons who have his great sensitivity—one is my stepson, one our adopted one—and generosity, and caring, thoughtful nature. We have two daughters who think their dad is great, and he has been a healthy role model for them.

It's useful to remember in times of crisis what we share—what our samenesses are, and not to dwell on our differences—as I restack the dishwasher after he's stacked it, so I can get twice as much in! And we have a very different opinion on what a "full load of washing" is! We remember that we have shared a lot of life together, thirty-six years, and what we have created in that time—our children, our family, our house and our garden, who we are, what we have become. We have had an enormous impact on each other, and also remember—more important to me than to him I suspect—that we are not symbiotic, that we are two people, that we can live separately, that being together is a choice. We can function without the other. I take frequent holidays, and times apart from him. I find this refreshes me, and he is always interested in what I have experienced. Likewise, he spends time with his siblings now that their parents have died. He also visited our son in South Africa for a month. He missed us, he said on his return, but his relationship with that son deepened as a result of my not being there.

We are different individuals, who are complementary to each other, and have made a conscious decision to stay together because we want to, because we love each other. We think the other is the "best thing since sliced bread," we make each other laugh, that's very important, and are proud of each other and our achievements, and especially of our children. We make a good unit, and have experienced a very interesting and stimulating thirty-four years together. Long may it continue!

Christopher John:

We got together on November 6, 1967, and began living together in September 1969, marrying soon after, when my divorce was granted.

My own parents' relationship was very good—they were good parents, got on well together, had fun, were mutually supportive, shared many interests. I went to private school and university, and when still a student met my first wife, who was wealthy, and her financial independence gave her the ability to do whatever she wanted, and basically be selfish. I think we were immature and the whole exercise of our marriage was a game. We did have children and the reality of it was too much for her. She was bored being a mother and wife and she wanted excitement, which she found by going off with another man, and our marriage broke down very shortly after the children were born.

I was left with these babies, a job, and still quite young. When Alice and I met, I wasn't looking for another relationship yet! Not to mention the fact that I was still married. I'd recently changed jobs too. I had a nanny for the babies, and when they were asleep, I went into one of the local hotel-restaurants for a drink. My aunt and uncle lived in the town and my aunt worked in the local estate agents. She'd told me about a young woman who'd stopped into the office looking for a furnished house, as she'd just returned from abroad. She said that she was temporarily living and working at a local hotel. Obviously my aunt had been pretty taken with this girl, as she prompted me to go into the restaurant and meet her. Which I did.

I wasn't going in with any intention of developing a relationship, but I liked her and a friendship did develop. Alice, during it, became privy to my marriage problems, and she provided support and comfort. After a bit Alice moved into a small farmhouse that she rented with a friend. There'd been no sex in the beginning, as we'd defined ourselves as having a "friendship," but after about five or six months I did visit her at her house one day, and her roommate was out, and nature took its course, and the relationship became more than friends!

We have always been best friends. We discovered early that we could, and have always been able and willing to, talk things through—even if I have needed pushing sometimes. We do, however, respect each other's privacies. We love kids—particularly our own. But in the beginning there was a real difficulty because the mother of the two youngest posed real problems then, which peaked within the first five years and remained uneasy for the first ten or twelve years. She had been expected to move to the Continent, but found that she wanted to return once she'd settled there. So she came back and became very resentful of Alice's relationship with the twins and with me. She saw the children for a weekend every month and alternative Christmases and Easters. It really resolved only gradually as the children themselves became more independent. But it didn't divide us as a couple.

Children can undermine partners very quickly. One must be alert to this. We developed a policy of consultation—to the extent that I appeared indecisive to the children until I had consulted Alice. The births of our children, the having of our children have been among the most delightful things of our relationship, despite the crises and dramas they have also provided, such as our baby's dehydration and near-death.

I made a good living but money was tight in the earlier years—especially since we'd decided that Alice wouldn't have a job, and instead would be the one at home with the children. I would feel very guilty about my failure to provide enough and would put off admitting it. But we'd discuss things. And once we had discussed the problem, it did seem to reduce and we worked out a strategy. For example, Alice did some part-time waitressing and babysitting and we also began to exercise some expenditure control. Over the years she did resent me being in charge of finances and controlling our financial priorities, especially as she has had a greater lack of earning power than I. Again, I hope I've listened, and have accepted her point that I've tended to control the financial priorities and I have tried to give Alice her rightful say.

In the beginning of our relationship, in particular, sex was terribly important, and it has, for me, remained important through most of it. Also, I think having sex sufficiently frequently—even if that fluctuates—over the lifetime together is very important, and we have done that, even now with my potency withering away. I have never been unfaithful, and I am aware that any infidelity would totally undermine our fantastic relationship. I haven't been tempted, either. Temptation, I think, occurs when two people are ready to be tempted—that the relationship isn't rock solid and that they're choosing to go for temptation.

At various times, but not all the way through, sex has been frequent and exceptionally satisfying. A long weekend in Morocco, on our own, and two weeks, again on our own, in the Mediterranean were particularly wonderful—with lots of frequent, mind-blowing, fun sex. But there has been a natural aging process and about seven years ago I began to have erectile problems. This caused anguish at first for us both until we found that we could manage without it. With regret, penetrative sex is on hold, but we have not totally excluded it and we do other things. We are both relatively fit and in good health, and so both share the attitude that minor ailments—we are in our sixties, and we do have minor ailments, like my erectile dysfunction and prostate, or Alice's bad hip, which limits movement during sex—should be ignored.

The period just after my retirement was very bad. I was totally unprepared for it, even though I knew it was coming. I was a pain to live with—boorish, and drinking too much, particularly at home, while my capacity for alcohol had diminished. But now we each have busy lives, independently, to the point that we have learned to negotiate and discuss, and try not to be greedy, about having time to do things for ourselves only, versus having time together. We have resolved this somewhat by having Wednesdays as our "together" day. We do various things—arts and crafts exhibitions, bike rides, gardening, for instance—on those days. That's not to say we don't also see each other and do things together on other days and evenings too!

We of course have rows, but whatever they've been, I myself have never lost faith and belief in our relationship. In fact, what happens is that regret occurs almost immediately after a row, and that is followed immediately by a realization that it was avoidable, and I think, "if only I hadn't done or said this or that." And then, of course, ultimately, after we're at that stage, we discuss, as we have always done. We have shared a love of our children and now grandchildren, and a way of bringing them up together, and we share a host of interests and values and attitudes, and we talk and are willing to talk difficult things through. We are still best friends!

Epilogue

The Noble Risk—The Widow's Story

MARY WATKINS

TO LOVE SO long and so nakedly almost inevitably means one partner is left, alone and grieving. It must be one reason, perhaps the deepest, that some people never take the risk of sustaining intimate love, but instead protect themselves by not remaining open to another, reserving great, meaningful tracts of their lives from another, indeed, perhaps never staying, but always moving on. For, isn't it just too painful to say good-bye, to be abandoned? To be left with only one voice for the shared memories?

The accounts in this book suggest that each partner carries a sense of the other partner "inside": by being shaped by the other's tastes or humor, through feeling "more than" just themselves as individuals. Internally they maintain an almost palpable sense of their partner when they are apart. And so it must be when death comes: the partner that has shaped their life stays, inside.

Mary Watkins is eighty-four. Her husband of sixty years died the year before she participated in the study. In her account she reflects on how her love deepened gradually, almost as if it came upon her by stealth. Last year her loss was sudden; its impact remains great. Yet in her story, her pride in and gratitude for having had such a partnership and having gleaned wisdom and pleasure from it overwhelm the profound grief that must always accompany the love these couples have created.

Mary Watkins:

We met on a blind date in 1940, parted due to war conditions, and then met again and stayed together. We had met for a drink, to make up a foursome, and had no intention of getting together. For one thing, he was too young for me to take seriously. But we met again about six months later, and for want of a better of idea, I started dating him; he was very persistent, and I went along with the tide. I had had another relationship in which we'd made a commitment—which ceased upon his death, due to enemy action during the war.

We had two daughters, one born during wartime. We set up home with a two-and-a-half-year-old daughter, took on a mortgage, and I stayed at home. My husband got and lost two jobs before finally getting a job which he kept for many years. For fifteen years I never had a holiday or visited a pub for a drink. Husbands went to work and went for a drink at the "local" at night; mothers stayed home with the children, not always willingly, but of necessity. There were no babysitters then! But by the time our elder daughter was at college, I had a part-time job and we had bought a nice house in a nice neighborhood and I bought myself a car; by that point we felt we had "arrived"—we had foreign holidays, played golf, and we had achieved a happy time.

In fact, sex improved, too. Sex, probably because of novelty, was important in the first few years, less so in the middle years, due to family and domestic duties taking first place in our lives. Then, after the menopause, sex became again quite important, due to the fact that no pregnancy was possible and therefore no precautions needed, and then again, not so important after the age of seventy, but still very pleasurable on occasions. Sex has an important place in any partnership but surely only a place . . . [For us] there were lots of other aspects of our marriage, or partnership: tolerance, honesty, sharing the physical work and effort of living and running a home or business of family, our children. Despite a certain amount of worry as they grew, and though when they were small I longed for freedom, more money, and more time for myself, I realize what an investment they were for us.

. . . There is an old saying, "Time is a great healer," and I do believe it to be true in all but the most resentful nature. After somewhat bitter personal rows all tempers cool and a great healer is an apology, even if the other party was probably more at fault. That's how we did it and that's how we "made up." My husband was quick-tempered and prone to leap at things. I was not, and in most cases I did the making up . . . My husband served seven years in the military doing war service, and he suffered but did not complain—we just "got on with it" like many of our generation and somehow overcame things; we were hand-in-hand in some respects regarding justice and retribution for enemies, and that's how we survived.

Something I learned after almost sixty years of marriage is that a sense of humor and to look at problems from all angles is most important for making a relationship successful. If possible, it's also good, I learned, to have a mutual hobby—we did golf, and gardening—anything that you can talk about and enjoy together. He needed to go out sometimes with his friends and I with mine. [I learned to let him] "go out with the boys" and I had a "girls' night" occasionally.

When I married, I realized that my new husband and I came from very different backgrounds. Mine was middle-class professional and his more working class. After the initial lovemaking and the pleasure of sex waned, there were many limitations on my part and, of course, feelings of inadequacy on his. We solved this by tolerance—mostly on my part, I must say. Small things can irritate to an enormous degree—for example, poor table manners, bad grammar in speech. But I have always had patience, and my husband did all he could to make our union happy . . . When we married, I was not passionately in love with my husband but I liked the idea of being a wife. I fell in love with him as time went by . . .

After our retirement, which lasted for twenty-six years, we became friends more, and enjoyed every day with a mutual sense of humor—we could get a laugh out of any situation . . . In fact, our best times were when our daughters had left home and we had more money and less responsibility. We traveled more, and for the first time we became friends, more than lovers, and enjoyed every day with a mutual sense of humor. We could get a laugh out of any situation.

Looking back I think it was happy in part because we didn't expect to be on cloud nine all the time, and we tried to make the best of our situation.

. . . His sudden death . . . has left half of me gone as well. No one can describe the feeling to another; the consolations are in looking back to a lifetime of happiness, of ups and downs, and of *living*.

Notes

1. Janet Reibstein and Martin P. Richards, *Sexual Arrangements: Marriage and Affairs* (London: William Heinemann, 1992). Published in the United States as *Sexual Arrangements: Marriage and the Temptation of Infidelity* (New York: Scribners, 1993).
2. Linda Waite and Maggie Gallagher, *The Case for Marriage: Why Married People are Happier, Healthier, and Better Off Financially* (New York: Broadway Books, 2000).
3. Robyn Parker, "Why Marriages Last: A Discussion of the Literature" (Australian Institute of Family Studies, 2002), www.aifs.gov.au/institute/pubs/parker2.html.
4. Erich Fromm, *The Art of Loving* (London/New York: Thorsons-Harper Collins, 1985).
5. Parker, "Why Marriages Last."
6. Mary Ainsworth, "Attachment and Other Affectional Bonds Across the Life Cycle." Colin Murray Parkes, Joan Stevenson-Hinde, and Peter Marris, Eds., *Attachment Across the Life Cycle* (London: Routledge, 1991).
7. Martin Seligman, *Authentic Happiness* (London: Nicholas Bradley Publishing, 2003).
8. John M. Gottman and Robert W. Levenson, "Rebound for Marital Conflict and Divorce Prediction," *Family Process*, Volume 38, No. 3, 387–292.
9. Janet Reibstein, *Love Life: How to Make Your Relationship Work* (London: Fourth Estate and Channel 4 Books, 1997).
10. Carolyn Page Cowan and Philip A. Cowan, *When Partners Become Parents: The Big Life Change for Couples* (New York: Basic Books, 1992).
11. Nathan Epstein, Duane Bishop, Christine Ryan, Ivan Miller, and Gabor Keitner, "The McMaster Model: View of Healthy Family Functioning." In *Normal Family Processes*, second edition, Froma Walsh, Ed. (New York/London: Guilford Press, 1993).

12. Reibstein, *Love Life*.

13. Donald W. Winnicott, *The Maturational Process and the Facilitating Environment* (New York: International Universities Press, 1965).

14. Judith S. Wallerstein and Sandra Blakeslee, *The Good Marriage: How and Why Love Lasts* (New York/London: Bantam Press, 1996).

15. Betty Carter and Monica McGoldrick, *The Expanded Family Life Cycle: Individual Family and Social Perspectives*, third edition (Boston/London: Allyn and Bacon, 1999).

16. Reibstein, *Love Life*.

17. Francesca Cancian, *Love in America: Gender and Self-Development* (Cambridge: Cambridge University Press, 1987).

18. Barbara Ehrenreich, Elizabeth Hess, and Gloria Jacobs, *Re-making Love: The Feminization of Sex* (London: Fontana/Collins, 1987).

19. John Gottman, *Why Marriages Succeed or Fail: And How You Can Make Yours Last* (New York: Simon and Schuster, 1994).

20. Reibstein and Richards, *Sexual Arrangements*.

21. Philip Blumstein and Pepper Schwartz, *American Couples: Money, Work, Sex* (New York: William Morrow and Co., 1983).

22. Reibstein and Richards, *Sexual Arrangements*.

23. Ibid.

24. Ibid.

25. Gottman, *Why Marriages Succeed*.

26. Epstein, et al., "The McMaster Model: View of Healthy Functioning."

27. John Gottman, "The Roles of Conflict Engagement, Escalation and Avoidance in Marital Interactions: A Longitudinal View of Five Types of Couples. In *Journal of Counseling and Clinical Psychology*, 6, 1, 6–15.

28. Ibid.

29. Ibid.

30. Parker, "Why Marriages Last."

31. Waite and Gallagher, *The Case for Marriage*.

Acknowledgments

The first person to thank for the existence of this book is Alexandra Pringle, my British editor and publisher. Alexandra had long been intrigued by the silent but powerful part of the relationship story, the one submerged under divorce headlines: happiness. She offered me the chance to try to decode what she herself called "the best-kept secret." For both her belief in and offer to me, I am deeply grateful, as I am to my agent, Araminta Whitley, who put us together so adeptly and intuitively. Karen Rinaldi, my U.S. editor and publisher, has championed me and my ideas, helping draw them out and clarifying them through our deep and excited discussions ever since I've known her. The teams of people supporting this project at Bloomsbury on both sides of the Atlantic have been sensitive, facilitative, and encouraging, and have turned what had seemed occasionally an unwieldy and daunting task into a manageable and pleasurable one.

To the numerous friends, relatives, journalists, contacts in organizations, and other researchers in the field who have helped, particularly in gaining access and paving the way to participants, I owe lasting gratitude. Not only are they too numerous to name, but many of them must remain nameless in the interests of both the confidentiality and anonymity guaranteed to the participants.

But it is to the participants themselves that I owe my deepest and most awe-inspired thanks. That people want to set the record straight and talk about their gratitude for what they see as their good fortune in finding happiness was made clear by the huge response I received when calling for participation in the study. The responses given were always thoughtful and generous, and sometimes so full that we would run out of cassette tape or paper and ink. This project filled me with a sense of honor: to be given access to the deepest, most private stories of people living with each other in a spirit of generosity, grace, and integrity was both affirming and humbling. I thank everyone who volunteered and shared their stories, many of which could not, in the end, be incorporated directly into the book, but all of which are in it indirectly, through informing my own conclusions and observations.

Finally, as in past projects and books, my own family's patience and help, as I traveled, researched, and wrote, was exemplary. So, to Stephen, Adam, and Daniel Monsell, once again, I say thank you. You three are the key elements of my own "best-kept secret."

A NOTE ON THE TYPE

The text of this book is set in Centaur. Centaur was designed by Bruce Rogers in 1914 as a titling font only for the Metropolitan Museum of Art in New York. It was modeled on Jenson's roman.